GCE AS Level

CW01617715

AS Level for **Edexcel**

Media

Communication and Production

Paul Baylis • Philip Holmes • Guy Starkey

Heinemann Educational Publishers
Halley Court, Jordan Hill, Oxford OX2 8EJ
Part of Harcourt Education

Heinemann is the registered trademark of Harcourt Education Limited

First published 2006

10 09 08 07 06
10 9 8 7 6 5 4 3 2 1

British Library Cataloguing in Publication Data is available
from the British Library on request.

10-digit ISBN: 0 435471 57 0
13-digit ISBN: 978 0 435471 57 6

Edited by Melanie Birdsall
Typeset by Tek-Art

Original illustrations © Harcourt Education Limited, 2006

Illustrated by Tek-Art

Cover design by Wooden Ark Studio

Cover photo © Alamy / RF

Picture research by Taryn Cass, Zooid Pictures

Tel: 01865 888058 **www.heinemann.co.uk**

Websites
Please note that the examples of websites suggested in this book were up to date at the time of writing. It is essential for tutors to preview each site before using it to ensure that the URL is still accurate and the content is appropriate. We suggest that tutors bookmark useful sites and consider enabling students to access them through the school or college intranet.

Contents

Acknowledgements

The authors and publisher would like to thank the individuals and organisations who granted permission to reproduce photographs, screenshots and text.

Images
Page 1, Getty Images.
Page 2 (Figure 1.1), Oliver Sugars.
Page 14 (Figure 1.10), Ragnar Schmuck / Zefa / Corbis UK Ltd.
Page 17 (Figure 1.12), Elaine Tuffery.
Page 18 (Figure 1.13), Rnt Productions / Corbis UK Ltd.
Page 19 (Figure 1.14), Gary Lee / UPPA / Photoshot.
Page 22 (Figure 1.16), Oleg Nikishin / Liaison / Getty Images.
Page 23 (Figure 1.17), Sipa Press / Rex Features.
Page 25 (Figure 1.18), Lewis Birchon.
Page 27 (Figure 1.19), Oliver Sugars.
Page 29, Sarah Urban.
Page 30, Katy McDonald.
Page 32, Philip Holmes.
Page 33, Philip Holmes.
Page 48 (Figure 1.36), John Powell / Rex Features:.
Page 51, Emap plc.
Page 53 (Figure 1.39), Advertising Archives.
Page 56 (Figure 1.42), Zooid Pictures.
Page 57 (Figure 1.43), Dezo Hoffmann / Rex Features.
Page 61 (Figures 1.46 and 1.47), Claro Cortes IV / Reuters / Corbis UK Ltd.
Page 62 (Figure 1.48), Keystone / Getty Images.
Pages 67 and 68 (Figures 1.54 and 1.55), Getty Images / PhotoDisc.
Page 69 (Figure 1.56 (left)), Bettmann / Corbis UK Ltd.
Page 69 (Figure 1.56 (right)), Empics.
Page 74 (Figure 1.59), Zooid Pictures.
Page 77, Getty Images.
Page 79 (Figure 2.1), Caren Firouz / Reuters / Corbis UK Ltd.
Page 80 (Figure 2.2), Yellow Dog Productions / The Image Bank / Getty Images.
Page 82 (Figure 2.5), British Board of Film Classification.
Page 85 (Figure 2.8), www.workthing.com.
Page 87, *PQ Magazine*.
Page 89 (Figure 2.11), *heat* magazine, Emap plc and asos.com.
Page 92 (Figure 2.12), Kerry Ghais / Rex Features.
Page 93 (Figure 2.13), Ofcom / MORI.
Page 97 (Figure 2.18), *The Bookseller*.
Page 98 (Figure 2.19), Vaughan Stephen Sygma / Corbis UK Ltd.
Page 99 (Figure 2.20), Paul Baylis.
Page 100 (Figure 2.21), Zooid Pictures.
Page 101 (Figure 2.22), Sony Ericsson.
Page 101 (Figure 2.23), Frank Micelotta / Getty Images.
Page 102 (Figure 2.24), New Line Cinema / The Saul Zaentz / AKG Images.
Page 104 (Figure 2.25 (right)), Getty Images / PhotoDisc.
Page 104 (Figure 2.25 (top left)), DPA Microphones A / S.
Page 104 (Figure 2.25 (bottom left)), Eyewire.
Page 106 (Figure 2.29), Oliver Sugars.
Page 107 (Figure 2.30), Sony Professional Solutions Europe.
Page 108 (Figure 2.32), BBC.
Page 109 (Figure 2.33), Paul Baylis.
Page 112 (Figure 2.37), Empics.
Page 113 (Figure 2.38), Fuji Photo Film Co. Ltd.
Page 114 (Figure 2.39), Grafton Marshall Smith / Corbis UK Ltd.
Page 115 (Figure 2.40), Getty Images.
Page 116 (Figure 2.41), Google Earth, Apple, Harcourt, DVD Studio Pro, Final Cut Studio, Shake.
Page 121 (Figure 2.45), Oliver Sugars.
Page 125 (Figure 2.50), Zooid Pictures.
Page 127 (Figure 2.52), STORM / UPPA / Photoshot.
Page 133 (Figure 2.56), Zooid Pictures.
Page 136 (Figure 2.59), Apple.
Page 136 (Figure 2.60), Landov / UPPA / Photoshot.
Page 137 (Figure 2.61), Oliver Sugars.
Page 138 (Figure 2.62), Getty Images / PhotoDisc.
Page 138 (Figure 2.63), Empics.
Page 140 (Figure 2.65), Paul Baylis.
Page 141 (Figure 2.66), www.google.co.uk.
Page 142 (Figure 2.67), Leicester College.
Page 145, Getty Images.

Text
Page 43 (Figure 1.30), ABC (left), NRS (right).
Page 44 (Figure 1.31), BARB, RAJAR, NRS.
Page 45 (Figure 1.33), RAJAR.
Page 46 (Figure 1.35), BARB.
Page 82 (Figure 2.4), Ofcom.
Page 83 (Figure 2.6), NRS.
Page 84 (Figure 2.7), NRS.
Page 86 (Figure 2.9), BARB.
Page 88 (Figure 2.10), RAJAR.
Page 91, *Case Study* courtesy of Channel 4.
Page 135 (Figure 2.58 (left)), www.thesun.co.uk.
Page 135 (Figure 2.58 (right)), *The Independent*.

Introduction

About this qualification

Welcome to GCE Media: Communication and Production. This is a relatively new qualification, which was launched in September 2005. As such, it reflects some of the very latest developments in production practices and technology in the dynamic media industry.

Understanding how the media work and about the various job roles and career paths in the media is becoming ever more important. This qualification isn't just for people who want to work in the media when they finish their education. Many of the techniques and skills needed for this qualification are *transferable* – they can be used in a whole variety of other situations. The planning, researching and organisational skills you will be developing through the work you do will be very useful in almost any profession or career. Sometimes, being able to present information in lively, engaging ways – such as through video, audio, interactive media or printed material – can be a real boost to a person's career.

Many students will go on to take the A2 in Media: Communication and Production. Some will take their studies of the media further – into higher education at a college or a university. Some, but not all, will get media jobs. However, the media play such an important role in everyone's life, even studying this qualification just to understand more about the media is a very worthwhile end in itself. We hope that, like many others, you enjoy your studies.

How to use this book

You will quickly see that the book, like the qualification, is clearly divided into three units. You must pass each unit, but you do not have to do the work in the order it is presented in the book if you do not wish to. Your teacher will advise you on the best approach, depending on the facilities and other resources available at particular times in your school or college.

It may be that you will start with some practical skills development in Unit 2, and then find out how the industry is organised from Unit 1, before moving on to extend and deepen your knowledge of the media industry by looking at careers and how the media make meaning for their audiences. You should certainly have a good knowledge of the media and developed some sound practical skills in pre-production, production and post-production before you tackle the externally set assessment brief for Unit 3.

We have tried hard to make the book appealing and engaging, so you'll want to learn more. Getting the best marks depends on doing your best to follow the guidance in the book, learning as you go and using those transferable skills to help you plan, produce and present your work as effectively as possible.

In some of the *Learning activity* boxes, you will see one, two or three ticks beside different activities that have been carefully planned to focus your work in the right direction. Three ticks indicate what you should do to get the best marks – but don't forget the one- and two-tick instructions, too! Throughout the book, you'll find questions to consider – and even debate – in class. You'll read some surprising facts in the various *Did you know?* boxes, and there are many other features in the book that are designed to make your work even more interesting and exciting.

Good luck!

Paul Baylis
Philip Holmes
Guy Starkey

Industries, texts and audiences

Unit 1

This unit contains four parts:

1.1 How the media industry is structured

1.2 How a media company is internally organised

1.3 How media texts are constructed in relation to their audiences

1.4 How audiences use media products

Unit 1 Introduction

Unit 1 is an important unit which explains some important principles about the way the media industry works. In it you will find lots of information about the different media you can choose to study for this qualification. Working in the media can be both stimulating and rewarding, and understanding how and why things happen is one of the best ways to learn how to do things yourself. Most media products are affected by the context in which they are produced (the type of company, how it is structured, its funding, etc.) and by the audiences they are intended for. Media producers usually have a good understanding of how their products will be consumed and understood by their audiences and will target their output accordingly. Some of the issues covered here relate to all the different forms of mass media communication which reach large numbers of people at the same time. Others are sector-specific, meaning that they relate quite specifically to one particular medium, be it moving image, audio, print or interactive media.

What you will learn in this unit

* The range of different organisations making up each major sector of the media industry – moving image, audio, print or interactive media
* How the organisations are structured and how they relate to each other
* How ownership affects media organisations in a sector
* How typical media companies are organised in terms of production processes and job roles

FIGURE 1.1 *The media industry produces a wide range of different products for different audiences.*

* How the output of the media industry is made for different audiences
* How audiences use and understand the industry's products

How you will be assessed

This unit is assessed internally, through one or more assignments set for you in class. You will have to make sure that you submit sufficient evidence of knowledge and understanding to meet the assessment criteria for the unit. You can present your evidence as written reports, illustrated presentations to class or in some other format appropriate to the media.

1.1 How the media industry is structured

Like many areas of economic activity, the media industry has developed in response to a combination of scientific discovery, audience demand and entrepreneurial investment. Initially, humans could only communicate with each other in person, by sending messages via couriers or by using signals – such as with smoke, beacons or flashing lights. The development of **mass media** enabled individuals to send messages to larger audiences, made up of people they will probably never meet.

Audience demand changes in response to the choices available to them. In the early twentieth century, attendance at music halls (at that time one of the most popular forms of entertainment) fell as the cinema became more popular. A few years later, radio brought popular entertainment into the home, and whole familes would gather around their one wireless set to tune in to their favourite programmes. The programmes they listened to featured many of the big music hall stars, who had transferred their acts to a new national 'stage'.

In turn, when television brought pictures into the home, radio suffered a massive decline in listening, and small single-screen cinemas in town centres also lost business – many closed down or were turned into bingo halls. Initially, television was restricted to a small number of analogue terrestrial channels, but satellite and cable companies, as well as the development of digital terrestrial television – Freeview in the United Kingdom – massively increased the amount of choice on offer.

The growth of the Internet and, most recently, broadband (which provides fast download times and the ability to access video and audio on demand) is challenging the more traditional means of distribution. In the media the term **convergence** has come to mean the breaking down of barriers between the original forms of distribution: increasingly text, images and audio are all becoming available via similar platforms.

Key terms

Media industry – the prime focus of the economic activity of this industry is on communication through the mass media

Media company – an organisation, either privately or publicly owned, which is mainly concerned with communication through one or more of the mass media

Audience – a group of people targeted by a media product because they share broadly similar characteristics and interests

Did you know?

1450s – Johann Gutenberg developed the first printing press, but it was two hundred years before the first daily English-language newspaper began.

1895 – Two brothers, Auguste Marie and Louis Jean Lumière, patented a projector they called the cinematograph and then opened the world's first cinema in Paris.

1906 – Experimental radio broadcasting began, using the new 'wireless' technology – first used to send personal messages from point to point.

1936 – The BBC began the world's first regular television service, but it closed down when World War II broke out.

1990s – Interactive media, which combined text, images, video and audio, developed worldwide in a range of disk-based formats and the Internet.

2004 – The term 'podcasting' was given to audio broadcasting through Internet downloads.

Types of media organisation

There are many different types of media organisation within each sector of the industry. Some can be broadly described as **producers**, creating content for audiences to consume. Others may be **distributors**, making another organisation's content available to their audiences. A third group consists of **regulators**, which make sure that the producers and distributors work within the laws of the land. Some organisations fit into two or even three of these categories, as shown in Figure 1.2.

You will notice that the BBC is one organisation that fits all three categories. That is because, when it first became the British Broadcasting Corporation, it was set up under a Royal Charter. This granted it powers, and also burdened it with some responsibilities to match. The most recent renewal of the Charter by the government was in 2006.

	PRODUCTION	DISTRIBUTION	REGULATION/SELF-REGULATION
BBC	Makes its own programmes	Operates its own channels	Ensures it works within the BBC Charter
ITV	Makes its own programmes	Operates its own channels	Its channels are regulated by Ofcom
Endemol	Makes programmes for broadcasters	Broadcasters buy and distribute Endemol's programming	Must ensure its products comply with Ofcom's codes of practice
GCap Media	Makes its own programmes	Operates its own radio stations	Its stations are regulated by Ofcom
News International	Creates content for its own newspapers and magazines	Owns and operates printing presses; organises distribution	Regulated by the Press Complaints Commission (PCC)
Walt Disney Pictures	Makes films	Depends on cinemas to show its output to audiences	Must ensure films will be passed by the British Board of Film Classification (BBFC)
Cineworld	None	Shows films in diverse locations	Regulated by the British Board of Film Classification (BBFC)
Amazon.co.uk	Creates sales and marketing information for the Internet	Operates its own website	Must comply with laws on fair trading with its customers

FIGURE 1.2 *Examples of media organisations that fit more than one category.*

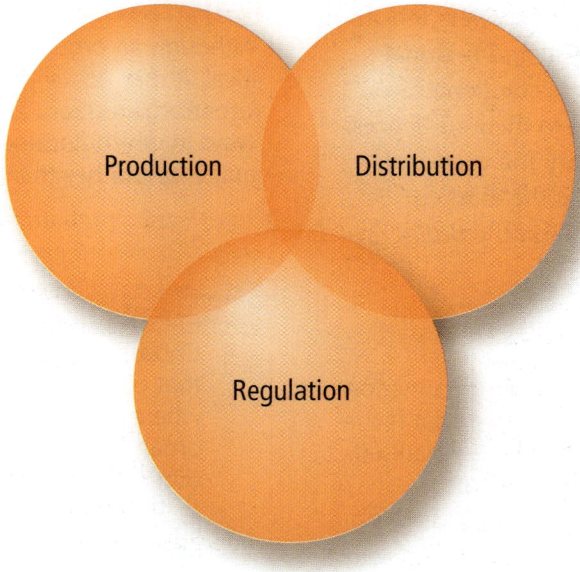

FIGURE 1.3 *Organisations can share some characteristics with others of different types.*

The size of a media organisation affects the scale of its operation. The BBC, for example, operates several television channels for both terrestrial and satellite distribution, over fifty different radio stations and one of the most visited websites in the world. There are regional studios and newsrooms in many different locations around the United Kingdom, providing alternative bulletins and documentary programmes that are broadcast in the local region for viewers of BBC ONE. BBC Wales has a major television and radio production centre in Cardiff, while Bush House in London is the home of the BBC World Service. Together with other national, regional and local services the Corporation provides, this all adds up to make it one of the world's most complex media organisations.

Key terms

Multinational – an organisation that operates in several countries at the same time, owning parts of the media in each one

Conglomerate – an organisation that is made up of several different parts, each of which may appear to be separate

Most media organisations are much smaller than the BBC. Channel 4 broadcasts a single analogue terrestrial television channel and a small number of digital-only channels, such as Film Four, More Four and E4. From its launch in 1982, Channel 4 adopted a 'publisher–broadcaster' role in that it made very few programmes itself, but commissioned other companies to make the programmes it wanted to broadcast. This encouraged the growth of many small television production companies, some of which have grown much bigger since then. Similarly, the introduction of the Welsh fourth channel, S4C, was the catalyst for the creation of several companies based in Wales and specialising in programmes in the Welsh language. They have to compete for commissions with BBC Wales, which also makes programmes in Welsh for S4C.

Although there are big groups of commercial radio stations, some are independently operated. That means that they are owned by a number of individual shareholders or perhaps small numbers of shares in them are owned by private companies – but no outside organisation has enough voting rights on the company board to have overall control. Community radio has been licensed in the United Kingdom since 2002. Small groups of enthusiasts have been allowed to set up and run not-for-profit stations aimed at specific communities that may feel under-served by commercial or BBC stations.

There are large groups of newspapers too – not just national titles, but also local and regional ones, which can belong to large conglomerates, however local they may seem to their audiences. For example, the largest, Trinity International Holdings, owns ten per cent of the market, including the *Sunderland Echo* and the *Belfast Telegraph*.

UNIT ASSESSMENT

Begin a detailed study of the macro-organisation of a major area of the media industry (that is the big picture of how your media area is organised). You should choose from the following:

- **Moving image** – television or film
- **Audio** – radio, talking books and guides or sound production for interactive media
- **Print** – newspaper or magazine publishing
- **Interactive media** – websites, video games or CD-ROMs

You will find it most interesting to choose the medium you will be working with in Units 2 and 3. You should aim to demonstrate a thorough knowledge and understanding of your chosen area, and use well-chosen examples to show how different organisations relate to each other. At the end of section 1.1 you will be generating evidence to meet assessment criterion (a). The learning activities throughout this section will help you to complete this task.

Learning activity 1

✓ In your chosen area of the media industry – moving image, audio, print or interactive media – identify the types of media organisation involved.

✓✓ Give examples and show how they relate to each other.

✓✓✓ Identify the scope and objectives of each one.

* Think very carefully about which area to choose, because you will be working on a number of different aspects of it in this unit. You might find your decision easier if you check the rest of the learning activities in this unit first to see what tasks you will be undertaking later.

Remember

Although an organisation might appear to be local, it may actually be a small part of a much larger organisation. There are many different ways in which 'localness' can be synthetic (or made up), rather than real.

Learning activity 2

✓ Choose a commercial media organisation that operates over a wide area, including where you live. Investigate whether that organisation operates independently of any other, or whether it is part of a large group.

✓✓ Identify the 'parent' company and how many other such organisations it owns.

✓✓✓ Now carry out the same analysis of another media organisation operating in your area, and compare the two. Present your findings and discuss them in class.

* The organisation needs to be big enough for you to present enough findings to get a good mark for your work. For example, a high street photographer probably wouldn't be part of a large enough organisation, and neither would a freelance writer or web designer, who works from home.

A number of small, independent film companies have successfully made feature films for screening in cinemas. However, it is the big Hollywood studios which dominate the film industry, because of the large amounts of money they are able to invest in film production. Aardman Animations first made its name through animated short films, and only later was its owner Nick Park able to invest in producing longer Wallace and Gromit features. The United States is a very large home market for Hollywood, but their output of commercially successful movies is also popular in many other countries around the world, and they are able to make huge profits from the most popular films. A big box office success can reward investors with profits worth many times their original investment – but sometimes films that look promising on paper can flop instead, losing money on a grand scale.

CASE STUDY

The British Broadcasting Corporation

The BBC has an annual budget of just under £4,000,000,000 (that's £4 billion). Most of this income comes from the television licence fee, but some of it comes from sales of programmes to cable and satellite channels, overseas sales, merchandising, subscriptions to its foreign cable channels and a grant from the Foreign and Commonwealth Office (part of the government) to run the radio World Service.

It runs national radio networks, Radios 1, 2, 3, 4 and Five Live, just over forty local radio stations and the regional services Radios Wales, Cymru (in Welsh), Scotland and Ulster. The analogue terrestrial television channels, BBC ONE and BBC TWO, are also available through satellite and digital platforms, and both broadcast slightly different versions with regional opt-outs from the national programming at certain times. The BBC is a partner in the Freeview digital terrestrial transmission network, and its digital-only services – BBC THREE, BBC FOUR, BBC NEWS 24, CBBC, CBeebies, BBC Parliament and BBCi – are also available on cable and satellite. A small number of local television services are being run on an experimental basis.

The corporation's websites, including bbc.co.uk and bbc.com are among the most visited in the world, and its publishing arm, part of BBC Worldwide, publishes the weekly listings magazine *Radio Times* and a whole range of themed magazine spin-offs from some of its most successful programming – such as *BBC Gardeners' World*, *BBC Good Food Magazine* and *Bob the Builder*.

The radio World Service, based at Bush House in London, broadcasts around the world using direct analogue and digital transmissions, as well as via partnerships with foreign broadcasters and the Internet. The television World Service is funded by advertising and subscriptions, and the entertainment channels BBC Prime and BBC America also earn income from subscriptions to overseas cable and satellite providers. Some programmes are produced for schools and the Open University.

As well as producing programming, the BBC also funds support services, such as advice lines for people affected by controversial issues in its programmes, and it actively campaigns on social issues, such as the environment, sexual health and adult literacy.

- Which parts of the BBC are the most expensive?
- Why does the BBC publish magazines and run subscription services abroad?
- Which parts of the BBC are most likely to be sold off some time in the future?

Income and outgoings

Without income, an organisation would have no money to spend on production. This means that, whatever the type of organisation and however it is funded, it simply cannot ignore the need to have a secure source of funding that will allow it to meet its financial obligations to all sorts of creditors. These include:

- rental or mortgage payments for the premises used for production and distribution
- fees and interest on loans for equipment hire or purchase
- staff costs, including pension contributions
- one-off payments to writers, artists, actors and freelancers
- fees to use copyright material, such as images, music, book serialisations, archive footage
- raw materials, such as newsprint, disks, and tapes
- transport costs and other expenses.

In the private sector, income has to come from clients buying advertising space, sponsorship by businesses wishing to closely associate their own products with the media product and sales to audiences. This income may be collected from copies sold or subscriptions paid to them. In the public sector, an organisation might be prevented from accepting advertising. Community radio groups often depend on donations from their listeners and funding bodies.

The BBC only receives income from advertising on some of its commercial services – BBC World television and its partnership in UKTV, for example. Its core funding for its main television channels and radio stations comes from the television licence fee that every household has to pay in order to receive television. Originally, the BBC was funded by a radio licence, too. Because the number of households with television doesn't change much, the BBC's income is relatively stable. When it feels it needs an increase to keep up with inflation, the corporation has to ask the government to raise the licence fee.

Private sector companies often feel aggrieved about the BBC's special income. They feel that, in contrast, they have to work hard for every penny they receive. However, if the BBC weren't so popular among the licence-fee payers, the government would be unlikely to agree to regular increases in the licence fee.

Learning activity 3

- ✓ In your chosen area of the media industry – moving image, audio, print or interactive media – identify the main sources of income.
- ✓✓ Identify which organisations are best able to earn this income.
- ✓✓✓ Explain how the income received affects the products made.
- * In a competitive market, some organisations are more profitable than others. Also, some markets are more lucrative than others – for example, more advertising income can be earned in London than in a small town in a rural area.

FIGURE 1.4 *Possible sources of income for a media organisation.*

CASE STUDY
Future Publishing

This magazine publishing company was founded in 1985 in the city of Bath, in the west of England, just as the home computer games market was taking off. Its first title was *Amstrad Action*, and editor Chris Anderson used a £10,000 bank loan to finance the launch.

Future Publishing pioneered the marketing gimmick of cover-mounted software giveaways (then on cassette tape), as well as using the latest DTP software for page layout and design – and the company quickly grew. Today, Future Publishing owns over 150 consumer magazine titles worldwide, runs a number of popular websites, and organises events such as Music Live.

- Why do magazine publishers include free giveaways with their main products?
- How many other types of magazine are there, in addition to computer magazines?

The advantages of size

There are many ways in which size really matters in the media. A large organisation is able to make cost savings by exploiting its assets to a greater extent than is possible in a smaller organisation. For example, a large organisation or group of companies can concentrate certain functions in one place, efficiently using specialists to 'service' each part of the business. Examples include:

* personnel – managing the recruitment of new staff and handling all the various administrative tasks relating to employing people
* accounts – keeping track of finances, preparing financial reports, invoicing clients for money they owe and paying bills and staff for work done
* advertising sales – selling advertising space or airtime, particularly to national clients who may be some distance away from local producers.

There are a number of ways in which pooling content can enhance an organisation's products. For example, national and international news can be gathered centrally and repackaged by each local company according to the interests of their own audiences.

Some commercial radio groups operate news 'hubs', in which a regional newsroom compiles bulletins for a number of different radio stations in the region, even covering stories for them. A single newsreader reads different news bulletins for several stations, recording them one at a time for each of the different stations to broadcast simultaneously. Very few listeners to a local station will realise that the same newsreader can also be heard on neighbouring stations that could be only thirty or forty miles away.

The BBC is able to exploit its content to great advantage. For example, reporters are able to produce news for radio, television and online use because the same information and recordings can be packaged and repackaged in different ways for different media, and different local, regional and national versions can be prepared within the same media.

Vertical and horizontal integration of activities within a single organisation, as shown in Figure 1.5, can lead to worries about it becoming too powerful. It can raise issues over ownership if, for example, the same company owns a film studio, the cinemas and television channels that show the films it makes, and other distribution outlets, such as a website or a DVD rental chain.

Key terms

Synergy – the advantages obtained by different parts of an organisation sharing resources and working together to enhance each other's output

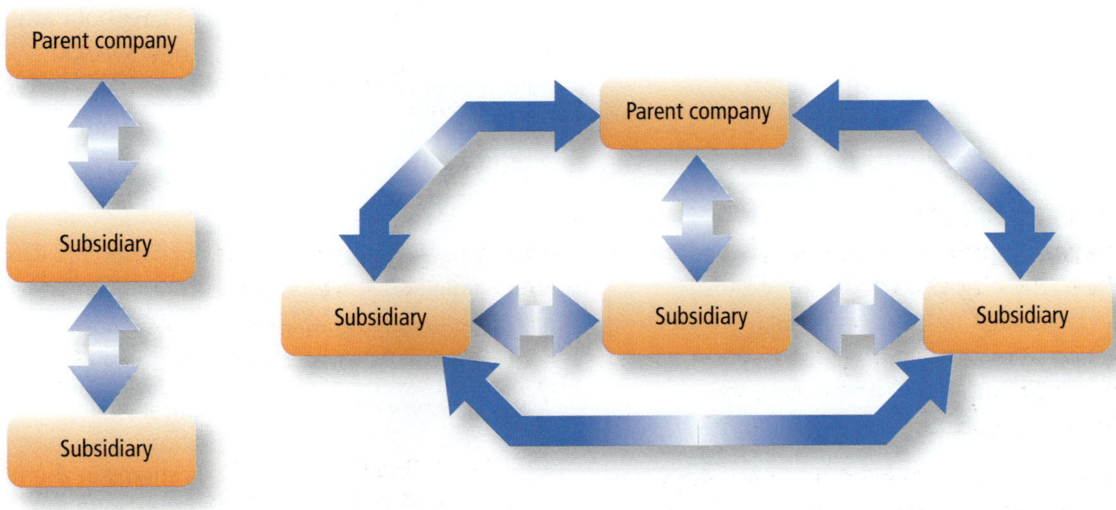

FIGURE 1.5 *Vertical and horizontal integration. The organisation represented on the left is vertically integrated, while the one on the right is both vertically and horizontally integrated as some departments work together and for each other.*

Ownership

We have seen that the media industry is made up of many different organisations. Most of them are **privately owned**, which means that individuals or other businesses have invested money in setting them up from scratch or in buying them from someone else. Usually this is done to make a profit. Companies which make a loss either go bust and close down or they are bought up by someone else who may or may not be able to make them profitable.

In some parts of the industry there are **publicly owned** organisations. That means that the state owns them on behalf of its citizens. Only in broadcasting is state ownership of the media very significant – and that is because in 1926 the Crawford Committee recommended that radio was too important to be left to private companies to run. There were very few frequencies available – which meant that not everyone who might have wanted to broadcast could do so. A small number of companies taking control of this new medium would have concentrated ownership in a few powerful hands and they might have used it to exert undue influence over the population.

So, in 1927 the British Broadcasting Company became the British Broadcasting Corporation, and it wasn't until 1955 that Independent Television (ITV) became the first official commercial competition that the BBC had ever had to face. Independent Local Radio (ILR) followed in 1973. Most people agree that having to compete for audiences has made the BBC more competitive and improved choice overall.

The press, the film sector and most interactive media companies have always been privately owned, because only broadcasting developed with a scarcity of basic resources.

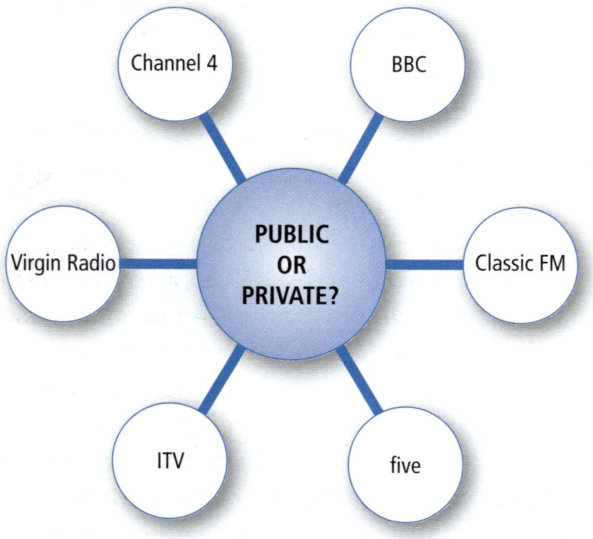

FIGURE 1.6 *Two of these broadcasting organisations are publicly owned and the others are privately owned. Which are publicly owned? You might need to visit their websites for more information.*

Learning activity 4

- ✓ In your chosen area of the media industry, identify patterns of ownership.
- ✓✓ Show who owns what and how and why the patterns change.
- ✓✓✓ Explain why ownership matters. You should think about diversity of opinion, choices available to audiences and what often happens to employees when their company is taken over by a bigger one.
- * The websites of many organisations have an 'About Us' page, which provides information about who owns them. Sometimes there will be a brief history of the organisation, showing when they were founded and if they have been bought up by another company.

Anyone with deep enough pockets can set up a newspaper, make a film or set up a website – although launching a daily or a weekly newspaper can cost many millions of pounds, without any guarantee of success. In 1987, a new weekly newspaper called the *News on Sunday* lost its owners £10 million and closed after just seven months. Fortunately, it costs only a tiny fraction of that amount to create and maintain your own website.

Remember

Public ownership means an organisation is owned **for** the public **by** the state.

Private ownership means an organisation can be owned, bought or sold by companies and individuals. In many cases shares in them are traded on the stock exchange. Foreign companies have invested heavily in buying media companies in the United Kingdom.

Because private media companies can be bought and sold at any time, it is impossible for any textbook to have all the latest details of who owns what. You will need to keep up to date with developments in media ownership by reading specialist magazines such as *Broadcast, Media Week, Screen International, UK Press Gazette* and *The Radio Magazine,* as well as the media pages of the national newspapers. There are also websites which report changes in media ownership – some of these are highly critical of the motives of the richest media moguls who own multinational conglomerates.

Not every media organisation is big and profitable. Even the biggest of them can lose money if their income falls short of their outgoings. In contrast, some small companies manage to make a profit on a very small turnover.

FIGURE 1.7 *Media ownership can make entrepreneurs rich and famous.*

Key terms

Income – the money earned through the organisation's regular activities. For example, from advertising, sales, subscriptions, fees and royalties

Outgoings – the money spent by an organisation in order to meet all its costs, including: wages, salaries and fees for staff, as well as rent, heating, lighting, vehicle costs, power, materials and taxes

Turnover – the total amount of money passing through an organisation's accounts in a year

Did you know?

Two of the biggest media mergers at the start of the twenty-first century were in television and radio.

In 2004 the separate companies Carlton and Granada merged to form ITV plc, in a multimillion pound deal. ITV began in 1955 as a network of separate companies, each broadcasting to one of fourteen different regions.

In 2005 it was the turn of the radio industry to be transformed by the merger of the two biggest groups of stations, GWR and Capital Radio. ILR had started out as a network of separate companies, then formed into a number of groups in the 1980s and 1990s, as the regulatory body and the government of the day loosened rules restricting ownership.

Macro-organisation refers to the way a whole industry – or a large sector of it – is organised. It may be dominated by one or more very large organisations, or there may be a wide diversity of large and small organisations, some in competition with each other and some working together. Some will be suppliers and others will be customers – much in the way that a feature film company may hire a specialist animation company to provide certain scenes or perhaps the opening and closing sequences of a production they are working on. The media industry makes great use of freelancers – individuals who work for organisations when they require their services, but who do not have a permanent job with them.

	ANNUAL TURNOVER, YEAR ENDING 2004
BBC	£3,752,600,600
ITV plc	£1,588,000,000
Channel 4	£841,400,000
GCap Media (as Capital and GWR)	£120,000,000
Daily Mail & General Trust	£2,109,000,000
Guardian Media Group	£634,800,000

Sources: annual reports

FIGURE 1.8 *Annual turnover of some of the UK's biggest media organisations.*

Regulation

Just as in 1926 the government thought that the new phenomenon of broadcasting was too important to be left to the free market to run, so governments today regulate various aspects of the media industry. One of the most important ways in which they do this is by using measures to prevent the media from becoming too dominated by one organisation – or just a few of them.

Regulation of ownership takes place in a number of ways. Broadcasting is very strictly controlled. Ofcom is the shorter name of the Office of Telecommunications, and one of its jobs is to ensure that there is a diversity of ownership of commercial radio and television in any particular area. However, since it was set up in 2003 it has already allowed the ITV and GCap mergers, and it has not discouraged greater foreign ownership of radio and television companies.

You might think that nobody could buy the BBC because it is publicly owned. In fact, an important part of its basic infrastructure was privatised in 1997, when its transmitter network was sold to Crown Castle.

Another way in which ownership is regulated is through the Competition Commission. This government body has powers to intervene in any industry, if a company takeover or a merger seems likely to adversely affect the operation of the sector. The Competition Commission only intervenes if a matter is referred to it for consideration. It would examine the media sector in similar ways to its investigations of food retailing and petrol distribution and sales, considering the effects of any proposals on the public.

Learning activity 5

- ✓ In your chosen area of the media industry, identify the regulations governing ownership. Is there just the Competition Commission, or is there an industry-specific regulator as well?
- ✓✓ Show how restrictions on ownership affect the operations of a major company.
- ✓✓✓ Explain whether the company would be able to grow in size through takeovers or mergers, or are they already so big that regulations would prevent them growing further?
- * Media regulators also have detailed websites, where you can find the regulations they enforce. If you find that there are no regulations on ownership in your area, you should explain why.

Remember

Macro-organisation is the big picture: how an area (or sector) of the media industry is organised.

Regulation does not just concern ownership. The media have such influence over a country's citizens that governments the world over have set up bodies that are responsible for overseeing different aspects of what media organisations do. In the UK, Ofcom's roles and responsibilities include:

- awarding licences to broadcast for commercial radio and television companies
- ensuring these companies keep to the terms of their licences
- setting rules over content – about taste and decency, for example, and over impartiality
- receiving and dealing with complaints about programmes and advertisements.

Ofcom's powers over the BBC are very limited as the BBC mainly regulates itself. From 1927 to

CASE STUDY

News Corporation

The Australian-born Rupert Murdoch's family business News Corporation has a wide range of media interests around the world. In the United Kingdom it is the parent company of News International, which publishes the *Sun* and *The Times* as well as the biggest selling Sunday broadsheet and tabloid newspapers: *The Sunday Times* and the *News of the World*. It has been alleged that the tabloid newspapers promote Murdoch's own political views, first supporting the Conservative Party and then switching to Labour in 1997. News International owns enough shares in BSkyB to control Sky Television, but as broadcasting is regulated more closely than publishing, it is required to be impartial over political issues.

News Corporation's interests in Australia include the country's only national broadsheet, *The Australian*. It also owns dozens of other titles and has control of sixty-eight per cent of the national and capital city newspaper market, seventy-seven per cent of the Sunday newspaper market and sixty-two per cent of the suburban newspaper market. In the United States, News Corporation controls the *New York Post* – the tighter regulation of press ownership in the US prevents the company from owning more newspapers there.

However, Rupert Murdoch's worldwide media ownership also extends to book publishing, magazines and various other terrestrial and satellite broadcasting companies, such as Fox in the United States and Australia, Star in Asia and Sky in Europe.

- Why do you think newspaper publishers might try to influence politics?
- In what ways do newspaper publishing and broadcasting complement each other?
- What might happen if one news organisation becomes too powerful?

2006 a single board of governors was responsible for the management of the BBC's operations, *as well as* ensuring it worked within the terms of its Charter. From 2006 a second governing body has had the job of regulating the organisation, leaving the management of the corporation to the original board of governors. It is called the BBC Trust.

The intention is to make the BBC both more accountable and better run. Until this split took place, the BBC governors had two roles that were sometimes in conflict with each other. Some people think it was this dual role that created the serious situation that occurred in 2003 – the BBC had a dispute with the government over a report by the journalist Andrew Gilligan that became so serious that the Chairman and the Director-General resigned in a blaze of publicity.

Think it over...

Until the roles of the BBC's board of governors were split between two separate bodies, how well could the board fulfil both aspects of its responsibilities?

The newspaper and film industries are self-regulating regarding their content. The Press Complaints Commission (PCC) and the British

FIGURE 1.9 *The size of the potential audience for a media product can seriously affect its profitability.*

Board of Film Classification (BBFC) were set up by these sectors of the media themselves, in order to respond to complaints and to decide what may be shown in cinemas – and to which age groups – respectively.

So, each part of the media industry has certain rules to comply with. An organisation which consistently breaks these rules can create big problems for itself. Commercial radio and television companies that breach their licences may be fined by Ofcom or they may even have their licences taken away. The PCC has few powers over newspaper publishers, though, and the worst sanction that could be applied by the BBFC to a film company that goes too far in terms of violence, bad language or sex in a film is to give the film a higher certificate. Of course, such a measure could still impact heavily on the film company, because if a film meant for teenagers is given an 18 certificate, the number of teenagers who could get into cinemas to watch it would be cut dramatically. That would reduce the box office revenue generated by the film and, in consequence, its profitability.

Did you know?

These are some of the biggest earners at cinema box offices worldwide (revenues are shown in US dollars):

Titanic (1997)	$1,835,300,000
Lord of the Rings (2003)	$1,129,219,252
Harry Potter (2001)	$968,600,000
Star Wars Episode I (1999)	$922,379,000
Lord of the Rings (2002)	$921,600,000
Jurassic Park (1993)	$919,700,000
Shrek 2 (2004)	$880,871,036

Source: www.amazon.com

Interactive media are the least regulated of all, as there is no official body in charge of them. The Internet grew from an academic network joining a small number of computers into the huge worldwide network we know today. Providing they have an Internet service provider (ISP), anyone with a suitable computer can connect to it. Anyone can own as many websites as they

FIGURE 1.10 *Even the smallest organisations must work within the law.*

can afford to run, and successful websites can be bought by other companies or private individuals without having to ask anyone's permission.

Anyone running a website, producing CD-ROMs and DVDs or involved in any other mass medium has to obey all the other laws of the land. For example, distributing child pornography, inciting racial hatred or encouraging other people to commit terrorist acts are all illegal, and serious penalties can be applied to anybody who is caught offending in this way. Broadcasters, film producers and publishers are also obliged to obey the general laws of the land.

Think it over...

Should the Internet be more closely regulated regarding content and/or ownership? What are the dangers of having no regulation at all? What kind of body would be appropriate for regulating the Internet? What sanctions could be applied to those who break the rules?

If an organisation is fined, or if a broadcaster loses its licence, its value will decrease considerably. Its shareholders – or a parent company – will be very concerned if the value of their investment falls dramatically as a result of someone making a big mistake or not following the rules.

Likewise, the value of an organisation that does well, winning new audiences, earning more advertising income or buying up a competitor, for example, can rise quite considerably.

Product range

Every organisation involved in production or distribution wants to succeed financially. That may require diversification, especially if growth is restricted in some way. For example, ITV may be unable to buy the BBC's terrestrial television channels or radio stations, but it thought it could increase its income by creating new channels of its own, using new digital technology.

ITV's first venture into digital terrestrial television was called ON Digital. Because viewers

CASE STUDY
Walt Disney Pictures

This company, famous worldwide for its larger-than-life characters, from Mickey Mouse to Shrek, began life as the Disney Brothers Cartoon Studio in 1921. Founded by two brothers, Walt and Roy Disney, it was Walt's animation genius and some early successes that turned a fledgling film studio into the giant multinational entertainment and communications empire that is the Walt Disney Company of today.

The 1937 feature-length animation *Snow White and the Seven Dwarfs* established Disney productions as firm favourites with audiences young and old, and the name has long been synonymous with good, safe family entertainment.

Long after Walt Disney's death in1966, the brand is still being used to develop activities in many different but related areas, including television production and distribution, theme parks, hospitality and merchandising. Innovations such as incorporating real actors and animals in animated features have been followed by computer-based animation. A relationship with the digital animators Pixar has brought *Toy Story*, *Finding Nemo* and *The Incredibles* to worldwide audiences.

The combined income of The Walt Disney Company as a whole in 2004 was just over 30 billion US dollars, and it has nearly 130,000 employees worldwide.

- What has made Walt Disney films so successful?
- Why would film companies want to develop theme parks?
- Why does the organisation use different methods of animation today?

were slow to subscribe to the service, it was rebranded ITV Digital in the hope it would have greater appeal. It collapsed because the income from subscriptions never managed to cover the massive investment ITV made in buying up rights to broadcast Champions League football matches. The BBC, Sky and Crown Castle stepped in to take over the digital frequencies and use them to launch Freeview, which was unexpectedly an outstanding success, reaching four million homes in two years. So, by the end of 2005, and keen not to miss out, ITV had set up four new free-to-air channels, all funded by advertising.

Television companies also sell their programming overseas whenever they can, because foreign channels pay very well for programming that their own audiences want to see. Often they will sell an idea or a format rather than the programme itself – for example, the BBC's *Fame Academy* is extremely popular in France, where it is produced by Endemol for the main commercial channel, TF1.

FIGURE 1.11 *Successful formats can be customised for use in virtually any market.*

Key terms

Brand – an identity, used to help people recognise a particular product and to encourage them to want more of it

Spin-offs – a brand can be applied to different products to associate them with the main one – for example, cartoon characters are used to sell such products as yoghurts aimed at children

Franchising – the selling of permission to use a particular brand on a product – for example, a production company might want to exploit a successful brand, but it wouldn't want to get involved in making yoghurt itself

A product range can be expanded in many ways, in order to exploit a popular character, scenario or format. Often, successful feature films are followed by 'spin-offs' such as television series. Successful series on television and radio, as well as films, can be marketed as DVDs, videos, CDs and audio cassettes. Most recently, pay-per-view video on demand has become popular through cable and broadband services, using the latest high-capacity technology to distribute content to consumers.

Learning activity 6

- ✓ In your chosen area of the media industry, select a large company and identify its main products.
- ✓✓ Explain how important each product is to the company's financial success. How does each product relate to all the others in the company's product range?
- ✓✓✓ Identify any possible future spin-offs from the existing product range, that could be used to increase the company's income.
- * Pay particular attention to products that are exploited by associated companies, either within the same organisation or through a licensing agreement.

Think it over...

As the number of media products increases, what will happen to the size of the audience for each one?

FIGURE 1.12 *Broadcasting House in London has long been the centre of the BBC's operations.*

Serving audiences

We have seen that the organisation of the media industry today is the result of several different factors:

* Technological development has opened up new possibilities for production and distribution that investors are keen to exploit.
* Audiences have demanded certain media products as they have become available, in order to be entertained and informed.
* Regulators (backed by governments) have set limits on development according to their own priorities and beliefs – for example, delaying the arrival of commercial radio for fifty years, and ensuring that levels of violence, bad language and sexual content are restricted according to the audience.

As the media industry has grown and the range of products has increased, audiences have become increasingly able to choose between alternatives. The development of the Internet, interactive media platforms and satellite transmission has enabled audiences here to access content from overseas – much of it free of content regulation.

Think it over...

How much further can the media industry grow? What will happen to the smallest companies if their audiences drift away to larger ones?

By 2012 the BBC plans to have moved hundreds of jobs out of London and to Manchester, in an attempt to make its output more relevant to audiences in the north of England. By contrast, since the merger of Carlton and Granada, ITV production has become increasingly centralised in the south-east of England. The networking of radio stations and modern print technology have both allowed production to become centralised, rather than close to regional audiences. Newspapers and magazines can be read via the Internet, too.

What is the effect of so much change on the audiences of all these media? Certainly, we are all becoming much more discerning about which of the media's offerings we choose to consume. The days when people could always discuss the previous night's television at school or at work are long gone, because now you are much less likely to find that everyone in the room has watched the same programme.

CASE STUDY
PMH Productions

This company grew from a single video and film producer working from home into a small multimedia production company. Much of the video and film production now appears on DVD or can be streamed on the Internet. For the company, this has meant regular updating of their hardware and software, as well as staff development in skills and digital techniques.

The company's client base ranges from blue-chip companies to small manufacturers in the pottery industry. New ways of working have been developed, including the use of DVCAM recording equipment, so that digital-quality images and sound can be captured on location and in the studio. The majority of recording by PMH Productions is done on location. They do not have a recording studio of their own, but they rent suitable studio facilities when they need them.

- What is it about this company that tells you it hasn't been operating for very long?
- Describe and explain the size of the organisation and how many people are involved in its work.

It is actually very difficult to tell what whole audiences think. Some sectors can get fairly reliable data about consumption of their products from ticket sales (cinema) or how many copies are sold (newspapers). Cinemas make returns to the film distributors, based on how many people pay to watch each showing of a film. This then feeds income back to the producers at the studios, and they will make the biggest profits on the films that attract most people into the cinemas to see them.

Newspapers, magazines and disk-based products are also sold in quantities that can be counted – if a lot are returned unsold, it can cost the producer dearly in terms of lost revenue. Pay television and Internet downloads are also measurable, as are hit counts on websites. Even posters for point-of-sale advertising can be judged for their effectiveness by considering whether sales have risen of the products they are promoting, and billboard advertising alongside roads and in streets is priced according to the volume of traffic known to pass by.

FIGURE 1.13 *Some audiences can be seen, and others cannot.*

It is broadcasters who face the biggest problems in measuring audiences and finding out which of their products are the most popular. We will explore how they go about this, and some of the problems they face in carrying out audience surveys, in section 1.3 of this unit.

Key terms

Quantitative data – information that tells us how many, how long or how often; it uses numbers to describe things, like the consumption of media products, and it can be presented in tables, charts or graphs

Qualitative data – focuses on people's feelings, impressions and reactions to what they have read, seen and heard

One major problem with quantitative data is that it doesn't tell us what audiences actually *think* about a media product – just how many people bought or watched it. Qualitative research that reveals how much audiences did or didn't enjoy something usually requires questionnaires or focus groups (see Unit 2). It is unusual for audiences to say what they would prefer from the media, because they usually find it difficult to imagine a new format or approach until they have seen or heard it for the first time.

The danger for producers of only looking at quantitative data is that they may just try to copy the most popular programmes and formats, never trying anything new. The fashion for 'reality TV' programmes was created by a small number of initial successes. Suddenly, because they proved a hit with audiences, every main channel had its own 'reality' shows, 'makeover' shows and variations on the *Big Brother* theme.

FIGURE 1.14 The Independent *changed to a smaller format in 2003 – other broadsheets have followed suit.*

The low cost of web production means consumers can create their own alternatives to mainstream print, audio and even television. Blogging and podcasting are two examples of how individuals can fill gaps in the mainstream media – but it is only if they get highlighted by television, radio, the press or the most popular websites that they will ever reach mass market audiences.

In the print industry, it can be easier to identify and respond to changes in audience demand, and redesigning a newspaper can greatly increase sales. The more serious newspapers used to be called 'broadsheet' because their size was much larger than the 'tabloids'. Sales of broadsheets had been declining for some years and the publishers felt something had to be done to revive their sales. In September 2003 *The Independent* became the first broadsheet to change to the smaller format, which could be easily read on public transport where people are often sitting in cramped conditions. *The Times* quickly followed, publishing large and small versions simultaneously for a while, before dropping the original broadsheet format altogether.

Because they wanted to distance themselves from the tabloids, these newspapers coined the term 'compact' even though they were now the same size as the *Sun*, the *Daily Mirror*, the *Daily Star*, the *Daily Mail* and the *Daily Express*. When the *Guardian* adopted its new 'Berliner' style in 2005, the flagging sales of this newspaper increased too, as old readers returned and new readers bought the newspaper for the first time to see what it was like. The move from broadsheet size to 'compact' was at least partly due to audience demand for a more manageable newspaper.

Think it over...

Where do new ideas for media products come from? How many new formats can the media devise?

CASE STUDY

GCap Media plc

In 1982 a small independent local radio company, Wiltshire Radio, began broadcasting to the Swindon area from studios in a small town called Wootton Bassett. It was so successful that it began buying other radio stations, starting with Bristol's struggling Radio West and rebranding itself as GWR. By 2005 GWR Group plc, as it had become, was one of the United Kingdom's two biggest radio groups. After merging with the other market leader, Capital Radio plc, the joint company became GCap Media, and its founder, Ralph Bernard, firmly established himself as one of the most powerful people in British broadcasting.

In 2006 GCap Media owned a vast range of radio stations, from the long-standing market leader in London, Capital Radio, to regional stations that carry the Century brand in the north east, the north west and the East Midlands – as well as dozens of local stations as far apart as Essex FM and Capital Gold in Manchester. It ran a number of digital stations broadcast on DAB and digital satellite, including Planet Rock, Core and Capital Disney.

Following the merger, GCap Media's share price fell dramatically because the country's economy slowed down and the advertising revenues the company depends on for its income dropped. Ralph Bernard announced that GCap would sell off some stations in North Wales and the West Country in order to meet its financial obligations, but he also reduced the amount of advertising on some stations, to make them more attractive to listeners. Cutting the amount of advertising, though, has the effect of reducing income even further unless the price of airtime is increased to compensate, and many industry observers considered this to be a risky move. But Ralph Bernard, who has had such huge success in building such a big media empire from humble beginnings, shouldn't be underestimated.

- Why would Ralph Bernard want to expand his original company?
- Which audience is targeted by Capital Disney?
- How does the price of advertising affect a radio station's income?

Up to a point, the 'free market' allows companies to spot a gap in the range of products available and fill it. The concept of the free market lies at the heart of capitalism, although the existence of regulation means it is not entirely free. Capitalist ideology is based on someone who owns something (capital) being able to exploit it in order to make more money, which can then be further invested in a spiral of continuing growth. Inevitably, the biggest organisations already have a head start, and so do certain countries, including the United States, whose domination of English-language cinema has resulted in Hollywood studios influencing film distribution internationally.

Although some people dislike the concept of rich people becoming increasingly wealthy – and often at the expense of the poor – in fact, the market for media products is becoming increasingly competitive and fortunes can be easily lost as well as won.

Key terms

Pluralism – the availability of a diverse range of opinions, perspectives and information – audiences have a wide choice and are not restricted to one dominant source or a small number of sources

Hegemony – the dominance of a society by a ruling elite – in media terms, this would mean mass communication being controlled by just a few powerful organisations, thereby restricting access to alternative views

Globalisation – the increasing concentration of political and economic influence in the hands of a few people, in a way that ignores international boundaries

Catering for the needs and interests of an under-served section of the population requires the investment of a lot of time and money – especially in the most expensive areas of the media industry. Setting up a new television channel or a radio station is much easier if it uses a digital platform such as Sky, Freeview or the Internet to reach its audience. Audiences that have little money to spend on advertisers' products are less likely to be catered for by privately owned, commercially funded media companies, whose main objectives are, after all, to make profits for their shareholders.

That is where the public sector can work for the good of the community, providing content that is either risky in commercial terms because of its experimental nature, or services for minorities that privately owned organisations wouldn't consider to be viable.

Think it over...

Do you think the BBC should only provide programming that is either new and experimental, or only of interest to small minority groups which a totally free market wouldn't serve?

How would the majority of people feel about paying the licence fee if the BBC only served minorities?

Learning activity 7

✓ For your chosen area of the media industry, carry out a survey of which products people choose to consume. Try to include as wide a range of people in your survey as possible. Identify first of all what they watch, listen to or read, and then ask the same people what they think of those choices.

✓✓ Find out how satisfied they are with those choices, and whether or not they would prefer something different instead. What would be their ideal media products in your chosen area of the industry?

✓✓✓ Now explain the results of your survey in terms of the earlier work you have done in this unit – how well does the way the industry is organised serve the audiences?

* It is very important to plan a survey properly before you carry it out. You should think about who to ask, where you are likely to find them and what to ask them. Keeping accurate records of your findings, and then presenting your findings is just as important.

1.2 How a media company is internally organised

Media organisations differ greatly even within the same sector, but they are generally organised according to the production processes involved in their operations. Understanding these processes will help you to make sense of the way they are organised. Your own interest in the media may lead to employment in such an organisation, and understanding how everything works could contribute to you having a successful career. Even if you never work in the media, you will understand more about the products you consume as part of the media companies' audiences.

UNIT ASSESSMENT

Choose a major company or organisation from your chosen area of the media industry. Investigate and report on its internal organisation. You should make sure that the organisation is big enough to provide you with a substantial amount of detail – a small, local company with just a few employees is unlikely to be suitable.

At the end of section 1.2 you will be generating evidence to meet assessment criterion (b), and the learning activities in this section will help you to complete this task.

In every case, production can be broken into three stages: pre-production, production and post-production. **Pre-production** is the preparatory work, including product development, content research, writing and making plans. The **production** stage involves creating the actual content, and then **post-production** is the finishing-off stage when the material is put together in the way in which audiences will experience it.

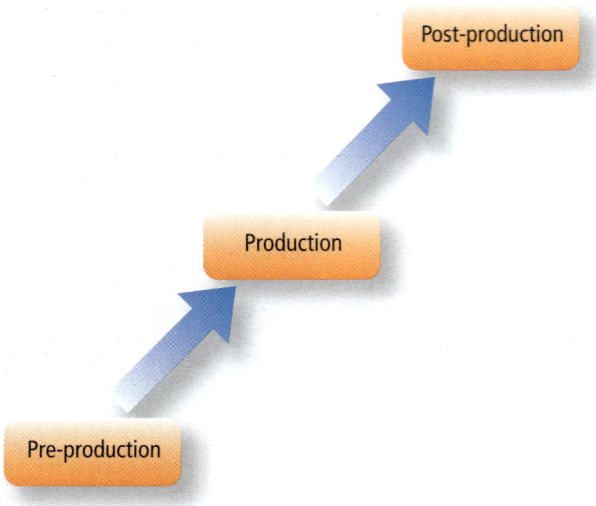

FIGURE 1.15 *The three stages of production.*

Moving image production

Television and film production begins with an initial idea, which may be entirely new or based on something which has been produced before. In order for production to take place and the idea to be turned into a finished product, somebody has to finance it. In the case of film production for the cinema, backers may have to be found, who will invest in many months of pre-production, production and post-production, before the film eventually starts to earn income at the box office and through television showings and DVD rentals and sales.

Sometimes, but certainly not always, those backers are handsomely rewarded with big profits because the income from the film greatly exceeds the cost of producing it. There is an element of gambling to this process, though, because if a film flops, large amounts of money can be lost.

Television has a huge appetite for new material – otherwise its output would consist entirely of repeats. News journalism must be carried out on an almost continuous basis – especially where the product is a rolling news service, such as BBC NEWS 24. Other forms of programming are often produced after a producer has made a successful bid to a TV channel for a commission to develop an idea, perhaps into a whole series.

Corporate video producers often respond to requests from companies to create promotional materials for their businesses.

FIGURE 1.16 *Before a television programme goes into production, many hours of pre-production will have taken place.*

Key terms

Commission – a formal request for a product to be made, in return for payment

Contract – a legally binding agreement for a commission, usually in writing

Recce (reconnaissance) – a visit to a location to check its suitability for the production work being planned

They usually have to make a 'pitch' (a proposal) to the company in order to get the commission to make the video.

Agreeing the finances is one of the first stages of pre-production – this can only be done once a budget has been worked out, based on what it will actually cost to make the product. Other pre-production activities include developing scripts, carrying out a recce of locations to be used, casting for actors and presenters, and arranging any logistical requirements. These include arranging transport to different locations, booking studios, equipment and a crew to do the work and organising catering. Drama productions may require many hours of rehearsals, costume design and production and make-up.

Production in studio or on location can be time-consuming, as there is often little chance of being able to go back and re-record something if it isn't right on the day. Actors may not be available at a later date, and locations may look different after a period of time. So everyone on the production team has to ensure that their work is carried out according to the script and the other production paperwork.

Live television production, such as news programming, has the added complication that mistakes cannot be covered over by re-recording and editing in a post-production stage. Luckily, television audiences largely understand that in live situations things can go wrong – and as long as it doesn't happen too often, they seem to tolerate, and even enjoy, such occasions.

With recorded programmes or videos and certainly in the case of feature films, there may be a lengthy post-production stage, in which different shots are edited together, mistakes are removed and scenes are placed in the correct order. Music can be added, and for big budget films that will be distributed internationally, additional language soundtracks are recorded. Special effects and subtitles can also be added at this stage. Films and television programmes then need marketing.

Did you know?

In the early days of television, location news work was shot on film, which had to be developed and edited in time for the evening news bulletin.

Audio production

Audio production includes radio, talking books and guides and sound production for interactive media. The biggest sub-sector is radio, which is now approaching its hundredth birthday. Although radio has been around for such a long time, some of the biggest changes in working practices have occurred since the early 1990s, with the introduction of digital post-production. Despite the changes, *pre*-production is still as important as it is for the moving image, and the nature of it depends greatly on the type of audio product being made.

Audiences often think radio is just about presenters chatting informally between songs. It all sounds so effortless, most people can't imagine the considerable preparation that goes into a 'sequence programme' like a breakfast show. Most music stations operate a central playlist, organised by a computer program, and the

FIGURE 1.17 *Production may take place in a studio or on location.*

individual programme teams have to work with the songs they are scheduled to play. Presenter chat is often the result of careful research, looking for interesting stories in the press, or seeking information on the Internet. Competitions need to be prepared in advance, perhaps because a number of songs have to be edited together, or questions and answers need working out for a quiz, for instance. There may also be guest interviews to arrange.

Did you know?

The first music sequence programme was launched in 1934, when Martin Block began presenting the *Make Believe Ballroom*, playing records on WNEW/New York.

Most radio stations run newsrooms, or at least contribute to news gathering for the region they cover. A three-minute bulletin is a compilation of several stories, some originating in the local area and some supplied by a national and international news service. Every news story requires careful research and the checking of facts, be it locally or far away, before it can be read on the radio. In some cases interview material and actuality is also included.

Commercial stations funded by advertising must first sell the advertising time to clients, who then commission either the station itself or an agency to produce the adverts. Writing copy for radio commercials requires imagination, creativity and also attention to detail, because they must be both catchy and memorable, as well as accurate in the claims they make and the offers they describe. Once completed, the advertising campaign needs scheduling, so each advert is played at the right time. Then the client needs billing for the airing of their advertisement.

The national BBC networks make programmes that local radio stations could not afford to produce. Comedy programmes such as the original *Little Britain*, science fiction series such as *The Hitchhiker's Guide to the Galaxy* and orchestral concerts by the BBC's own orchestras require vast resources and big budgets to support them. Any programmes requiring large numbers of people – for example, drama, light entertainment or panel discussions produced as outside broadcasts, such as Radio 4's *Any Questions* – require planning, varying amounts of scripting, and, if on location, obtaining permission from the site owners. Transport, catering and security need to be planned for and arranged in advance.

Radio work demands great professionalism – especially when microphones are live – no matter how informal the programme may sound. Recorded programmes can be edited and re-mixed if necessary in post-production. Non-linear editing software is used to remove mistakes, to edit together material that was recorded at different times, and to add music and effects where appropriate.

Key terms

Copy – script material for news or commercials

Actuality – real sound from a location, which helps listeners to imagine a scene or illustrates what is happening

Non-linear editing – this is done using computer software, instead of by cutting audio tape and sticking it back together

Talking books and guides require careful planning, too. Scriptwriting, booking studios and actors and actresses, arranging permission to record copyright material, as well as finding music and sound effects can all be very time-consuming. Inlay cards for the CD cases need to be designed and printed before the finished product can be distributed. Audio production for interactive media purposes uses many of the same processes as talking books and radio, depending on the nature of the sound, how it is to be sourced, and the way it is to be used.

Print production

The print area of the media industry is involved in the production of promotional and advertising materials – such as posters, leaflets, DVD and book covers – as well as the publication of newspapers, magazines and comics. Despite the increase in online information, there is still a huge market for printed products and the print industry will continue to be an important part of the media. For example, the UK book market saw an increase in volume sales of twelve per cent in 2003 with an overall value of over £2.5 billion, and the UK's magazine market has seen a 6.6 per cent year-on-year rise in the number of copies purchased, with more new titles being added each year.

Key terms

Copy – the written content of news reports, magazine articles, etc.

Layout – the way different items are positioned on a page

Image manipulation – the use of computer software to alter images so they look their best on the page

Did you know?

The print industry as a whole employs over 185,000 people in over 12,000 companies throughout the UK.

There are four key stages to the production of any print product. The first is **pre-production**, and in the case of work done for a client, this stage begins with the publication being commissioned. Of course, regular publications continue to be produced on a daily, weekly or monthly basis, depending on how frequently they appear. Every publication has to start somewhere, though, and the first edition of a magazine or a newspaper undergoes an initial period of research and development before its design and content are finally agreed.

After the research and planning stages, **print production** involves the generation of words and graphics, the putting together of these into the desired layout and design, and then the actual printing and collation of the completed product. The original words used in a print product are called copy. Images and graphical information are as important as the copy in communicating the right message and ensuring that the correct target audience notices the product in the first place. For example, there are literally hundreds of magazines on display in most newsagents, and having an image-rich front page that communicates the right message to the potential reader is an important marketing strategy.

Traditional photography, using film and chemical processing, has been largely replaced by the production of digital images using

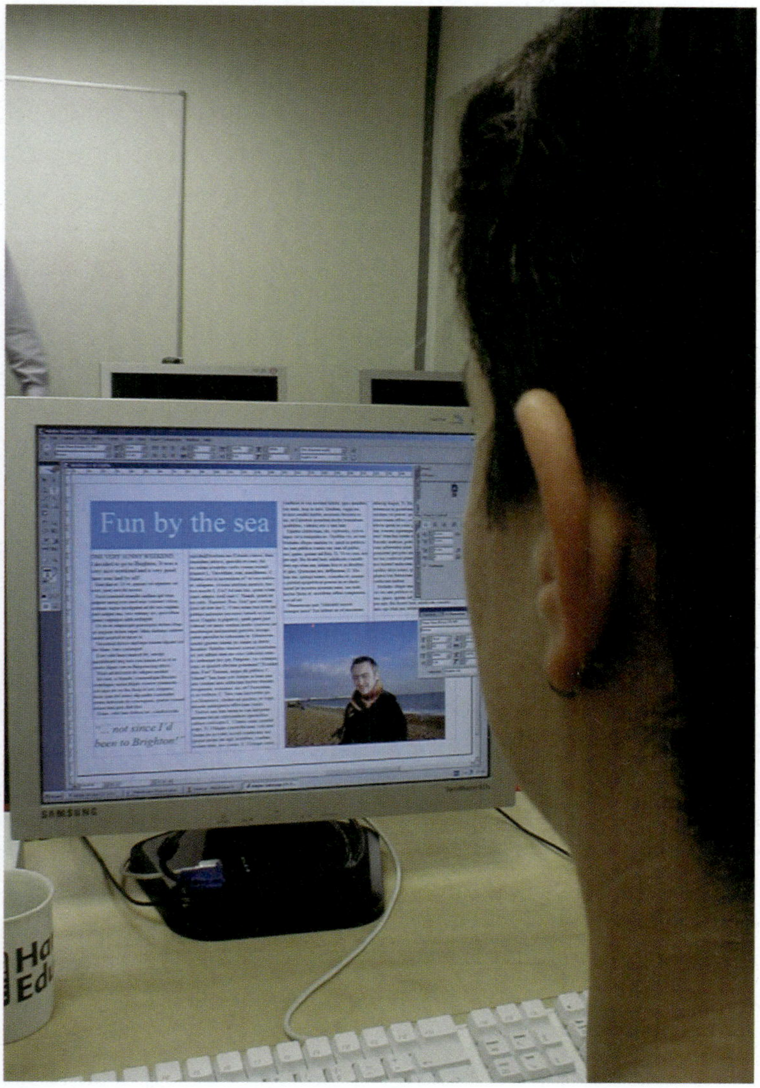

FIGURE 1.18 *Page layout software enables a single person to write copy and lay it out on the page with photos or artwork.*

increasingly powerful digital cameras or scanners. These digitised images can then be imported into image manipulation software, such as *Adobe Photoshop*, to be resized and enhanced according to the specific requirements of the job.

Did you know?

Until the 1980s, page layout was done by typesetters, working by hand to lay down metal letters and spacing according to the editor's instructions.

Pre-press is the generic term for all of the design and layout work that takes place before the product can actually be printed. As in other areas of the media industries, the traditional labour-intensive methods of pre-press layout have been replaced by desktop publishing software packages. This has meant that the hand-crafted skills associated with cut and paste methods have been superseded by the design and software skills needed to operate DTP and design software such as *Adobe InDesign* and *QuarkXpress.*

Print finishing is the final stage in print production. It involves trimming and cutting the pages to the correct size, folding and collating them in the right order, and then using some form of staple or stitching to bind them together in a finished product.

Interactive media production

Websites, video games and CD-ROMs all begin with an initial idea, which has to be fully worked through as an initial proposal, indicating how that idea will look, read and sound to the consumer. This may be in response to a request from a client, in the form of a brief, or it may be an original idea intended to make money from sales or subscriptions – or to promote another product or cause. Usually developed further in a treatment (a detailed description of the content of the proposed production), the product will be carefully targeted at a particular audience or market.

Companies usually want a website to communicate with new and existing customers, while clubs, societies and pressure groups – who may want to change government policy over a particular issue – may want their website to publicise what they do or believe. The purpose of DVDs and CD-ROMs can be to entertain, persuade or to inform – and some do all three. Video and computer games are usually written in order to exploit the vast home enterainment market. Whether on disk or the web, often the purpose is to sell, with cataloguing and purchasing functions that enable customers to view products, select from those most likely to appeal to them and buy them online.

Content production can be simple or complex, depending on the nature of the product. It may include writing, shooting and editing video material, finding and editing audio or creating and manipulating entirely new images, as in the case of video games. These processes are all described in detail in the sections on moving image, audio and print production, so you can read up on them there.

Key terms

Editing – selecting from one source, or from a number of different ones, an appropriate amount of material that fits the brief and enhances a finished product

Authoring – assembling an interactive media product – for example, pulling together the various features in a CD-ROM or a DVD

Putting the various parts of an interactive media product together requires careful selection of the best and most appropriate material, in order to create a quality product that fits the brief. Games need to be extensively tested before release, to identify any problems with them and bugs in the software. They must also be given a rating by the self-regulatory body, the BBFC, which will decide whether they are suitable for children or not. The sales and marketing stages come next, aimed at getting the product to as many members of the target audience as possible.

FIGURE 1.19 *A range of interactive media products.*

Did you know?

One of the first personal computers, the Sinclair ZX80, was plugged into the back of an ordinary television set. It needed extensive programming by the user to perform even the simplest of tasks – such as displaying a simple clock on screen.

Remember

The pre-production and post-production stages are usually just as important as the more glamorous work done in the production stage.

Learning activity 8

✓ Identify the production activities that take place in your chosen company or organisation.

✓✓ Explain which are the 'core' activities – those which are most important to them – and which are secondary.

✓✓✓ Explain why the core activities are the most important ones.

* The production activities may be among those listed in this section of the book, or they may include other, related activities, depending on the organisation and the media area you have chosen.

Working in media organisations

The larger the organisation, the more specialised the people who work there tend to be. They have quite specific jobs in which they become expert. Other parts of the production process are performed by other people, who can bring their own expertise to the next stage. In smaller organisations, staff tend to be spread across more different job roles. This is often because there isn't enough work in one specialised field to keep one person fully occupied all the time. Each person may become expert in a number of roles, as a small organisation probably could not afford to employ people who weren't very busy.

Some very specialised roles are carried out by freelancers who are brought in to perform a particular task for a one-off fee. For example, most actors and actresses get work in broadcasting for a short period of time – it would be uneconomic to employ them to sit around waiting for a suitable part in a drama or commercial to come along.

Key terms

Multi-skilling – having enough expertise in a number of different roles to be able to do all of them to a satisfactory standard

Freelance work – casual or one-off work that is paid on a per item basis

Learning activity 9

- ✓ Identify the different jobs in your chosen company or organisation.
- ✓✓ Explain who performs each activity, who is responsible to whom and why.
- ✱ The following pages will help you to understand the different roles. Remember that some people may carry out a number of different job roles if they are multi-skilled.

Jobs in television and film

Producers are effectively the team leaders, and they report to **executive producers** or the owners of film studios, or in television to **network controllers** who commission the programmes they produce. In the case of corporate video production, the producer may be the owner of the company – and he or she may simply hire freelancers to do other jobs, as and when they are required.

In film production, although the producers are important people in the process and without them a production would not even take place, it is usually the **director** whose name becomes most closely associated with the production. This is because it is the director's job to turn the script into a finished film by interpreting the script, deciding how it should be shot and edited and directing the actors – these are big creative decisions which determine whether or not the film will be a success.

Not surprisingly, the Walt Disneys, Martin Scorseses and Steven Spielbergs of the film world become very famous because of the importance of their roles in creating box office successes. Their successes, though, wouldn't be possible without large numbers of other people performing a number of roles which are specific to the pre-production, production or post-production stages.

Pre-production

Researchers perform some of the most important work, finding out historical facts to be included in a script or researching locations before recces can take place. **Scriptwriters** turn initial ideas into the detailed set of words for presenters and actors to speak, as well as instructions for the people responsible for costume, props, make-up, camera, sound and lighting.

Scriptwriters often become famous too, because when audiences like their stories they will want to see more of their work. It is unusual for any of the other people involved in pre-production, production or post-production to become celebrities.

In news production, **journalists** usually work on their own news stories, but sometimes a number of them may work together on a big story – and they often use researchers to help find out facts or get footage from an archive to be able to show past events as background to something that has just happened.

Production

A television programme in production involves several people, simply because of the large number of tasks that have to be performed simultaneously. Each camera needs a **camera operator**, who will follow instructions from the director in the gallery. A **lighting director**, a **vision mixer** and a **sound mixer** will each follow the requirements of the script and the instructions from the director, to ensure operations run smoothly. On the floor of the studio a **floor manager** will also receive instructions from the gallery, and make sure they are carried out – giving **actors** or **presenters** cues to begin, for example.

A **sound recordist** is an important part of a location team when shooting drama, and **boom operators** can be as necessary away from the studio as in it if microphones have to be kept out of sight. **Runners** perform odd jobs, carrying messages and getting last-minute items to where they are needed On location, **reporters** take crews with them, to operate a camera and make sure the sound is broadcast or recorded correctly. Sometimes they need **interpreters** and even **minders**, too.

Post-production

The various post-production jobs are carried by **editors**, **special effects designers** and **musicians**. **Foley artists** create overlays of sound to produce particular effects and mixes.

Jobs in audio production

As in television and film, **producers** in radio and in audio production studios are effectively the team leaders on each individual programme or project. They report to the owner of a production company or, in the case of a commercial or a BBC local radio station, to the **programme controller**. The title may differ slightly between organisations – some call them **programme directors** and many local BBC stations have **programme organisers**. BBC networks each have a **controller**, who decides on its general direction and sound, commissioning programme proposals from producers and **department heads**. Above them will be **managing directors**, **managing editors** (in BBC local radio) and ultimately a board of **directors** or the BBC's **board of governors**.

CASE STUDY

Sarah Urban

Sarah Urban studied for four years at university doing a Media Production degree. Although her main interest was radio, the varied nature of the course enabled her to develop knowledge and skills in a number of different areas of the media.

Because she did regular work experience for several independent television production companies on reality TV shows, when a first job as a runner came up, she took it immediately and found it very interesting and enjoyable.

Sarah is developing contacts and gaining valuable experience on a temporary contract, while watching out for further opportunities to develop her career.

- What are the main job functions in this role?
- What skills are needed to perform this role successfully?

Sarah Urban

Then there are a number of roles which are specific to the pre-production, production or post-production stages.

Pre-production

Researchers work to a brief from a **producer**, investigating a topic and arranging interviews to be recorded or broadcast live at a later date. Often it will be the producer who does this work, if the programme team is small or it is working to a tight budget. Producers also book studios, hire actors and make the logistical arrangements needed to make a production a success. At the news desk, it is the job of a **reporter** to research and write stories, often preparing reports or 'packages' that use interview material and actuality to add interest. The **editor** then selects stories for inclusion in the next bulletin. A magazine programme might also use a reporter to prepare recorded items or even to report live from an event that will be of interest to the audience.

Scriptwriters work on drama productions, researching facts as they need them – for a historical drama, for example, or one set in the medical world. Music will be scheduled by the **head of music**, who decides what songs should go on the station playlist, and which should come off it, how often they should be played and at what time of day.

Sales executives sell airtime, while **copywriters** write the advertisements for commercial radio stations. Some stations contract out this work to production houses that produce hundreds of commercials each week for several stations at a time. Scheduling the commercials is the job of the **traffic manager**.

Production

Producers usually want to be in the studio – or the control room – while a programme is in production. They can make sure things run smoothly and to time. **Presenters** link different items together, whether music or speech, and carry out live interviews with studio guests or 'down the line'. A complicated programme, like a drama or a magazine, might have a **technical operator** or an **engineer** operating the equipment (a **studio manager** or a **broadcast assistant** in the BBC).

CASE STUDY

Katy McDonald

Katy McDonald is a radio journalist. She studied for a Media Production degree at the University of Sunderland, and stayed on there for a further year to complete a post-graduate course – an MA in journalism.

Katy McDonald

As a student, she did some work experience at Sky Television, and then talked her way into Metro Radio in Newcastle, where she began by working for free. After a short while she was being paid to do the technical operation on the Saturday afternoon sports programme and a five nights per week phone-in on Metro's sister station, Magic 1152.

As soon as she got her qualifications in journalism – including the National Council for the Training of Journalists (NCTJ) certificate – Katy got a full-time job on the news desk, where she quickly became morning news editor, compiling and presenting bulletins on Metro and Magic.

- What are the main job functions in this role?
- What skills are needed to perform this role successfully?

Studios producing talking books and guides and anyone undertaking audio production for multimedia use will employ people with similar job titles because their roles are so similar.

Commercials are made by **creative producers**, who take the script that has been agreed by the client and use **voiceover artists** to record them. Often in radio there will be a **station sound producer** in charge of recording jingles and station promotions, mixing items for competitions and producing other features for use in sequence programmes.

Post-production

Any pre-recorded item can be edited and mixed or remixed with other audio in post-production, so depending on the type of product, it could be the **producer**, the **creative producer** in the case of commercials, a **reporter** or a **studio manager** who puts the finishing touches to it.

Jobs in print production

Editors are effectively the team leaders in print production, and they report to a **publisher** or, in the case of many newspapers, a **proprietor**. This person is the owner of the company – some newspaper proprietors lead colourful lives that make them the subjects of news stories, while others are rarely heard of because they choose to live discreetly, away from the limelight. In this sector of the media industry, there are a number of roles that are specific to the pre-production, production or post-production stages.

Pre-production

Planning the design, style and layout of a new publication – and in the case of many leaflets, brochures and catalogues, that means every commission – is the job of specialised **designers**. They have to make sure the look and content of the finished product meets the commission brief.

Production

Journalists are employed by the newspaper and magazine industries, and **copywriters** by the advertising and promotional industries, to produce the words that will help communicate the product's message to its target audience. Journalists and copywriters often work under a lot of pressure and to very tight deadlines, and need to be creative and skilled wordsmiths with a good, broad knowledge base. Sometimes their work will require the assistance of specialist **researchers**, and the biggest newspapers employ **librarians** to manage their in-house libraries of information, past editions and cuttings.

In newspapers and magazines it is the **editors**, and **sub-editors** under them, who check and refine the copy produced and manipulate it if necessary to fit the space available. In reality, most newspaper editors simply don't have the time to be involved in the production of every page, and they will delegate a lot of this work to **section editors**, each of whom will take responsibility for a section of a publication, such as the travel, motoring, gardening, business or entertainment pages.

A few of the larger companies still employ in-house **photographers**, but most now use freelance photographers with the skills required for particular projects, or they buy images from a photographic agency.

It is the role of the pre-press **designers** and **art workers** to ensure that the words, images and layout devices are combined in an effective manner.

The final stage in production is the printing. Digital printing methods are replacing the more established methods such as offset litho and gravure, and this is having an impact on the number of **printers** needed by printing companies to run the presses and on the skills that they require.

Post-production

Once the product has been printed, then the **print finishers** ensure that sorting, folding, and packaging are carried out according to the brief.

CASE STUDY

Dan Walker

Dan left school with a love of drawing, colour and graphics. He had done well in his GCSEs and his careers officer suggested a career in printing. Dan started as a trainee print manager at a local print company and attended college on a full-time basis for three years. He then spent two years on day release at college while working for the print company and learning skills on the job.

Dan Walker

Now Dan runs a multimillion pound digital printing press that prints a wide range of products. He has to work to tight deadlines and accurate colour tolerances. His everyday work includes printing posters and tour books for bands such as Coldplay, DVD box set covers such as for *Lord of the Rings*, cartons for packaging and leaflets for major companies.

Dan uses his skills to colour-match exact customer requirements for a print product. He has ultimate responsibility for ensuring that the print product he produces matches the design provided by the graphic designer. Dan's skills have been developed through working on a wide variety of print products and training both on the job and through his college course.

- What are the main job functions in this role?
- What skills are needed to perform this role successfully?

Jobs in interactive media production

People who work in interactive media production tend to be so multi-skilled that they can perform most functions themselves. Many of them work to a brief from a client, either as a freelancer or working within a section of a large company – for example, a public relations department. One of the biggest interactive media production centres is BBC Online, which provides web support for a vast range of the corporation's television and radio programming. The BBC website is one of the most visited websites in the world – producing such a large quantity of relevant and up-to-date material for people to download involves large numbers of **content producers**, **bulletin board editors** and **designers** who work in teams that report to the **producers** of individual programmes. Some specialise in turning audio and video produced for broadcast into web downloads.

Pre-production

Because much of the content has been originated for other purposes, writing copy, for instance, may have been the job of someone unconnected with the organisation's interactive media operation. Radio or television reporters may bear in mind that the stories they are researching and presenting will be reused on the website, but this is unlikely to be their main concern – especially when they are preparing to speak live 'on air'. The tri-media nature of the BBC's many newsrooms means that almost any story can be exploited in different ways for the different media outlets the corporation operates.

The PR department of a non-media organisation may produce a printed in-house newspaper, marketing leaflets and press releases. The same copywriters could be working on both print and online materials.

The process may be overseen by an **editor**, or the **copywriters** may simply report to the **head of marketing**, a **director** of the company or someone else who occupies a senior, but apparently unrelated, position.

However, a lot of interactive media production is original, and CD-ROM and DVD content is very often produced for sale or for marketing purposes to specific audiences. The production process will begin with an idea being explored by a **commissioning editor** or a **publisher** – the product will be proposed and researched and then contracted out to **authors** to write, in the same way as is done for new books. An **editor** may control quality, organise **proofreaders** and commission a **picture editor** to find appropriate illustrative material – which could of course include video or audio material created by specialised **producers**.

Production and post-production

As multi-skilling is very common in interactive media production, it may be difficult to distinguish between production and post-production. A **web designer** may create the 'look' of a site or a page and then hand it over to someone else to administer, while a **web master**'s role is ongoing, managing a site on a continuous basis.

DVD and CD-ROM production also depends heavily on design. The authoring process carried out by the **producer** includes gathering and editing material, then physically positioning it within the product. Packaging material, such as inlay cards and accompanying booklets and manuals, will be the responsibility of **designers**, **proofreaders** and **copywriters**.

Conditions of employment

Unlike students who undertake work experience in order to gain experience and who are prepared to work for free initially, most professionals in the media industry do expect to be paid for their skills and knowledge, ideas and creativity, and time and effort. Although the work is often fun and exciting, as in any career, it can become routine

CASE STUDY
Thomas Holmes

Thomas attended a college in Nottingham to take a National Diploma in Media. He was interested in computers, photography and video production. After finishing the National Diploma he went to university to complete a Bachelor of Arts degree in Media Production (Video and New Media).

Thomas now works as a freelance web designer, producing material for a wide range of clients. He works from his office at home and uses broadband technology to communicate with clients. He uses a wide range of hardware and software to produce high-quality web designs. He is also working in the area of DVD menu design and authoring for a DVD production company.

Thomas Holmes

Now Thomas is developing his own web hosting facility, to ensure he has control of his web designs from initial design to integration into the worldwide web. His business is growing because clients have seen the quality of his work and recommended him to their colleagues. Thomas is considering taking further courses to keep his skills up to date with developments in technology and software.

- What are the main job functions in this role?
- What skills are needed to perform this role successfully?

FIGURE 1.20 *Not everyone who wants to present a programme will be suitable.*

and the initial thrill of a job that uses the latest technology and perhaps involves working with celebrities can soon wear off. That is especially so if you are underpaid and have difficulty in affording life's essentials and the kind of treats we all need from time to time. Some work in the media can be dangerous, too, for example when a reporter is covering a war or the aftermath of an emergency, and at times like that media workers will feel a particular need to be valued by the people they work for – and paid properly.

An obvious exception is community radio, where volunteers work for free, but they can usually only manage to do so because it is not their main occupation, and they have another job which provides an income. Some community radio stations are staffed by people with particular social needs, such as refugees or the homeless, and those who become involved with the station on a regular basis may be supported by state benefits in some way.

Types of contract

As we have already seen, paid work is undertaken by staff or freelancers. Even unpaid volunteers may have to sign a contract, agreeing to keep to certain rules or codes of conduct. In a media organisation, paid staff may be either full-time or part-time, meaning they work for the organisation either all week or just for part of it.

Key terms

Staff contract – a legal document between an employer and an employee, which sets out the employee's set hours, pay and conditions and annual leave entitlement

Freelance contract – a legal document agreeing a fee for the completion of a particular task or project

Their relationship with the company is formally established by a contract of employment, which they will have had to sign when they first accepted the job. In the contract will be information detailing their obligations to the organisation and the organisation's obligations to them. These obligations are most likely to include pay, holiday entitlement, hours to be worked and where the work is to be done, and any pension contributions to be deducted from the pay. Current good practice includes referring to a job specification that was sent to all applicants for the job when it was first advertised – as well as listing the duties of the post, this will indicate who the employee's line manager is.

There may be other specific terms, such as rules about not smoking at work and perhaps about complying with rules on equal opportunities and the regulators' codes of practice. There will be a period of notice which the employee must give the employer if they want to leave the organisation – for example, to take up a better or more highly paid job elsewhere.

Staff contracts may be either permanent or temporary. A temporary contract means that the employment is for a fixed term only – perhaps to cover someone else's absence on maternity or paternity leave, for example. The employee cannot expect to be employed after the end of the contract, unless he or she is offered a new contract – this could be for the same job or for a different one.

There are considerable advantages to having a full-time contract, rather than a temporary one. The most obvious is that you can decide when *you* want to leave the organisation, rather than your job finishing at a predetermined time when you might not have found a new job to go to. A full-time contract will often allow you to join a company pension scheme and some employers give employees longer holidays once they have worked for them for a certain length of time. Working on temporary contracts, even if these are renewed over several years with the same organisation, means you may miss out on benefits such as these.

Key terms

Human resources department – the part of an organisation that deals with staffing issues, such as recruitment, employment contracts, pension contributions and pay

Trade union – an organisation formed to protect the interests of staff when dealing with their employers. Members pay monthly fees and then may benefit from a range of services, including help in any dispute with their employer. Some employers choose not to recognise trade unions, or they may have a preferred union that they deal with on an exclusive basis

It is worth reading a contract of employment very carefully before signing it, and raising any queries with the personnel (or human resources) department of the organisation – or even seeking specialist advice from a solicitor, your local Citizens' Advice Bureau or a trade union.

Freelance contracts relate only to the performance of specific tasks, and a typical freelancer might be working on different contracts for more than one organisation at the same time. Freelance work offers no job security or benefits beyond what is specified in the current contract so, again, it is important to check the contract before signing.

Some people working in the media like the flexibility of working on temporary or freelance contracts, because they can move around different organisations and choose when they work. Sometimes, because the work is less secure than a full-time staff post, organisations have to offer higher rates of pay in order to attract the right people to do the work. In broadcasting, for example, presenters may be hired for only a single series of programmes, but be paid very generously – especially if they are already famous names.

Not everyone who works freelance manages to find work all the time. There may be some long periods of unemployment. However, busy freelancers are able to pick and choose between different jobs, turning down work that doesn't pay so well and discriminating between interesting and less interesting work, or people they do and don't want to work with.

Moving around the industry certainly means meeting and working with a greater variety of people, and one way to further your career is to build up a long list of contacts – people you have worked with in the past, who might be helpful when you are looking for more work. This is called 'networking' because over time you develop a network of supportive contacts.

Michael Foan, *Broadcaster and Writer*

Income and expenditure account for the year ended 30th April 2006

	£
INCOME FOR WORK DONE:	22068
Deduct: EXPENSES	
Motor running costs	2011
Telephone (business use)	291
Work clothes for professional appearances	301
Stationery, postage & sundries	274
CDs & DVDs purchased for professional use	451
Reference books, etc.	101
Computer expenses	30
Use of room as office	230
Accountancy fees	180
	3869
NET SURPLUS OF INCOME OVER EXPENDITURE:	18199

FIGURE 1.21 *The accounts of a freelance writer and broadcaster.*

TYPE OF CONTRACT	TEMPORARY STAFF	PERMANENT STAFF	FREELANCE	VOLUNTEER
Paid	✔	✔	✔	
Medium- to long-term stability		✔		
Increased choice for worker	✔		✔	
Greater likelihood of variety	✔		✔	
Greater opportunities for networking	✔		✔	
Better holiday entitlement		✔		
Sick pay	✔	✔		
Access to company pension scheme		✔		
Best chance of trade union assistance		✔		
Self-employed accounts needed			✔	
Career development opportunities		✔		
Good experience for beginners	✔	✔	✔	✔

FIGURE 1.22 *The advantages and disadvantages of different types of contract.*

Another disadvantage of working freelance is that you have to keep accounts and file tax returns for your own 'business'. Many freelancers pay accountants to do this for them, and this cost to their business can be offset against tax they owe, as can other costs that they incur in their work.

Everyone who works has to pay National Insurance. This is a scheme run by the state, which helps to finance sick pay when you are ill (does not apply to self-employed people), medical treatment when you need it and a basic old age pension when you reach retirement age. It is wise to contribute to a 'top-up' pension as soon as you can afford to.

Did you know?

Several of today's top radio and television presenters worked for free as volunteers in hospital radio or at their local radio station, helping out behind the scenes.

Many media organisations arrange work experience for school pupils and students.

Career development

Very few people begin working in the media industry in senior positions. Most begin in low-paid, low-status jobs and work their way up their own personal 'career ladder'. This is fine for young people who don't yet have mortgages and families to provide for.

Climbing up the career ladder doesn't happen automatically, though, and it is important to develop the skills to identify opportunities and submit a successful application in order to benefit from them. Networking helps, but so do being well qualified, learning new skills and getting to grips with changes in technology and working practices as soon as possible.

Portfolios and demos

In most media jobs, maintaining a portfolio of your best work means you will be able to demonstrate your suitability for promotion or an opportunity in another organisation without delay. This might mean keeping cuttings of stories written for printed publications, keeping recordings of moving image or audio work,

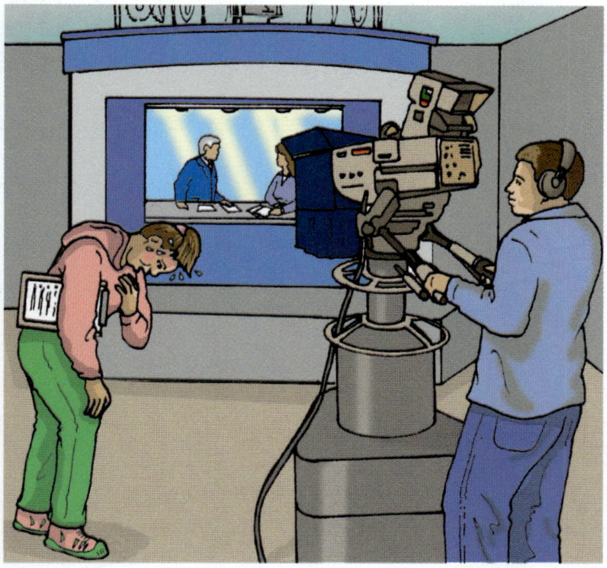

FIGURE 1.23 *A good way to start working in television is as a runner.*

or keeping examples of interactive media that you have worked on. Unless a specific job advertisement asks for more, audio and video demos should be short, three to four minutes maximum, because the people who will be deciding which applicants to put on a shortlist for interview will probably be very busy, and they won't be able to set aside much time for trawling through lots of material that has been sent in.

Only include your very best work in your demo or a portfolio – the moment the selectors come across anything of a poor standard, they will almost certainly move on to the next application. And only submit copies, not your original work. Presentation is crucial. Your covering letter and any application form must be very well set out. Disks and tapes must be neatly and clearly labelled with your name and contact details, in case they become separated from the rest of the material, and work on paper or card needs special protection to prevent it getting spoilt.

Remember

This is an introductory-level course, and studying the media for longer in higher education (for a degree or an HND) will greatly increase your employability.

Preparing a CV

Most job adverts require an up-to-date CV and it is a good idea to have one ready in case an opportunity comes up unexpectedly. Your CV should contain all the following information, laid out clearly and neatly and without any errors of spelling or grammar:

- name and contact details
- education
- qualifications
- work experience
- employment history
- training undertaken
- hobbies and interests.

The last section is particularly important when you are just starting a career and don't have much work experience to include, as having a number of interests outside your studies shows that you are a well-rounded individual who is more likely to relate well to others in the workplace. As people get older and more experienced at work, the earlier years become less important. Employers may be concerned about any unexplained gaps in your history, though. They might think you are hiding something. Be truthful when applying for jobs, or you risk being caught out at interview or, even worse, being caught later and dismissed.

Key terms

CV – *stands for curriculum vitae*, which is a Latin term for a detailed list of information about your life so far

Being interviewed

Getting an interview is often quite an achievement in the very competitive media industry, because many jobs are hotly contested. However, a lot of people who apply for media jobs may not be particularly well qualified or experienced, so having a strong educational background and relevant experience will make you stand out from the crowd.

CURRICULUM VITAE

Name:	Michael Foan
Age:	24
Qualifications and dates:	B.A. (Hons.) in Media Production (Television & Radio) 2/1, University of Sunderland, 2004 Advanced GCE in Media (A) 2001 Advanced GCE in English (A) 2001 Advanced Subsidiary GCE in History (C) 2000 GCSE English (A) 1999 GCSE Maths (C) 1999 GCSE History (A) 1999 GCSE French (C) 1999 GCSE Geography (B) 1999
Employment history:	Presenter, Oldtown FM, June 2004-present, evening show Station Assistant, Oldtown FM, September 2001-June 2004, working on Saturday sports & music show Work experience at Oldtown FM, 2 weeks in August 2001 Shelf filler, Bestco supermarket, Oldtown, January 1999-August 2001

Interests:	Music, sport and writing. I have written four magazine articles for the music press, as well as my first novel (currently available for publication).
Other experience:	Duke of Edinburgh's Award (Silver) Oldtown orienteering club member since 1999

FIGURE 1.24 *A typical CV.*

An interview is a chance to show yourself at your best, so prepare for it – even practise being interviewed – and try to anticipate the kinds of questions you will be asked. Even very experienced workers have to revise their interview technique if it has been a long time since they applied for a job.

Did you know?

A 2001 survey of workers in broadcasting, multimedia and film found that:

- 60% had joined the workforce since 1994
- 50% were working on a freelance basis
- 30% were graduates in media subjects
- 30% had a post-graduate qualification

Source: Skillset and the DCMS AV Industries Training Group

Getting started

The survey quoted above also asked employers in the industry what they wanted from new recruits. They said they wanted them to:

* distinguish themselves from the pack
* be multi-skilled where relevant (for example in newsrooms), but specialised for many other roles
* maintain a willingness to learn, work hard and be flexible over working practices
* be enthusiastic and not arrive thinking they know it all
* be disciplined
* balance common sense with creativity.

Reasonable employers will understand that you cannot be expected to know everything at the start of your career. But they will expect that you understand the contexts within which you will be working and know how you will fit into the bigger picture of the organisation and the wider industry around you.

It does seem that employers in the media industry want a lot from their workers – but you have a right to be treated fairly in return. That means not being exploited, having equal opportunities whatever your gender, your ethnic and social background and whether or not you have any disability. Fairness at work also means others have the right to expect the same from you.

Even very experienced graduates with media degrees may find adapting to the world of work challenging. For a start, they are expected to turn up punctually every day, and to stay behind late if something needs finishing off for a deadline. It can be a big shock, too, to have only four weeks of holiday a year, plus bank holidays or days off in lieu of weekends or evenings worked.

Learning activity 10

✓ Investigate the conditions of employment for the main pre-production, production and post production jobs in your chosen company or organisation.

✓✓ Present your findings in detail.

✓✓✓ Explain any differences you find between roles or departments.

* You may find it helpful to interview some of the workers in the organisation, asking about their conditions and what they think of them. You may want to ask questions that will help you with Learning activity 11 at the same time.

Career pathways

Depending on where in the production processes you begin, there are a variety of different pathways that are possible in each sector of the media industry. Sometimes a freelancer working from home will be tempted to join the staff of a company. Equally, permanent staff may decide to go freelance – this tends to happen when companies run into financial difficulty and have to make a number of employees redundant. This can be very distressing at the time, but sometimes a forced change of career path can open up new opportunities. Often there is financial compensation for redundancy, which is sometimes enough to purchase equipment and make the first few months as a freelancer easier financially.

Figures 1.25 to 1.29 illustrate some typical career pathways in a selection of different types of media organisation. Some have been simplified for reasons of space. Of course, some people make what are called 'sideways' moves into a different field or a parallel process, either because they want a change of scene or direction, or because they are being flexible and responding to change in order to make themselves more employable. There are, of course, no guarantees that you will make it to the top – especially as there tend to be fewer senior jobs than junior ones.

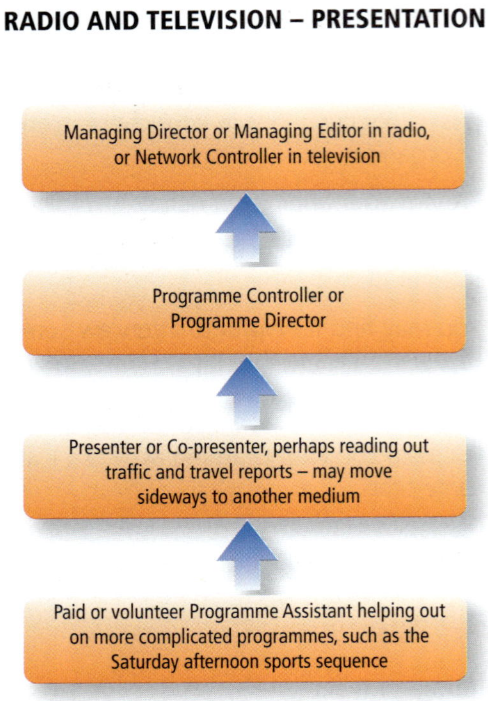

FIGURE 1.25 *Career paths in radio or TV presenting.*

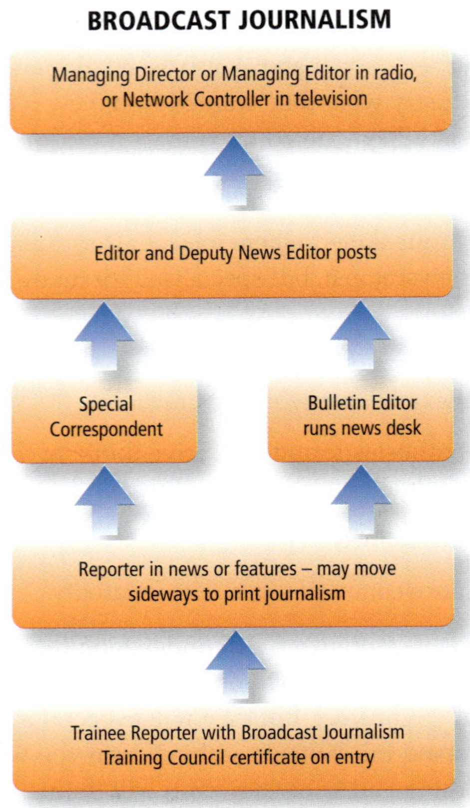

FIGURE 1.26 *Career paths in broadcast journalism.*

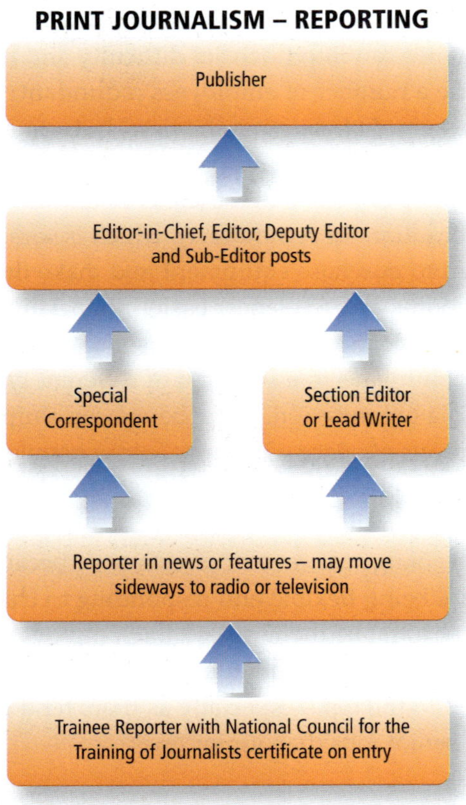

FIGURE 1.27 *Career paths in print journalism.*

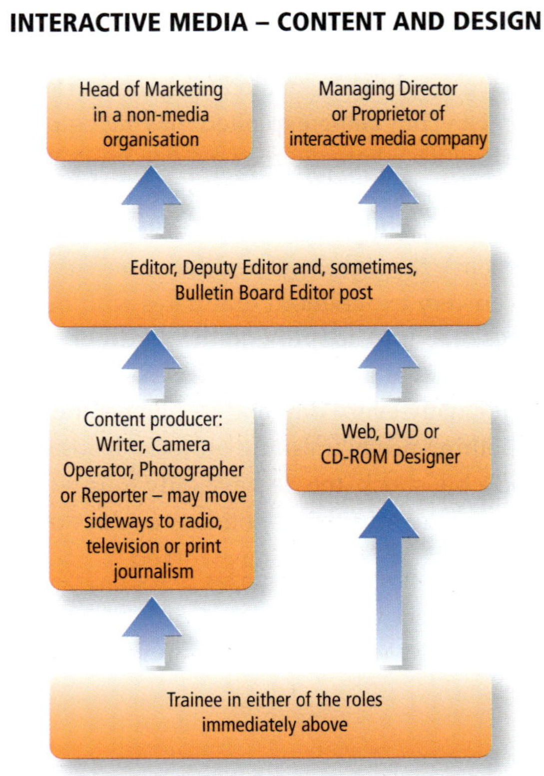

FIGURE 1.28 *Career paths in interactive media content and design.*

MOVING IMAGE PRODUCTION – TELEVISION AND FILM

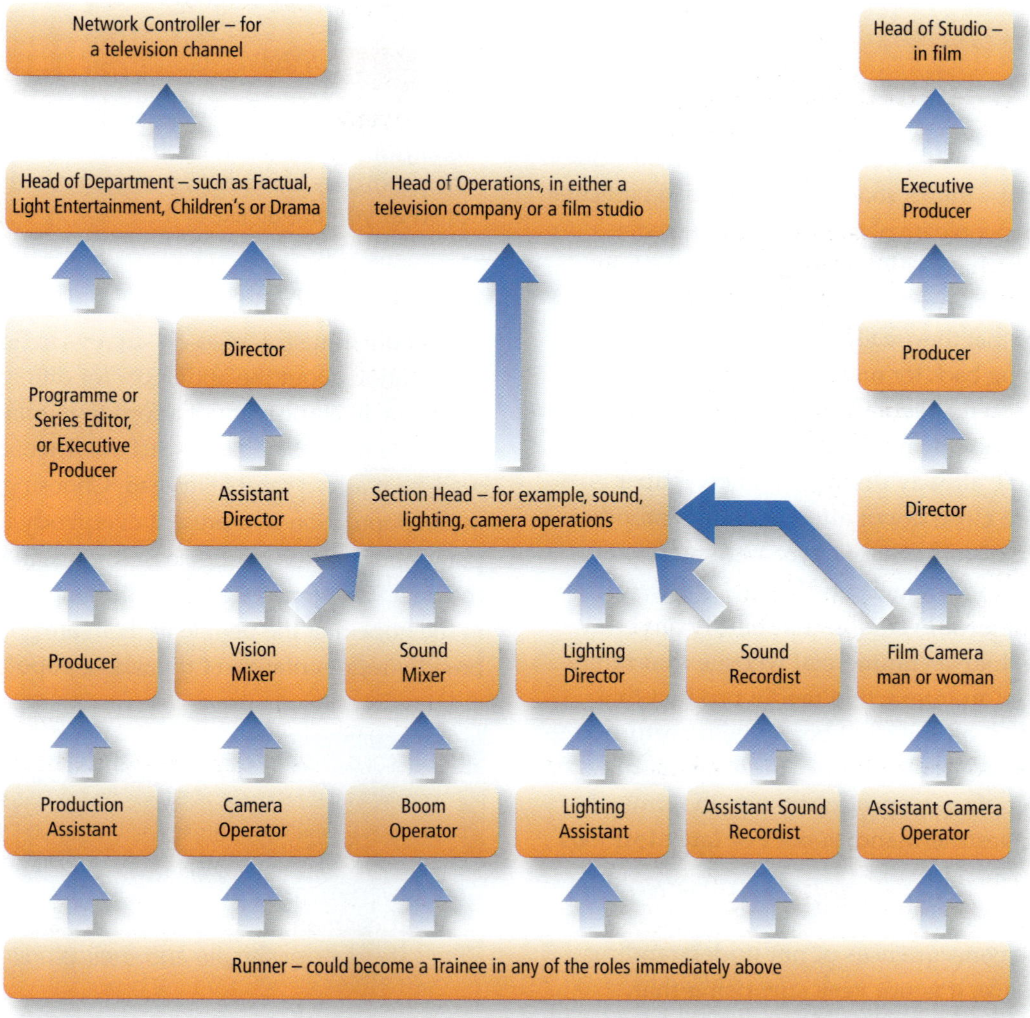

FIGURE 1.29 *Career paths in moving image production.*

As people climb higher up the hierarchy in an organisation, they usually earn more with each promotion. That is a considerable incentive for most people to develop their careers. Unfortunately, getting a management post often means leaving behind the kind of interesting production roles that originally attracted people into the media industry. By contrast, some television and radio presenters earn many times more than their managers do.

Learning activity 11

- ✓ Complete your study of employment in a media company or organisation by identifying and explaining the main career paths through it.
- ✓✓ Use examples of actual people working there now, and people who have left, to add detail to your investigation.
- ✓✓✓ Find out and show how a number of people plan to develop their careers.
- * Your interviews for Learning activity 10 will help you complete this task.

1.3 How media texts are constructed in relation to their audiences

The media industry – that is, the people who work in it and run it – thinks about its audiences in particular ways. The people involved in making a media product of whatever kind have to think carefully about who will want to consume the product and make sure that they really will like it and want to keep coming back for more. As we have seen, if audiences do not want the products, the organisations which produce them will soon go out of business.

We have already discussed a newspaper that had to close down after just a few months. Imagine a film that earns very little money at the box office, a television channel with very few viewers or a radio station that hardly anybody listens to. Like a commercial website that rarely gets hits or an interactive media product that collects dust on the shelf before being returned to the distributor's warehouse, these are all disasters for the people who produce them, in terms of wasted investment and, sooner or later, lost jobs.

Thinking about audiences

Given the consequences of not understanding the audience, it is not very surprising that media producers try very hard to know as much as possible about their audiences. One major problem is that most audiences are invisible at the time of point of consumption. Some audiences can be physically counted – attendance at a football ground, the number of people who pass through an art gallery or how many cars pass by an advertising billboard, for example. But we simply don't know how many people tune in to a television or radio programme or how many people read a single copy of a newspaper. It may be bought and read by just one person, and then dumped or recycled – or it may find its way into the waiting room of a doctor's surgery, and then be read by dozens of people in the course of a normal day. Consumption of interactive media products can be measured up to a point, but once an item has been sold or downloaded from a website or over a mobile phone, it is difficult to detect any secondary use of it by people it is subsequently passed on to.

Think it over...

How often do you watch television with your family or with a group of friends? How would the producers know how many of you there are, or what you are all like?

Audience surveys

The media industry relies on surveys to find out information about the audiences for different products. It simply cannot afford to regularly ask everyone what they have watched, listened to or read, so it asks a sample instead. Choosing a sample of the population to represent everybody in the population results in huge cost savings in collecting the data. The samples are usually carefully chosen in the hope that the people in them are going to be broadly representative of the whole population.

Did you know?

The only time anyone tries to count the whole population of the United Kingdom is every ten years – for the National Census. In 2001 it cost the government £255 million to find out who lives at each address, how old they are, whether they are male or female and their ethnic origin.

The four most important audience surveys are carried out on a regular basis by the following four organisations:

* BARB – the Broadcasters' Audience Research Board uses set-top meters in a sample of homes to measure what everyone who lives there watches on television and for how long.
* RAJAR – Radio Joint Audience Research finds out what a sample group listen to on the radio and for how long.
* ABC – the Audit Bureau of Circulations checks how many newspapers and magazines are *sold*, how many are given away free and how many are returned unsold.
* NRS – the National Readership Survey interviews a sample of people in order to find out if they have *read* any newspapers or magazines.

The different functions of the ABC and NRS address the fact that more than one person might read a single copy of a publication, as discussed earlier. More information about all these organisations is included in Unit 2.

Learning activity 12

✓ Use a search engine to find the current websites of the four research bodies listed above, and use information from the websites to explain what they do.

✓✓ Choose the one that is most closely related to the industry sector you have been studying and use the audience data on the website to draw conclusions about the products in that sector. For example, which are the most popular, and which are the least popular?

✓✓✓ Using the information in this section, consider what the main problems with the way the organisation collects data might be. Explain any positive aspects as well.

* Audience research data can seem complicated because there is so much detail. There is some more detailed information on the next few pages to help you understand it.

Another major problem, though, is that nobody knows how accurate these surveys actually are. NRS and, until recently, RAJAR have relied on interviewing people about what they have read or asking them to complete a 'listening diary'. This method relies entirely on people's powers of recall, and some people may be too forgetful or too careless to provide very accurate data. You might think that electronic meters are very accurate, but sometimes people fall asleep in front of the television, when they would still be counted as watching the programme tuned in to. When a participant in this data collection method enters the room with the TV in it, they are supposed to key a personal code into a handset to tell the meter they are present, and then to sign out when they leave the room for whatever reason. If they forget to do this, the data will be inaccurate.

RAJAR tested several types of audio meter, which are worn by the sample group – each designed to look like a wristwatch or a pager or built into a mobile phone. The meters detected some radio stations the 'listeners' couldn't

Title(s) (Publisher)	Average Net Circulation
News of the World (News International Newspapers Ltd) 27-Feb-2006 to 02-Apr-2006	3,457,436
The Sun (News International Newspapers Ltd) 27-Feb-2006 to 02-Apr-2006	3,110,999
The Daily Mail (Associated Newspapers Ltd) 27-Feb-2006 to 02-Apr-2006	2,397,768
The Mail on Sunday (Associated Newspapers Ltd) 27-Feb-2006 to 02-Apr-2006	2,270,874
Daily Mirror / Daily Record - Group Certificate (Trinity Mirror plc) 27-Feb-2006 to 02-Apr-2006	2,076,459
Daily Mirror (Trinity Mirror plc) 27-Feb-2006 to 02-Apr-2006	1,634,584
Sunday Mirror (Trinity Mirror plc) 27-Feb-2006 to 02-Apr-2006	1,447,150
The Sunday Times (News International Newspapers Ltd) 27-Feb-2006 to 02-Apr-2006	1,356,042
The Daily Telegraph (Telegraph Group Limited) 27-Feb-2006 to 02-Apr-2006	901,491
Sunday Express (Express Newspapers) 27-Feb-2006 to 02-Apr-2006	894,364
The People (Trinity Mirror plc) 27-Feb-2006 to 02-Apr-2006	849,123

Source: ABC

Average Issue Readership Latest 12 Months-Jan05-Dec05		
	Total	
UNWEIGHTED SAMPLE	35937	
EST.POPULATION 15+(000s)	47771	
	000s	%
Daily Newspapers-6 Day AIR		
The Sun	8138	17.0
Daily Mirror/Record	5322	11.1
Daily Mirror	4148	8.7
Daily Record	1234	2.6
Daily Mail	5635	11.8
The Daily Telegraph	2159	4.5
Daily Express	1977	4.1
The Times	1811	3.8
Daily Star	1778	3.7
The Guardian	1222	2.6
The Independent	705	1.5
Financial Times	391	0.8
Racing Post	254	0.5

Source: NRS

FIGURE 1.30 *Audience data for newspapers, from the ABC (left) and NRS (right).*

remember hearing, and some people in the sample forgot to pick up the meters when they woke up in the morning and wear them in the bathroom.

As well as the measuring system used, the sample itself can cause problems. If there are too many people of one 'type' and too few of another, their responses will distort the data collected. Because each person in the sample represents many other people, even one person making uncharacteristic choices actually misrepresents large numbers of people.

Did you know?

In the 1990s, radio listening was only measured using special 'diaries', which respondents completed over a fixed period, noting down all their radio listening. More recently, electronic devices have been used to identify which radio stations respondents have been exposed to, and store the data for experts to analyse. Unfortunately for RAJAR, the different methods produce very different results, so knowing which to trust presents particular problems, and highlights the unreliability of much audience research.

The table in Figure 1.31 shows how the bigger the size of the sample – and the greater the cost of doing the survey – the fewer people each person surveyed has to represent. For example, in 2003 the BARB survey used 11,614 people, so each one surveyed represented 4,806 of us.

	BARB	RAJAR	NRS
Size of sample	11,614	226,185	34,931
Ratio of population size to sample size	4,806:1	217:1	1,357:1

Sources: BARB, RAJAR, NRS websites, 10 October 2003

FIGURE 1.31 *The size of a sample in audience research affects how many of the whole population each participant represents.*

RAJAR's audience survey is one of the biggest and most complicated in the world. Also in 2003 another organisation was researching radio and television together, using a device they called the 'audiometer'. Its sample was only 2,080, so each person in it represented 21,652 of us.

For all the problems of audience research, it is much better to have some even moderately reliable information about audiences, than to have none at all. Most people in the media industry take the audience data that are produced very seriously and are prepared to spend a lot of money on collecting and processing the data. They have to invest in audience research in order to demonstrate the size of their audiences to potential advertisers.

The most easily accessible audience research data, which you will by now have found on the Internet, use certain key terms that you will have to learn to make sense of it all. **Reach** and **share** relate to the size of the audience and, of course, broadcasters also want to know how long their audiences are watching or listening to their output for. The longer they are listening, the bigger the share of the market the station or channel has – that is partly because when someone is listening to Radio 1, for example, they probably aren't listening to another station at the same time. So that means more hours for Radio 1 and fewer for everyone else. This makes the industry very competitive. Every time a TV channel or radio station increases its share, someone else's share goes down to make room for it, because the total must always add up to one hundred per cent.

FIGURE 1.32 *Some types of audience research are more reliable than others.*

Key terms

Respondent – someone who provides responses in a survey

Reach – how many people the product 'reaches' – this could relate to a single issue or programme or it could relate to a whole radio station or television channel over a fixed period, such as a week or a month

Average hours – how long the station or channel is consumed over a fixed period – this figure indicates how long audiences are listening or viewing

Share – put simply, how large a slice of the market that product takes – the bigger the share, the better!

Audience research organisations provide their paying customers with much more detailed information than they release to the public on their websites and in publications such as *Media Guardian, Screen International, Broadcast* and *The Radio Magazine*. Television producers can get 'overnight' figures from BARB, showing how popular – or unpopular – yesterday's programme was. In contrast, audience figures for print products take a long time to arrive.

Just before they receive the figures can be a very tense time for media employees, as unpopular programmes or presenters can be quickly shunted into off-peak parts of the schedule. Whole series can be cancelled and presenters can be fired if they perform very badly. Sometimes the management of the organisation might be replaced, if the parent company or the shareholders feel the results are disastrous. Newspapers and magazines also suffer financially if their circulation figures fall, or their readership drops significantly, because they, too, depend on advertising. Advertisers buy both space and airtime on the basis of the cost per thousand viewers, readers or listeners.

We will be revisiting the subject of audience research in more detail in Unit 2.

Think it over...

Privately owned companies need audience data to show to advertisers. But why does the BBC, which isn't financed by advertising, also invest in audience research? You can find the answer in section 1.1!

STATION	PERIOD	ADULT 15+ (000s)	WEEKLY REACH (000s)	%	AVERAGE HOURS Head	AVERAGE HOURS Listener	TOTAL HOURS (000s)	SHARE OF LISTENING %
BBC Radio 1	Q	49,377	10,294	21	2.0	9.5	97,446	9.2
BBC Radio 2	Q	49,377	13,252	27	3.4	12.8	170,049	16.0
BBC Radio 3	Q	49,377	1,973	4	0.3	6.4	12,694	1.2
BBC Radio 4	Q	49,377	9,318	19	2.5	13.4	125,100	11.8
BBC Radio FIVE LIVE	Q	49,377	5,721	12	0.9	7.8	44,740	4.2
BBC Radio FIVE LIVE (incl. SPORTS EXTRA)	Q	49,377	5,777	12	0.9	7.9	45,618	4.3
FIVE LIVE SPORTS EXTRA	Q	49,377	460	1	–	1.9	878	0.1
BBC 6 Music	Q	49,377	354	1	–	5.4	1,911	0.2
1Xtra from the BBC	Q	49,377	352	1	–	4.3	1,527	0.1
BBC 7	Q	49,377	600	1	0.1	4.8	2,902	0.3
BBC World Service	Q	49,377	1,353	3	0.2	5.7	7,705	0.7
BBC Asian Network UK	Q	49,377	420	1	0.1	7.8	3,268	0.3

FIGURE 1.33 *Radio audience data from RAJAR for the third quarter of 2005.* Source: RAJAR/IPSOS-RSL

FIGURE 1.34 *Electronic measurement of audiences can sometimes present problems.*

Remember

Audience research may not be perfect – in fact, sometimes it may be misleading – but it is far better for the media industry to have some knowledge of audiences than to have none at all.

Demographics

Audience data can be broken down into *demographic* groupings, so that different sections and sub-sections of the audience can be identified and catered for. Demographics relates to a number of variables concerning the way people can be described. The media industry uses the following categories to distinguish between different groups of people:

* age
* disability
* ethnicity
* gender
* sexual orientation
* social class.

Most or all of these terms will already be familiar to you. We have presented the list in alphabetical order in order to avoid suggesting that any of the categories is more important than the others. Ethnicity can be difficult to define, because it depends on so many different factors. This area can be sub-divided as follows:

* colour
* country of birth
* race
* region of birth
* religion.

Social class is also difficult to define. As recently as forty or fifty years ago, in the United Kingdom, it seemed perfectly appropriate to define people as upper, middle or lower class. Lower class was more politely called working class – not because people in the middle class didn't work, but because the lower class did the more manual, the dirtier and the more physically demanding jobs, such as working down mines or in heavy manufacturing industries

CHANNEL	AVERAGE DAILY REACH		WEEKLY REACH		AVERAGE WEEKLY VIEWING	SHARE
	000s	%	000s	%	HRS: MINS PER PERSON	%
ALL/ANY TV	41,938	75.2	51,893	93.0	25:15	100.0
BBC ONE (incl. Breakfast News)	28,449	51.0	46,972	84.2	5:34	22.0
BBC TWO	15,916	28.5	37,229	66.7	2:15	8.9
Total BBC ONE/BBC TWO	31,743	56.9	48,358	86.7	7:49	31.0
ITV (incl. GMTV)	24,092	43.2	43,839	78.6	5:03	20.0
CHANNEL 4/S4C	17,616	31.6	39,472	70.7	2:26	9.6
five	11,208	20.1	29,989	53.7	1:30	5.9
Total/any commercial terrestrial TV	31,849	57.1	48,521	87.0	8:59	35.5
Other viewing	24,150	43.3	36,297	65.0	8:27	33.5

FIGURE 1.35 *BARB audience data for television viewing, week beginning 24 April 2006.*

such as steelworks and shipbuilding. There was little *mobility* between classes, because young men tended to follow their fathers into similar jobs, and many women didn't work at all.

Now, many more women work and there is much more upward mobility through the class structure. Greatly increased educational opportunities and a shift from heavy industry to a greater number of jobs in the service sector, banking and retail industries have led to children of working-class families growing up to fit the description of the old middle class.

Today, audience research – and as a result, the media industry in general – uses a more detailed way of considering social class, which was devised in the 1950s and is based on the profession of the main earner in the household. Families are grouped into categories using the labels A, B, C1, C2, D and E (see Unit 2, page 83 for more details). Group A is considered more 'upmarket' than B, B than C1, and so on.

People are sometimes very surprised when they see which group this method puts them in. The different categories relate quite closely to family income – the better paid jobs tend to be in category A – but don't reflect the most important people in terms of who we need in emergency situations, for instance, when there is a leak or our house is on fire!

Another problem with grouping people in this way, is that *within* ethnic or social groups, people simply are not all the same. Most of them have had different experiences of life, which may have affected their attitudes to a whole range of different issues. Because of that, we simply can't say that all white people share a long list of characteristics and interests, that all black people share another, and those of Asian origin another. Often, the similarities between individuals in different ethnic or social groups are greater than the differences between them.

With age groups, things are often a little easier. A whole generation of people who grew up at the same time, had their first date in a particular decade and witnessed particular milestone events, such as the first landing on the moon or England winning the World Cup, will share memories and a feeling of nostalgia for certain moments in history.

Learning activity 13

- ✓ Choose two or three media products from the company or organisation you have been studying, and describe the demographic group each one has been produced for.
- ✓✓ Interview some members of those demographic groups, and find out what they think of the media products made for them.
- ✓✓✓ Explain how well the producers of the products have thought about their audiences. For example, if your sample is enthusiastic about the products, does this mean the producers know their audience well?
- * As with your previous survey, plan carefully who to ask, where to find them and how to structure your questions.

How products are tailored to audiences

Radio stations that play 'oldies' from certain decades, such as the sixties, the seventies or the eighties, try to exploit nostalgia by targeting particular age groups. So do television programmes that recreate particular eras and books and magazines that feature particular events. While some magazines are intended for a wide range of readers – such as the *Radio Times*, which lists television and radio programmes that would interest all sorts of people – most of them aim for a specific market 'niche'.

One of the most recent market niches to have been discovered by magazine publishers is young males. Magazines such as *Loaded*, *Front* and *Maxim* target their market with lots of pictures of young women and articles about fast cars and gadgets. Until they came along, there was very little aimed at young males except for the 'girlie' magazines usually found on the top shelf of the newsagents, which used sexually provocative images to appeal to men. It is much more socially acceptable to be seen reading one of the new breed of men's magazines in public.

FIGURE 1.36 *Newsagents group together magazines aimed at different niche markets, so customers can easily find a range of magazines that are of interest to them.*

TARGET AUDIENCE	SOME OF THEIR INTERESTS	PRODUCT INTENDED TO SATISFY AT LEAST SOME OF THOSE INTERESTS	MARKETING
Young (perhaps single) men	Cars, having fun, daring activities, young women, weird phenomena	Bravo (television channel)	In magazines and on other TV channels owned by the same company – for example FTN
Young women	Celebrity lifestyles and gossip, fashion, keeping fit, shopping, beauty, going out	*Cosmopolitan* (magazine)	Television advertising, other magazines owned by the same company
Middle-aged men	Rock music, going to gigs featuring classic rock artistes	Planet Rock (digital radio station)	Specialist press
Middle-aged women	Real-life stories, cooking, fashion and beauty, health, soaps	*Woman's Own* (magazine)	Television advertising, other magazines owned by the same company
Book buyers of all demographic groups	Buying books for study, entertainment and finding out information	Amazon.com	Internet pop-ups and banner advertising and radio advertising

FIGURE 1.37 *Different products single out particular interests within their target audiences and aim to satisfy them. Some target audiences are very narrow, and others are very broad.*

Key terms

Market – the area in which customers for a media product may be found

Segment – a part of a market

Niche – a specialised, and sometimes very narrowly defined, market segment – the smaller the niche, the more difficult it may be to make money from it

A slightly different new niche area is the men's fitness market. *Men's Health* differs from more mainstream lads' mags by including content about getting and keeping fit, as well as more medically orientated health issues. Of course, men have always bought magazines specialising in such topics as computing, motoring, fishing, racing and football. However, until the arrival of the lads' mags in the 1990s there was no male magazine genre that could be described as an equivalent of the women's interest magazines, which range from *Woman's Realm* to *Cosmopolitan*.

Magazine companies are quick to follow a successful formula in a newly discovered market in order to get a share of the action. When *Hello!* launched successfully as a women's magazine focusing on celebrities and royalty, instead of the traditional formula of fashion, cookery and relationships, *OK!* magazine soon followed.

The principle of appealing as much as possible to the shared interests and values of a particular group of people is used throughout the media industry. In order for a product to be successful, its producers need to do four things well:

1. Identify the market segment (or niche) that they are going to target.
2. Find out what people in that segment (or niche) are most likely to be interested in.
3. Make a product that people in that market segment (or niche) will find attractive and interesting in some way – so much that they will want the product.
4. Communicate to the market segment (or niche) that the product is available and how to get it.

Stage four, communication, is called **marketing**. Marketing products is a specialised activity, and often it is not the media producers who do this, but separate marketing departments within the organisation – or even external agencies which have the necessary skills to do this important job well. Even media organisations which advertise other organisations' products and services, will happily pay a specialised marketing or advertising agency to market their own products.

The key to successful marketing is knowing the market segment and how to reach the people in it. Sometimes the best way to market a new product is through an organisation's existing product range. That could mean selling to the same people twice, three times or even more, if the brand is attractive enough to the audience.

Learning activity 14

Find a wide range of different media products from your chosen area of the media industry.

- ✓ For each one, identify the target audience. It may be either a demographic group or based in a particular geographical area.
- ✓✓ Explain how each product is intended to appeal to the target audience.
- ✓✓✓ Explain how the marketing of each product is intended to persuade the target audience that they must consume the products.
- * Concentrate on the way the media organisation tries to get as many people as possible to consume its products.

FIGURE 1.38 *What will be the next niche market to be discovered?*

Media products can be marketed in many different ways, including:

* advertising in print, on radio and television, in cinemas, via websites and on DVDs and videos
* trails between or during programmes on radio and television and trailers in cinemas
* features within programmes on radio and television or included within copy in print and on web pages.

You will have noticed that guests on television chat shows and radio programmes are often only there in order to promote their latest book, album or film.

Did you know?

A good example of a brand used to sell more than one product to the same people is Virgin. Originally a record label in the 1970s, the Virgin brand has been extended to high street retailing through Virgin Megastores, travel by Virgin Trains, soft drinks called Virgin Cola and financial services also carrying the Virgin name and logo. Not all of these products are used by all the same people – but where their different markets overlap, it could be that the brand has helped attract more custom to the group. Originally, Virgin Radio was also owned by the founder of Virgin records, Richard Branson. He made his personal fortune through successfully exploiting the brand – which involved a lot of hard work in the early stages, as well as having the vision to spot opportunities.

CASE STUDY

BBC Radio 1

Target audience

This radio station targets its audience of fifteen-twenty-four-year-olds very carefully. If anyone who is outside this core audience doesn't like the programmes very much, this is unlikely to worry the network controller. Of course, other people do listen, and some of them are much younger than fifteen or older than twenty-four. They are, of course, very welcome to listen, but their views on programming won't be taken much into account.

Main product

The station concentrates hard on serving its core audience with a mix of mainly current and new music linked by presenters who have lots of 'street cred'. Because of its public service obligations, Radio 1 makes sure there is a well-resourced news team providing regular bulletins that are strongly targeted at the audience, as well as documentaries that are mainly about music. Radio 1 features some unsigned bands and specially recorded sessions in order to promote the development of new music and ensure that as a station it remains at the cutting edge of the music scene.

Associated products

The station's popular website features background information about the programmes and audio downloads so listeners can listen to certain programmes again, or catch them online if they missed them on air. There is advice for the target audience on issues that concern them.

A second radio station, 1Xtra, is targeted even more finely at black audiences within the age group, because the main network has to cater for a wider range of tastes in music. This niche audience has to access the station via digital platforms, because the station does not have an FM transmitter network to broadcast from.

- Why does Radio 1 concentrate on its core audience?
- What distinguishes Radio 1 from its main competitors?
- Explain the advantages and disadvantages for Radio 1 of having associated products.

CASE STUDY

The Hits

Target audience

This digital-only television channel secured a valuable slot on the surprisingly successful platform Freeview, as well as being one of a large number of music channels available on Sky and cable. Its prominence on Freeview enables it to reach a larger audience of young people than would be the case if there were more competitors on the same platform.

Main product

The output is mainly current hits, chosen to form a playlist of videos that appeal to the target audience. There are also interactive features such as dial-in requests, downloadable ringtones and on-screen text messaging, themed around relationships and dating.

Associated products

A radio station of the same name was launched soon afterwards, using a similar playlist to target a similar audience via DAB radio, Freeview and the Internet. The parent company, EMAP, developed a range of other brands, including the Smash Hits television channel and radio station which themselves capitalised on the popularity of the pop magazine of the same name.

- Why does The Hits concentrate on its core audience?
- What distinguishes The Hits from its main competitors?
- Explain the advantages and disadvantages for The Hits of having associated products.

Representing the audience

The media industry represents its audience in different ways. The most obvious one is the way it 'sells' its audiences to advertisers. Every commercial channel, website or print product that is financed by advertising does this, as do cinemas when they sell advertising time before the film starts. The industry talks about selling space on the page or website or time on the radio station or television channel. But advertisers only want to buy that space or that airtime in order to reach the audiences that come with them.

So, in effect, it is the audience that is being sold on to the advertiser. Naturally, advertisers want to know what – or whom – they are buying. Most are sophisticated enough to realise that there are different audiences out there that are specific to the particular media product, and that not all of those audiences will be interested in buying the products they have to sell.

For example, young people are unlikely to have the kind of income needed to buy an expensive new car. Older people wouldn't be interested in downloading ringtones, so it would be a waste of money for an advertiser to try and market the latest chart hit ringtones on Saga Radio or in *Saga* magazine – which are both targeted at the over-fifty-fives.

Did you know?

Advertising time or space is often priced on a 'cost-per-thousand' basis. That is how the media organisation sells its audience to advertisers. It also enables advertisers to understand the size of the audience and how effectively their money will be spent in trying to reach it.

Advertisers want demographic information about the different audiences, so they can make up their own minds about which are the best products to advertise with. They will use quantitative data, of the kind we looked at earlier in this unit. In the case of the main television and radio channels, the demographic make-up of their audiences changes from programme to programme. An advert shown during the *Channel 4 News* will be seen by a very different audience to one shown during *Big Brother*, for example.

When media companies are trying to persuade advertisers to buy airtime or space, or to provide sponsorship, they have to be persuasive. Part of being persuasive is sounding positive about what you are selling. So, EMAP's website described the audiences to their FM radio stations in the following way:

> *They are spirited, independent, sociable and confident and metropolitan. They lead an active social life reflecting their main agenda, which is to have a good time.*
>
> Source: EMAP website

As we have already seen, it is most unlikely that *everyone* who listens to these radio stations is going to be exactly as they were described. At best, this kind of general description is an *indication* of what the listeners are most likely to be like, according to the data gathered through audience research.

Learning activity 15

- ✓ Find out how the organisation or company you have been studying represents its audience to others. This will probably be on an advertising rate card, or it might be on a web page for advertisers. Describe the audience in your own words and explain how it might be attractive to a number of different advertisers.
- ✓✓ Consider how correct an impression this might be of the audience, bearing in mind the problems with gathering accurate audience data discussed earlier in this unit.
- ✓✓✓ Evaluate how much this representation of the audience sounds like it has been exaggerated in order to have more appeal to advertisers. Explain your reasons.
- * This information may be quite easily available from the orgnisation's website. In some cases you may need to make contact and ask for it to be sent to you, either over the Internet or by post.

Representing other social groups

The media represent social groups in many different ways, sometimes fairly and sometimes unfairly. Often, the only way to know whether representations are unfair, is if you belong to such a group, or know someone from within the group very well.

The way groups of people are presented is very important because it is very common for people to develop attitudes to others through what they see, read and hear in the media. In some parts of the United Kingdom there are very few people with a skin colour other than white. A white person living in such an area might have difficulty separating misleading media representations from the reality they would find for themselves if they lived in an area of the country with more ethnic diversity.

In many ways the media industry has grown up a lot in the past twenty to thirty years. The representation of women and ethnic minorities has improved a lot – women are no longer mainly depicted as housewives and it is no longer acceptable to poke fun at people because of their ethnic origins.

Examples of racial stereotyping were once very common, and it was very unusual to see or hear people from ethnic minorities in any positive roles. In the 1960s the BBC's *Black and White Minstrel Show* featured white dancers with their faces blacked up in a stereotyping of black people that many people later found offensive.

Think it over...

Imagine how it might feel to be the only person who is different to everyone else in some very noticeable way. Now imagine also being surrounded by negative images in the media of people that share that difference with you.

At the same time, all the serious programming on radio and television – and the continuity announcements before and after them – featured voices which spoke using 'received pronunciation', a kind of English spoken in parts of Britain. Forty or fifty years ago just having a northern accent made some comedians seem hysterically funny in the minds of producers and audiences alike. Comedy shows such as *The Clitheroe Kid* were hugely sucessful on radio and television in the 1960s, mainly because the northern characters were made to appear stupid and confused by everyday events.

Today, many people still speak in a way that could be described as 'received pronunciation', but a wide range of other accents are also heard on radio and television in a variety of positive, authoritative roles.

Homosexuality has also been the butt of much humour in the media. Early television portrayals of gay men concentrated on how their appearance, dress, manner, speech and behaviour was perceived to differ from that of heterosexual men. They were openly called offensive names.

Lesbians appeared only very rarely in the media. When they did, they were more likely to be represented either in erotic roles to appeal to heterosexual men or as very unattractive characters, rather than in realistic and positive roles that reflected their true place in society. The media representation of gay men and lesbians has improved considerably over the last twenty years or so, reflecting the greater acceptance and visibility of homosexuality in society as a whole.

FIGURE 1.39 *Some people still don't seem to realise that many people in the world are very different from them.*

Although the representation of minority groups in general has improved, many people consider that there is still a lot of room for improvement. In 2001 the Director-General of the BBC described the Corporation as 'hideously white', meaning that non-white people were still under-represented. Some of the press coverage after the London suicide bombings of 2005 gave rise to concerns that revenge attacks might be made on Muslim communities.

The Internet is still awash with pornographic depictions of both straight and gay women, which many consider to be demeaning because women are characterised as objects whose only purpose is for male gratification. Although the *Daily Mirror* abandoned topless photography some time ago, the *Sun* and, to a far greater extent, the *Daily Sport* still use images of near-naked women to sell copies to men.

FIGURE 1.40 *The Internet is widely used to sell and distribute pornography, most of it degrading to women and some of it illegal.*

Many people believe that news coverage of natural disasters in other parts of the world is detrimental to the image of black people. News reports about Africa are often about famines, droughts, poverty or disease, rather than more positive stories. The Africans depicted in these news reports are often shown as sick, hungry or destitute, rather than in more active and positive roles.

You could argue that people only become newsworthy when their lives are disrupted by some very dramatic change to their circumstances – such as occurs when disaster strikes. However, editors and producers throughout the media are actively choosing the stories they cover and the material they use to illustrate them, and it is rare for them to choose 'good' news stories from certain parts of the world.

Did you know?

The BBC's first female television news reader, Angela Rippon, may be best known for showing her legs in a dance routine on the *Morecambe and Wise* comedy show in 1976.

It is more difficult to gauge the representation of minority groups such as gay men and lesbians. The sexuality of the participants may not be relevant to the subject of many news stories or TV programmes, for example, so it cannot be known whether any of the people depicted are gay or not. Gay couples are increasingly being given more positive coverage, as they are often presented in the same way as heterosexual couples.

	POSITIVELY REPRESENTED	NEGATIVELY REPRESENTED
White males		
Old people		
Women		
People with an obvious disability		
Lesbians, gay men, bisexuals		
Working-class men		
Non-white people		
People born in different countries		
People from regions other than the south-east of England		
People wearing religious clothing or insignia		

FIGURE 1.41 *Checklist for monitoring the representation in the media of people from different social groups. Some people represented may fit more than one description, so you will need to tick more than one box for them.*

The depiction of religious groups is also quite difficult to gauge, given that members of a religious group may not wear special clothing or insignia. As they do with other social groups, today's media tend to present people from different religions in a less biased way than was previously the case. The media both reflect and help to form people's views about different groups. Stereotypical images are no longer seen as acceptable by a large proportion of the population and this comes across in the media. In our diverse society, differences between people are respected more than they were in the past, and the concept of 'normality' is less narrowly defined.

It is selection processes that most directly affect the representation of different social groups in the media, including both the selection of material for inclusion in media products *and* the selection of the people who work in the media. There are now laws preventing discrimination against people on the grounds of their ethnic group or gender, as well as for any disability they may have. These laws are to stop barriers being put in the way of people having equal opportunities in life, simply because they come from a minority group – or, in the case of women, because they may need to take a break in their careers at some time in order to become carers.

Learning activity 16

- ✓ Use the checklist provided in Figure 1.41 to monitor the representation of different social groups in the media.
- ✓✓ Report on your findings, explaining why you think certain groups may have been represented more positively and/or more frequently than others.
- ✓✓✓ Explain how the representations you have studied might have been made fairer *or* what the producers have already done to represent social groups fairly.
- * You will find it easiest to carry out this work if you consider the different areas of representation one at a time. For example, you could begin with gender. Some aspects may seem more important to you than others.

Representing social issues

The media don't only represent people in their products, they also represent issues that matter to us all. It follows that as well as sometimes misrepresenting people, they can also misrepresent issues on occasion. One aspect of regulation that applies to the broadcast media – radio and television – is that of impartiality. In simple terms, impartiality means not being biased one way or another, especially when there is a controversial issue under discussion. Sometimes broadcasters are accused of showing bias towards one political party or pressure group, for example.

Unlike broadcasting, the press and interactive media sectors are not regulated in this respect at all. The owners of newspapers and magazines can decide to use them to support political parties if they wish. Nobody can prevent them from doing so unless, of course, readers and customers or web users stop consuming products because they object to the bias in the presentation.

Key terms

Balance – equal emphasis given to all sides of an argument, so no one side has an unfair advantage over the others

Bias – an unequal stance or representation, which gives one side an advantage over another

Impartiality – the state of being unbiased

Propaganda – material designed to persuade people that one or other side of an argument is correct

Political parties and pressure groups can and do set up their own websites, where they can put across their own points of view on almost any issues they like. They can also make and distribute tapes, DVDs and CD-ROMs to help promote their message. Politically inspired leaflets and posters are almost as old as the printing press itself. They are a very effective way of getting a message to an audience without journalists 'mediating' or altering it in any way – by asking awkward questions or putting across alternative points of view, for example.

FIGURE 1.42 *Political literature can come in all shapes and sizes depending on its purpose.*

In the UK, the main political parties have a right to free airtime on the main television channels and radio stations. Some of this is allocated to them during election periods, but they may also choose to schedule a small number of party political broadcasts at other times. In some countries, such as the United States, political parties must pay for any advertising they do on radio and television. In this country they can buy advertising space in newspapers, magazines and the websites of other organisations.

Did you know?

When John Major was re-elected Prime Minister of a Conservative government in May 1992, the *Sun* newspaper's headline was 'It's The Sun Wot Won It!'. Five years later in 1997, the *Sun* had changed its support to Labour and, when Labour won a landslide victory, the paper's headline was 'It's The Sun Wot Swung It'. Many political commentators agree that the *Sun*'s support was crucial on both occasions. Others think the newspaper was just reflecting a change of mood in the country.

All sorts of social issue are covered in the media. A decent argument – or, more politely, a heated debate – over an issue lots of people feel strongly about can make good listening or viewing on radio or television, and this is reflected in the number of chat shows and phone-ins. Newspapers and magazines print letters, e-mails and texts from readers on controversial issues; bulletin boards, blogs and podcasts are the Internet's contribution to this type of material.

Media producers know that their audiences will agree with some of the comments sent in and disagree with others – perhaps enough to send in their own. A full postbag, a busy telephone line or a large text or e-mail response can indicate that a programme or a feature is very popular, and is getting the audience's attention. Some topics crop up time and again, either because an issue often occurs in the news or simply because producers know a certain topic will provoke a response.

Think it over...

When do you think it is OK to put across two sides of an argument without saying either one is right? When is it better to indicate support for one view rather than another?

Smoking

Every year a group called Action on Smoking and Health (ASH) promotes a National No Smoking Day. There are clear health reasons for not smoking, which have been demonstrated in countless medical studies. Smoking damages the lungs and makes lung and heart disease more likely, as well as cancer and many other diseases. It is also important not to smoke near others, because secondary smoking can be almost as harmful, particularly in children. The popular entertainer, trumpeter and television presenter Roy Castle died from lung cancer, despite being a non-smoker. He had too often filled his lungs in smoky venues in order to play his trumpet, and the smoke he had inhaled from other people's cigarettes killed him.

Yet some people view the pressures not to smoke as interfering with their personal freedom, and a rival organisation, the pressure group Freedom Organisation for the Right to Enjoy Smoking Tobacco (FOREST) was formed. On National No Smoking Day, media producers regularly pit members of ASH and FOREST against each other in interviews, written features, chat shows and other staged confrontations designed to produce emotive debates that will interest their audiences.

This type of media debate represents a kind of 'balance' because each side has an equal chance to express its point of view, each argument is made in turn and the audience can make up their own minds on the issue. On the other hand, giving both sides equal time could be seen as unfair – the medical evidence overwhelmingly supports the ASH side of the debate, and presenting smoking as an equally desirable alternative to not smoking could be viewed as irresponsible on the part of the producers.

In recent years this issue has re-emerged whenever bans on smoking in public places were being considered by politicians, when people have sued tobacco companies for damaging their health, and when tobacco advertising and sponsorship have been banned in some sports and not others.

FIGURE 1.43 *Popular entertainer and presenter of BBC1's* Record Breakers, *Roy Castle died as a result of breathing other people's smoke.*

Remember

The way a subject is treated in the media is not always the correct way. Often, subjects are represented in ways that are irresponsible or morally wrong. Even worse is exploitation, where someone is wrongly treated so the media can make money.

The MMR vaccine

The MMR vaccine – against measles, mumps and rubella – has been the source of great controversy in recent years. The overwhelming medical evidence that a triple vaccine given to very young children was safe was 'balanced' repeatedly in the media with the views of a very small number of experts who thought it wasn't. Most of the medical community, including the

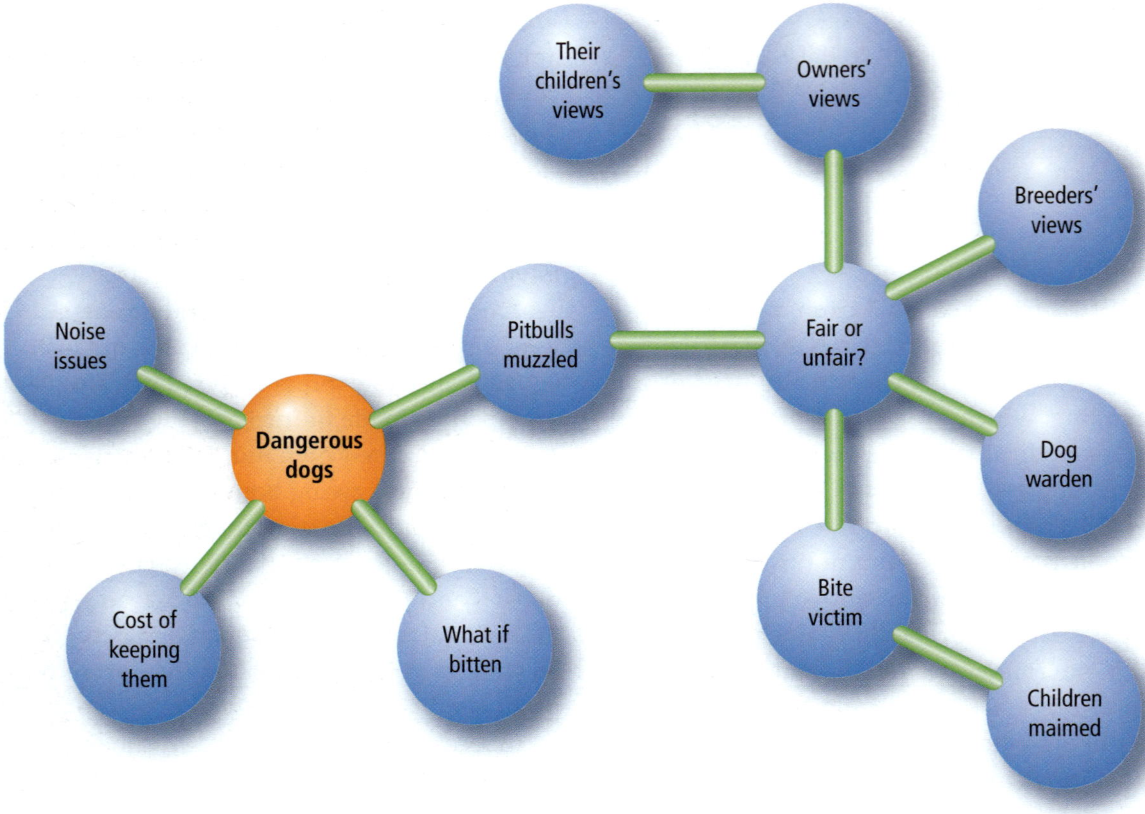

FIGURE 1.44 *Issues can be portrayed in many different ways, depending on the points of view the producers decide to represent.*

government's Chief Medical Officer and the National Institute for Clinical Excellence, have considered MMR to be safe since the beginning of the controversy in 1998.

Because one researcher claimed the MMR vaccine could cause autism in children, many worried parents began to demand separate vaccines for measles, mumps and rubella. Several doctors began offering separate vaccines, either because they had their own doubts about the safety of MMR or because it was better to vaccinate children in this way than not at all.

Very soon there were lots of people on both sides of the debate for the media to interview, and it became widespread practice to give both sides equal coverage – even though there still wasn't any hard scientific evidence linking MMR to autism.

Racism

In Britain a law called the Public Order Act of 1986 made it illegal to incite other people to racial hatred. This made media debates involving people with strongly racist views a risky venture for producers to attempt. Some people may feel that their freedom of speech is restricted by this law. But this has to be balanced by the reality that protecting people from racist crimes is more important than giving every side of the argument a platform for airing their views.

Gun crime

When an activity is illegal, it may not be desirable for the media to include all points of view in its coverage – examples of such activities are crimes involving violence, bullying, drug taking, grafitti, stealing and carrying illegal weapons. The growth of gun crime in recent years has been a cause for concern for police, schools, parents and, of course, victims. Yet some young people say they carry illegal weapons because they feel unsafe and they need them to protect themselves.

This subject can be attractive to some media producers because it plays on people's fears – of danger to themselves or of the possibility of becoming innocently caught up in someone else's fight. Some parts of the media might want to appear 'cool' rather than siding with the police on matters such as this. A 'balanced' presentation including the views of those who do carry illegal weapons may actively encourage those who already break the law to carry on and other people to join them.

Certain types of media coverage of illegal activites have caused complaints of irresponsibility. Many media producers go home to safe neighbourhoods when they finish work, and the dangers they show in other people's neighbourhoods may not trouble them at all on a personal level. Some critics of the media will say that rising levels of violence over the past forty years are a direct result of the glorification of violence on television, in films and in popular music.

Learning activity 17

✓ Identify a range of social issues, such as the ones discussed in this section of the book, that are represented in the area of the media you have been studying.

✓✓ Describe the different ways in which they are covered.

✓✓✓ How fairly or unfairly do you think each issue has been covered? Explain your answer carefully.

* There are all sorts of social issues you could investigate. Choosing ones that particularly interest you will help you to produce your best work.

Issues are everywhere

It's not just in news and documentary programmes or on the news pages of websites that you will find controversial issues being represented. Issues such as the ones we've explored here can crop up almost anywhere in the mass media, for example the widespread use of guns in dramas on TV and in films.

Some types of media product you might like to investigate include:

* soap operas on radio and television
* problem pages in magazines
* feature films and film shorts
* local talking newspapers for the blind
* web pages
* presenter links in radio programmes
* interviews with celebrities
* music videos and song lyrics
* blogs and podcasts
* drama series and serials
* sport reports.

1.4 How audiences use media products

We have spent some time investigating the way the media industry thinks about its audiences. Now let's consider what happens when audiences consume media products – that is, when audiences read, watch or listen to some of the industry's output.

You will need to know key terms that are used in media studies to describe what is happening when audiences use media products. For example, every media product is considered to be a **text**, in the same way as novels, plays or poems are called texts in English lessons. Consuming a media text, and making a meaning from it, is often referred to as **reading** it – even if the 'text' is a film, a DVD, a website, a radio show or a television programme.

> **Key terms**
>
> *Text* – any media product that is 'read', or consumed, by an audience. A text may include written copy or it may consist entirely of sounds and/or images
>
> *Reading* – the act of making meaning from a media text, for example, forming an understanding of what is happening in a radio play, or making sense of events described in a news report

Reading media texts

If you have ever watched an obscure film and been unsure what it was all about, or simply argued with friends about the ending of a film and what it meant, you may have realised that meaning in media texts is not always the same for everyone. Some film directors deliberately leave endings ambiguous, to encourage each member of the audience to think about what might happen next. At other times, media producers may try hard to make sure everyone in the audience understands the text in the same way.

Based on a single image on the front cover and the detailed descriptions and dialogue in the text, the reader of a novel has to work quite hard to imagine what all the characters and scenes look like. The more description there is in the novel and the clearer the description is, the more likely it is that every reader will create images that are similar to the ones the author had in mind when writing the book. If the descriptions are not very detailed or clear, it is more likely that every reader will create different images from the ones in the author's mind. Even with very clear descriptions, what each reader imagines will be coloured by their own life experiences, so each reader will have an entirely unique reading of the novel.

In fact, all media texts are open to different readings. In the case of a radio play, the words of a text are spoken out loud by actors' voices, and there are sound effects and probably music. Each sound in the play provides the listener with a little bit more information to use when building up a mental image of what is happening.

FIGURE 1.45 *Different individuals are likely to make different readings of the same text, even when descriptions are very unambiguous.*

> **Key terms**
>
> *Preferred reading* – the meaning the producer intended the audience to make from the text
>
> *Alternative reading* – a meaning that is different in some significant way from the producer's preferred reading
>
> *Anchorage* – a means of 'tying down' the meaning of some part of a media text

> **Did you know?**
>
> In 1978 a radio play by Andrew Sachs was broadcast without any words at all. Consisting entirely of sounds depicting places and action, *The Revenge* was about a man on the run. Without any dialogue, listeners had to work out for themselves what was happening from start to finish. If you are able to listen to a recording of the play in class, preferably with the lights dimmed, try stopping the play from time to time to discuss what everyone thinks is happening. Sometimes readings of the play are very different from one person to the next.

If the radio play is subsequently adapted for television, images will be added and each viewer will receive a lot more information about what is happening. The audience doesn't have to imagine the images because they are there in front of them. Likewise, in other areas of the media industry such as print and interactive media production, audiences are given images to look at, and there are fewer gaps in their understanding of what is happening to fill using their own imagination.

It follows that the more information given to each member of the audience (and therefore the less each one has to imagine), the more likely different people are to read a text in similar ways – that is, to make very similar readings of it. Some media producers want individuals in their audiences to make different readings of a text, while others want them to understand the text in the same way. However hard producers may try to impose their own 'preferred' readings on their audiences, in practice this is very hard to achieve.

Anchorage

One way of fixing a particular meaning to part of a media text is by adding some extra information that is designed to make the audience understand it in a particular way. Throughout this book, for example, the images have captions underneath them. They have been added to explain their significance or to make sure the image tells you something in particular in order to develop your understanding.

In many cases, changing the caption would change the way you think about the image – that is, you would make a different reading. Consider the way the different captions under the image below alter the meaning of the same picture. Even though the picture is unchanged, the second caption encourages you to think about it in a completely different way.

Learning activity 18

- ✓ Choose a media text that can be read in different ways and make your own reading of it. Now compare your reading with the readings of others.
- ✓✓ Explain how the different readings could have been made from the same text – in other words, what did people interpret differently, and why?
- ✓✓✓ Explain how the producer could have encouraged audiences to make a preferred reading.
- * Try this activity using a story with an ambiguous ending – everyone has to make up their own minds about what is most likely to happen next.

FIGURE 1.46 *Animal conservationists assist endangered species to reproduce in safety.*

FIGURE 1.47 *Life in captivity often causes distress and anxiety to the animals.*

Now try and imagine other captions which could alter the meaning again. The possibilities are endless, because your imagination and that of other people reading this book can range far and wide to bring an infinite variety of different ideas to the task. Because this activity can be quite good fun, newspapers and magazines sometimes run caption competitions, inviting readers to suggest new captions for photographs that are already quite amusing. The funniest in the opinion of the editor is the one that wins. Of course, different people find different things funny, so if you change the editor, somebody else will probably win the prize.

Many people find the front covers of *Private Eye* magazine amusing because they usually feature a photograph of one or more politicians, with 'speech bubbles' added to them. By mischievously putting words into the mouths of the politicians, the meaning of the photograph can change quite dramatically, making an ironic or satirical point about the people pictured and their views.

Signification

Anchoring meaning with a caption or some other 'qualifying' device is just one of the ways meaning can be produced in media texts. What you have been doing with the images on the previous page is **decoding** them. Just like someone receiving a secret message, you have been using your own knowledge of the way books are laid out in order to make sense of the images. After all, you already knew that a line of text under an image is meant to be read in connection with that image. Someone who has never read a reference book before might not realise that at first.

The way people learn to decode media texts, through experiencing lots of them over time, is very like the way someone learns a code, such as Morse code or semaphore. In some parts of the world, groups of people have communicated effectively for many centuries using smoke signals or drums, which are also types of code.

Media producers **encode** meanings into their products, just as we have written captions for all our images, and divided the text of this book into sections, adding headings to help you find your way around the book, and so on. We also chose which information about the wide and varied world of the media to include and – because of the shortage of space – which information to leave out.

In making these decisions about what went into the book and how we put it together, we were encoding large amounts of information for you to decode. For example, by now we hope you will have realised that inside the 'Did you know?' boxes you will find interesting and useful further information to help your understanding and develop your knowledge of the subject even further.

Did you know?

One of the earliest ways of sending information over long distances was by using Morse code. This code uses different combinations of short and long bursts of sound to represent the letters of the alphabet. As long as both the sender and the receiver know the code, they can communicate effectively, if rather slowly. Morse code is still used to send messages, but advances in voice, image and data transmission have made more user-friendly forms of communication possible.

FIGURE 1.48 *During World War II, Morse code was used to send top secret military information across long distances. By agreeing in advance to swap the letters and the 'dots and dashes' representing them around, a sender and receiver could encrypt messages in a way only they could understand.*

There are all sorts of ways a media text can make meaning. Just as a book could consist entirely of writing (as novels often do), relying on the words alone to tell the reader everything the author wants to encode, a radio programme could consist of just words, all spoken in a flat monotone voice that doesn't give anything away in terms of emotion, mood or action. A television programme could also feature a single person reading aloud from a book – and there have been very successful programmes that have done just that. Likewise, a print or multimedia product could use only text to communicate to its audience.

Such unadventurous use of these different media would quickly become boring for their audiences, because the producers wouldn't be exploiting the opportunities they offer to the full. Adding a picture to a page, some variations in voice tone and sound effects to a radio play, and moving images to a story reading not only makes the text more interesting, but the combination of different elements within the text can start to work together to create meaning. By juxtaposing two different elements – like the picture and the caption – new meanings can be created while others become impossible.

For example, the sound of a lion roaring could make radio listeners think that the scene is set on the African savannah – until they hear a loudspeaker announcement warning visitors that the zoo is about to close. A picture of a young man running towards an old lady might make television viewers think he is going to rob her – until another shot reveals that he is running to intercept a heavy object that is falling towards her. In the print media, many different typefaces can be used – from traditional to scary to futuristic. Choosing the right one for the type of headline or story involved can add extra meaning.

Think it over...

If the saying 'a picture paints a thousand words' is true, how many words does a moving picture paint? What about an interesting sound? Or a combination of the two?

Did you know?

Although the mass media can easily encode meaning for audiences to decode using their sight and their hearing, it is rare for them to use touch, smell or taste. There have been experiments with 'smellyvision', when producers have distributed scratch cards that release particular smells to TV viewers. The viewers then follow instructions as to which parts of the card to scratch at different moments in the programme. Cinemas have sometimes used devices under and in front of seats to move people at particular moments in a film or to spray them with water.

Key terms

Element – a constituent part of a text

Juxtapose – to put two or more dissimilar elements together in a text, in order to produce a more sophisticated meaning from the combination that results

All the different elements used to create images in media texts are in fact **signs** or signifiers which carry meaning. Audiences recognise the signs and understand some of the meanings they are intended to send. **Signification** refers to the way in which signs work in media texts.

One of the key academics to have studied signification, Roland Barthes, suggested that this sending of messages happens in two different ways: one on a very basic, obvious level, and the other on a higher, much more sophisticated level. He called the first level **denotation**, and the second **connotation**. For example, the word 'red' denotes a colour most people can visualise. If someone says 'red', another person might just imagine the colour itself, as if thinking of a colour to paint a room. So in this case the word 'red' simply *denotes* a colour.

On the second level, though, the same word 'red' may also suggest a number of more abstract things, such as facing danger, being in debt, being angry. The word 'red' can also make people think of the communist or socialist political systems. The interpretation will depend on any anchorage of the word's meaning – such as the context in which it is used and what is said before or after it.

Learning activity 19

✓ Read through the lists of signs that follow in this section – especially the one for the media area you have been studying. Then make a list of examples of your own from actual media texts.

✓✓ Explain why each signifier you find works as it does. You could put the information into a table.

✓✓✓ Suggest other ways in which these meanings could be produced. Explain your answers, also using a table if you wish.

* You should choose texts that have lots of different signifiers. The simpler the text, the harder you will find it to get a good mark.

Remember

Different people may read the same signifier in different ways, depending on their own perceptions and experience. Their readings could also be affected by how they are feeling at the time – happy, sad or perhaps alone and frightened.

FIGURE 1.49 *Making the sound of horses' hooves with coconuts is similar to encoding words into Morse code. Listeners hear this sound and think of a running horse.*

There are many different ways in which elements within texts can work to create meaning. The tables in Figures 1.50 to 1.53 give just a few examples for each area of the media. The relationship between the signifier and what it signifies can be very complex – sometimes depending on the listener having encountered the signifier before.

Signifiers in audio

The first set of examples are from radio, but they could also apply to the production of any audio product. Radio has been called the 'blind' medium because listeners have only sounds from which to work out what is happening. This can be very confusing if the sounds are unfamiliar or unexpected. For this reason, radio producers have

SIGNIFIER IN AUDIO	WHAT IT CAN SIGNIFY
A car horn in a jingle	A traffic and travel report is beginning
The words 'Where in the world?' sung to a certain tune	An advert for PC World
Fade down of speech in a drama	The end of a scene
Fade up of speech in a drama	The beginning of a new scene
Jingle	It's time for the weather forecast
Coconut halves being knocked together	A horse walking or trotting
A siren gets louder, then quieter, in a drama	A police car is passing
Crunching gravel	Someone is walking on a gravel drive
The 'pips' (also known as the 'Greenwich time signal')	It's time for the news

FIGURE 1.50 *Some examples of audio signifiers and what they might signify.*

to be very careful to use sounds in a way that aids understanding, rather than confuses listeners.

Talking books often dramatise stories, and they use similar signifiers to those used on radio. This is because listeners use the same techniques to decode talking books as they do to make sense of radio programmes. Because they are recorded, though, instead of being broadcast live, talking books can be rewound and listened to again.

Signifiers in print

Print products use signifiers to help their audiences make meaning from the collection of photos, text and artwork they see. In a newspaper, for example, the main words on the front page are large and eyecatching, so readers' eyes are drawn towards them. In this way, the main headline on the front page is shown to be one of the most important parts of the day's newspaper. It is certainly meant to persuade people to pick up a copy and buy it.

SIGNIFIER IN PRINT	WHAT IT CAN SIGNIFY
Large words covering half the page	Today's 'lead', or most important, story is below
Small-sized text under an image	Further information about the image
White words on a red panel	The name of the newspaper
Thick, glossy paper	An expensive or luxury product
An image by a reporter or a columnist's name	This is what the reporter or columnist looks like
Words printed in a box within a magazine article	This is some further information about the subject
Words from an article, repeated in much larger type among the rest of the words	This is a highlight to encourage you to want to read the whole article
A single image on the front cover of a novel	This represents a highlight or the main theme from the story told inside
A large gap between lines of words in a novel	A change of scene or flashback follows or some time passes

FIGURE 1.51 *Some examples of print signifiers and what they might signify.*

SIGNIFIER IN MOVING IMAGE	WHAT IT CAN SIGNIFY
Large words on screen during a film	The beginning of the film
Small words on screen during a film	The end of the film
Suspenseful music is played while an otherwise unremarkable place is shown	Something dramatic or even frightening is about to happen
Fast-paced music is played while a car chase is shown	The action on screen is very exciting
Long shot of a location	This is where the action you are about to see takes place
Close-up of a frightened face	Something scary is happening
A cowboy on horseback rides towards the setting sun	That is the last we will see of this character
A fast-moving sequence of images, sound and the word 'next'	These are highlights of the next episode or the next programme in a series

FIGURE 1.52 *Some examples of moving image signifiers and what they might signify.*

SIGNIFIER IN INTERACTIVE MEDIA	WHAT IT CAN SIGNIFY
Words underlined	This is a hyperlink to another web page
Images on a DVD inlay card	These are scenes from this film or programme
A still background with several images and words arranged around it	You can choose between these menu items
A pop-up box with an image and a message within it	This is an advert for goods or services and by clicking on it you may find more information
The words 'special features' on an inlay card	There is extra material available on this DVD, which you can access interactively
A logo showing Uc, U, PG, 12, 12A, 15, 18 or R18	This is an age restriction relating to the suitability of the content for children
A small box with a cross through it	An image intended to be shown here is missing
The sound of a click is heard	The computer has registered your mouse click

FIGURE 1.53 *Some examples of interactive media signifiers and what they might signify.*

Signifiers in moving image products

Moving image products usually use audio signifiers as well as pictures and graphics on screen. They will often work together, in the way that a loud and fast-paced piece of music can make a car chase seem more exciting. Incidental music tries to capture the essence of the action taking place on screen.

Signifiers in interactive media

Because interactive media products require their audiences to navigate around them, among the most important signifiers are those which indicate where to click a mouse button or the remote control of a DVD player. As with moving image products, sound can work with images and text to produce sophisticated meanings in the audience's readings of them.

In any media product, the way signifiers work can be on a very simple level – or it can be much more sophisticated. The scientist and philosopher C.S. Peirce categorised signifiers into three levels: icon, index and symbol. An **icon** conveys meaning at the simplest level. A **symbol** operates at the most complex. Between these levels of complexity is the **index**.

Even words can be signifiers, and onomatopoeic words are those which sound like what is being described when you say them.

Key terms

Icon – the most basic type of signifier. For example, on radio the sound of a siren could be an icon representing a police car, simply because that is a sound police cars sometimes make; or in visual media, a picture of smoke is iconic of smoke

Index – a secondary level signifier. The sound of the same siren may *suggest* police officers are present, not because officers sound like sirens, but because a siren often indicates their arrival; an image of smoke may indicate that there is a fire

Symbol – the third level of signification. The siren may be symbolic of crime – not because crime has a sound like a siren, but because police sirens are generally associated with criminal activity; smoke may symbolise danger

For example, 'whoosh' sounds like the noise it is meant to describe. Meanings can be very sophisticated, and sometimes they rely on both encoder and decoder agreeing on their meaning. The word 'dog' neither looks nor sounds like a four-legged animal, but English speakers all agree it refers to such a creature, and so the word serves us well as an index for our canine friends. The word has other possible meanings,

FIGURE 1.54 *Does this picture mean something good is happening – or something bad? Turn the page to find out!*

too, which may be difficult for a non-native English speaker to understand – in the saying 'you can't teach an old dog new tricks', for example, the word 'dog' actually refers to a person.

Remember

Signifiers often work together to create complex meanings. In making their own readings of texts, audiences consider all the relevant information they notice.

Codes and conventions

Codes

When signifiers work together, each one acts as part of a code – in any code, each symbol is of little use without the rest. In the example of Morse code, without a complete set of symbols to work with, it would be impossible to spell out a whole word or message.

In the same way, media texts rely on whole systems of signifiers working together, in order for producers to construct them and for audiences to read and understand them. Codes in media texts have evolved – that is, they have developed over time. They weren't created from scratch in one sitting, as may have been the case when Morse wanted to devise a code for sending messages over long distances.

An example of how a media code develops over time is the way news is presented on television. Many of the very first news broadcasts on television didn't feature a visible newsreader – instead, scripts were read out while still images or a newsreel were shown on screen. The newsreader's presentation manner had already been developed in radio – very formal in order to connote the seriousness of news, but sometimes sounding more cheerful over a lighthearted news item.

Once newsreaders began to appear on screen, their dress, seating position and 'look' towards the camera all became important. The first audiences watching television newsreaders had to make sense of these images. Now, though, we are all so used to this way of presenting television news that we subconsciously read these codes without having to think about them.

We usually know we are watching a news programme the moment we tune into a channel, because the various signifiers that work together to encode meaning into the programme do so immediately: we see a desk, one or two presenters, some on-screen headlines and perhaps a screen showing a reporter talking to the presenters. If we tune in before the programme begins, the opening title sequence tells us immediately what kind of programme is going to follow – the theme music is pacey yet sounds important, and a series of images show us glimpses of people and places that are often in the news.

Tuning in to a foreign news programme involves that instant recognition, even though we cannot understand what is being said – the music, the use of images, the set design and so on all tell us what type of programme this is. You wouldn't need to look for very long at a foreign newspaper, either, before you realised what it was! There are bound to be differences between it and our own newspapers, but the similarities between them are probably much greater.

FIGURE 1.55 *This photo shows the same smoke as on the previous page. Now what do you think the smoke indicates?*

Codes can at times be **symbolic** or **technical**. Symbolic codes suggest meaning through the choice of content – for example, using the colour red might suggest danger in a vampire movie, because it is the colour of blood. In another context, red can suggest passion or love, so an article about St Valentine's Day may have a red border or a red background. The facial expressions of actors in a drama, presenters, interviewees or contestants in a game show are also symbolic codes, suggesting the emotions they are feeling. Voice can portray emotion, too, and it is particularly important on radio, where faces cannot be seen and have to be imagined.

Technical codes include the use of graphics on screen and in print and interactive media products, the framing of an image, the use of soft focus to romanticise a scene or to hide someone's true age. Filters, lighting, camera angles, special effects and sound processing are other examples of ways in which the technical aspects of a production can be put to work to create particular meanings.

Some media products try to convey a moment in history. In order for the illusion to be convincing, all the different elements have to be right. The scenery or the backgrounds in any images have to reflect the time period. The costumes, tools, transport, buildings, what the people are doing and even the way they speak all have to seem authentic – otherwise there will be conflicting meanings in the text. If everything in the picture – and of course the sound – fits the time period, the most likely audience reading will be that the events shown are actually taking place then, rather than today.

Key terms

Code – a system of conveying meaning to audiences without having to use words to explain what is happening

Convention – an accepted, even expected, way of doing something – in the media industry this means the usual way of creating a particular type of product

This is why film and television producers make great efforts to make sure there are no television aerials or satellite dishes visible when they are shooting a scene for a Charles Dickens adaptation.

Learning activity 20

- ✓ Identify a range of different codes used in a number of media products of your choice. Find some symbolic codes and some technical codes. Say which category each set of signifiers fits into.
- ✓✓ Explain how each code works – how does it make meaning?
- ✓✓✓ Suggest alternative ways of encoding the same meanings into those texts. Explain how and why you think they would work.
- * It will help you to be sure in your own mind of the difference between technical and symbolic codes.

Conventions

When producers and audiences have particular ways of doing things, these are called **conventions**. The signifiers we have just used to describe television news are all conventions of television news. That is, they are the usual ways of encoding the same meanings into those texts. Until the television channel Five launched, it had been usual in this country for television newsreaders to sit behind a desk. Originally they had scripts on the desk, and more recently they have had keyboards or laptops.

One of the more interesting aspects of *Five News* when it launched was that, instead of sitting behind a desk, Kirsty Young would move around the studio, perching on the edges of desks while talking to the camera. This was done deliberately to connote a younger, more active 'feel' to their news, because channel Five wanted to appeal to a younger audience. It would not have seemed so sensational in Germany or the United States, for example, where television newsreaders have been standing up to deliver their bulletins for a long time.

When channel Five began presenting the news in such a very different way to the convention, it was being groundbreaking: showing how something can be done differently without the media product losing its credibility with the audience. Innovation and creativity can be very

FIGURE 1.56 *The conventions of television news presentation have changed over time.*

good things. They can bring a breath of fresh air to an area of the media, and often one new idea is followed by another. Certainly, it is much more common now for newsreaders to get up and walk around the studios while presenting the news. What starts out as breaking a convention, sometimes becomes a new convention, as it is copied by others who also want to seem new, fresh and exciting. The way the broadsheet newspapers changed to compact size in a relatively short space of time is a very good example.

When a comedy programme wants to satirise television news, it begins by using the conventions of news presentation and then makes something unexpected and funny happen. Spoofs of different media products are made in similar ways – for example, a newspaper front page using many of the conventions of layout, language and image, but with some surprise element that makes it funny.

One of the best ways to understand conventions in the media is to ask yourself what a media product would be like if the producers did the opposite of the usual convention. For example, if the newsreader had his or her back to the camera while presenting the news or was seen only in profile. What would audiences think if a serious newspaper had the sport news on the first few pages instead of the usual news? In the recent past, *The Independent* has broken with convention by printing comment on the front page, instead of factual reporting.

Here are some more ways in which conventions could be broken:

* Placing captions above, instead of below images.
* Reading serious news in a lighthearted way.
* Beginning news bulletins with the 'funny' story and leaving the most important news until last.
* Allowing listeners to present radio programmes, while presenters sit at home.
* Playing music or music videos at the wrong speed.

Some of these examples of breaking conventions in the media would not be read as groundbreaking, challenging or innovative by their audiences. They would be thought of as mistakes – and even worse, if there were too many of them, the producers might be thought of as amateurish. That would bring about a loss of credibility, and the audiences for those products would decline.

FIGURE 1.57 *What does the front page of this newspaper tell you about its content and target audience?*

FIGURE 1.58 *Breaking conventions may be seen as amateurish.*

Much has been written and broadcast about how the late John Peel occasionally played records at the wrong speed over his thirty-seven years as a presenter on BBC Radio 1. Far from discrediting Peel, because he was so well respected as a presenter and his ability to spot promising new musical talent made him so distinctive, such mistakes were seen by most of his audience as endearing rather than amateurish. There are few people in the media who are so well respected that they can get away with making many mistakes, though – and beginners have to try very hard to get things right at first.

There are plenty of other examples of conventions being broken on purpose. Radio stations usually have news bulletins on the hour, but BBC Radio 1 has them on the half hour. That makes the station seem different from the rest, even though the reasons for it are historical: in the 1970s the station shared newsreaders with Radio 2, and they couldn't read different bulletins on different stations live at the same time!

New ideas often revitalise the print industry. The *Guardian* brought in a feature called 'Notes and Queries', in which readers provided answers to other readers' questions, instead of featuring an 'expert' who apparently knows the answers to everything. Soon many other publications had similar features – although for copyright reasons they would be reluctant to admit they got the idea from the *Guardian*. Every clever idea had to start being used somewhere – imagine people's surprise the first time a magazine stuck a free gift onto the front cover in order to increase sales. Now it's almost expected.

On the web, hyperlinks are usually images or text with underlining, but there is no rule or any technical reason why this should always be so. As developments in technology make the delivery of media products possible in more and more different ways, the products themselves are likely to evolve. That means more conventions will be broken and new ones will become established.

Think it over...

When do you think a new idea ceases to be a groundbreaking challenge to the usual conventions, and it actually becomes a convention itself?

Did you know?

RSS began as recently as 2004 to enable audiences to pre-select the kind of news they want to receive over the Internet from different providers. Until then, it was rare for audiences to be able to predetermine the content of the news they received. The conventions of RSS content and presentation developed very rapidly. Do you know what RSS stands for?

CASE STUDY

Private Eye

Private Eye is a satirical magazine that creates a lot of its humour by making fun of the conventions of newspaper and magazine journalism. Some of the magazine's content is serious, as well, but reading *Private Eye* regularly is a good way to become familiar with many of those conventions, while enjoying yourself at the same time.

The conventions that *Private Eye* ridicules include the following – see if you get the joke by reading the latest edition:

* Headlining the lead story on the front cover – but adding funny captions to it
* Continuing a story on another page – in *Private Eye* all continuations are on page 94!
* Printing poetry on a topical issue – usually signed E.J.Thribb (aged 17½)
* Writing editorial comment in a very conversational style – under the heading 'The Sun says'
* Printing many pages of in-depth coverage on subjects likely to increase sales
* Printing by-lines for reporters that suggest they have a particular expertise in a subject area
* Having a pictured personality columnist – *Private Eye* regularly features the fictitious Glenda Slagg, who writes in a very colloquial style
* Headlining regular features with clever titles – for example, 'HP Sauce' covers politics (and the Houses of Parliament) and 'Ad Nauseam' covers the advertising world
* Showing photographs of people who appear to look alike – *Private Eye* deliberately mixes them up as if they are so alike they are indistinguishable
* Carrying small ads for gifts and services – theirs are often made up and very expensive so nobody wants to try and order them. For example, there was the Pav-Nav, an 'on-head satellite navigation system for pedestrians' that looked like a miner's helmet with a small satellite dish on the top it.

- Explain how *Private Eye* makes fun of different conventions.
- What examples are there of these conventions being followed in the mainstream press?

Learning activity 21

✓ Choose a range of products from the part of the media industry you have been studying and explain the use of a number of conventions. What meanings do they create?

✓✓ Explain the likely effect of doing the opposite of each of those conventions.

✓✓✓ Explain how those conventions compare to others in the same products – for example, which are the most important and why?

* Again, the simpler the product, the less you will be able to find and explain. Choose products that use a variety of styles and techniques, rather than being similar from start to finish.

Genre

This word is the French word for 'type'. In media studies it is used in a particular way to group together all the media products of one type, in order to help us to discuss and understand them.

For example, we have considered television news programmes in some depth over the last few pages. Television news is, in fact, a particular genre – other genres in the medium of television include game shows, makeover shows, weather forecasts, drama and situation comedy, which is often referred to as the 'sit-com'. Within genres, there can be sub-genres, too, where types within types can be identified.

Drama is a very broad genre, so it can be much more helpful to use a sub-genre and describe a programme type as 'comedy drama' when it is meant to be funny or 'period drama' when it is set in a particular historical period. 'Soap opera' is another drama genre, used to describe a long-running series with a large number of different characters simultaneously involved in plots that intertwine and twist and turn over time, some stories beginning while others are ending.

Some types of media product mix different genres together – in film, radio and television it is quite common to find docu-drama, where something that happened in the absence of microphones and cameras is re-enacted in the way the producer thinks it happened. A responsible producer will go to great lengths to check facts and avoid presenting fiction as fact – but this isn't always successful. Reconstructing a crime for *Crimewatch* on BBC ONE depends on piecing together the known information about the crime – but there may be vital facts about it that are not known at the time to the police or the producer.

Each area of the media industry has its own set of genres – and as people come up with new ideas, new genres are formed. Makeover shows weren't particularly common until the 1990s, and wouldn't originally have been called by that name. Reality TV is a genre that many people think began in the 1990s, but in the 1970s a 'fly-on-the-wall' documentary (as the genre was then known) broke a number of previous conventions of documentary making – a camera crew was placed in a family's home and the most 'interesting' bits of the family's daily lives were then edited together.

Key terms

Genre – a type of media product within which most examples share a large number of characteristics

Sub-genre – a sub-division of a wider genre

What makes a genre? A media text belongs to a particular genre if it shares a large number of characteristics with others in the same genre. That is, they use the same – or very similar – codes and conventions in order to make meaning. They tend to be structured in similar ways. For example, the whodunnit is a common sub-genre of drama in radio and the moving image, and whodunnits almost all feature a murder or some other crime and an investigator from the police, a private detective or an enthusiastic individual who likes to solve a mystery. There are a number of possible suspects and, at the end, the investigator unmasks the real criminal.

The following boxes list some of the most popular genres within the different areas of the media industry. These lists are not exhaustive – there are other genres and sub-genres which are not listed. You will probably be able to think of some better or more recent examples.

TELEVISION GENRES WITH EXAMPLES
News programme – *Channel 4 News*
Documentary – *Panorama*
Comedy sketch show – *Little Britain*
Situation comedy – *Two Pints of Lager*
Science fiction – *Dr Who*
Reality TV – *Big Brother*
Period drama – *Bleak House*
Chat show – *Parkinson*
Soap opera – *EastEnders*
Drama series – *Waking the Dead*
Children's magazine – *Blue Peter*
Teen magazine – *T4*
Cartoon – *Scooby Doo, Where Are You?*
Rolling news programme – *Lunchtime Live with Kay Burley*

RADIO GENRES WITH EXAMPLES
News programme – *Newsbeat*
Documentary – *File on Four*
Comedy sketch show – *Dead Ringers*
Situation comedy – *Clare in the Community*
Science fiction – *The Hitchhiker's Guide to the Galaxy*
Soundscape – *The Twin Towers: A Memorial in Sound*
Period drama – *Classic Serial*
Chat show – *Midweek with Libby Purves*
Soap opera – *The Archers*
Drama series – *Afternoon Theatre*
Breakfast show – *Chris Moyles*
Children's magazine – *Go For It*
Sequence programme – *Steve Wright in the Afternoon*

PRINT GENRES WITH EXAMPLES
Compact newspaper – *The Times*
Tabloid newspaper – *The Sun*
News magazine – *The Economist*
Free sheet – *Metro*
Regional newspaper – *Western Daily Press*
Local newspaper – *Liverpool Echo*
Women's magazine – *Cosmopolitan*
Lads' magazine – *Nutz*
TV listings – *Radio Times*
Music magazine – *Smash Hits*
Classified advertising – *Exchange & Mart*
Special interest – *Boat Owner*
Fiction – *True Romances*
Children's magazine – *Bob the Builder*
Pre-teen magazine – *Girl Talk*
Comic – *Beyblades*

INTERACTIVE MEDIA GENRES WITH EXAMPLES
Website – *amazon.co.uk*
DVD – *Van Helsing*
CD-ROM – *World Atlas*
Computer game – *The Sims*
Game console game – *Crash Bandicoot*

Sometimes a media text will fit more than one genre – and this may be because a suitable genre label hasn't been thought of yet to describe it adequately. You may also find a genre that seems to have quite different texts within it. For example, the label 'reality TV' is given to programmes that follow people around in what are supposedly their everyday lives – such as *Airline*. But these programmes are very different in style, content and purpose to programmes like *Big Brother*, *I'm a Celebrity, Get Me Out of Here* and *Fame Academy*, in which groups of very different people are put together in a confined location, observed constantly through live feeds, voted in, voted out and voted winner.

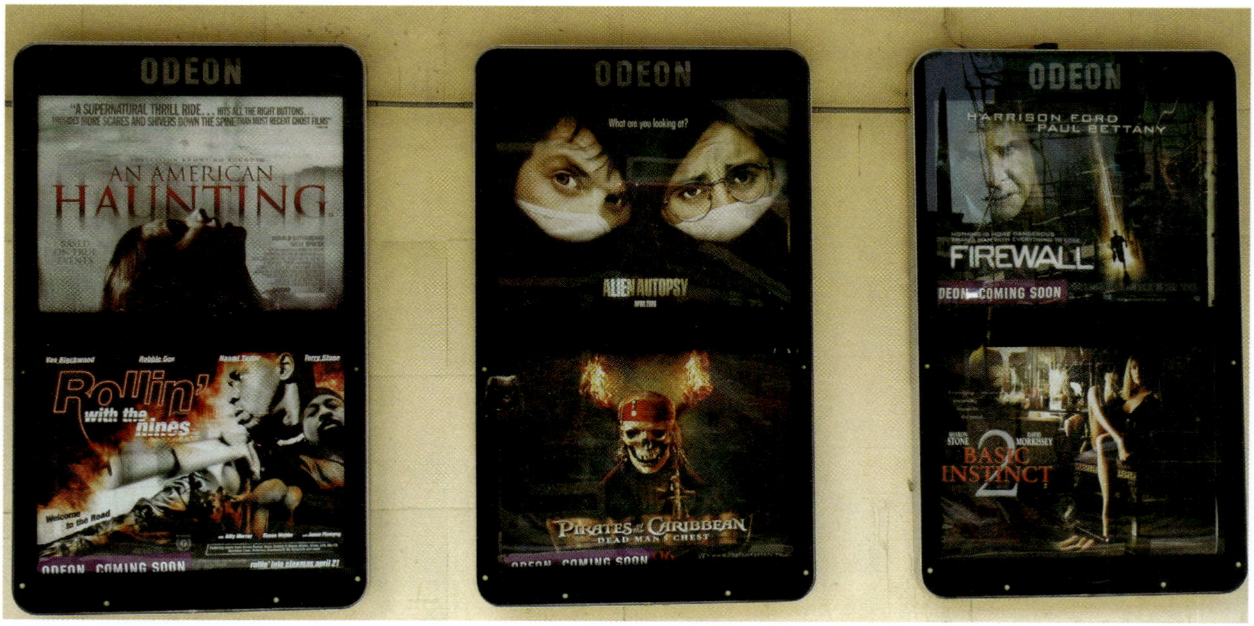

FIGURE 1.59 *The marketing of a media product often reveals a lot about its genre.*

Remember

It is usually the codes and conventions in a media text that indicate most closely which genre it fits into. Listen out for the laughter track in a sit-com, for example – it is used to reinforce the humour in the dialogue and the action. It suggests there is a studio audience, but often it is just dubbed on afterwards for effect, in post-production.

Learning activity 22

✓ Choose a range of products from the area of the media industry that you have been studying and categorise each one by genre.

✓✓ Explain what characteristics of each product make them fit those genres, and why.

✓✓✓ Suggest ways in which each product could be transformed to make it fit another genre or a sub-genre of the original genre. Sometimes only a few changes will be necessary to make quite a difference to the genre a product fits into. And some of those changes might seem very minor.

* You can include images, text and audio in your evidence, as appropriate, as long as you explain why you have chosen them and what they show.

Skills for media production

Unit 2

Unit 2 Introduction

Media products do not simply happen. The films and television programmes that we watch, the radio programmes that we listen to, the newspapers and magazines that we read and the websites and computer games that we interact with have all been researched, planned and produced by teams of people using some form of technology.

Media products are often very expensive and time-consuming to produce, and there is a lot of pressure on the people who plan and produce them to get them right. A major Hollywood film such as *Titanic*, which cost over £120 million to produce, needs to attract a large cinema audience to begin to recoup these costs, and also earn additional revenue from DVD rental and purchase sales. Similarly, the companies that have paid money to have their products and services advertised, in a lifestyle magazine such as *Marie Claire* or a prime-time soap such as *Coronation Street*, expect and demand a quality product that will deliver to them the desired audience.

Because of these pressures and demands, media companies put a lot of time and effort into thoroughly researching a product to ensure that it will attract the right audience and that this audience will react in an appropriate way to it. They also plan the production process thoroughly, and make use of the latest technology and techniques, to ensure that their product has the desired production values to compete effectively in the media market and is able to communicate in the right way to the right audience.

What you will learn in this unit

* The research methods and techniques that are used within the media industry
* The different purposes that this research is used for
* How to develop your own research skills
* The range of production technology available for different forms of media production
* Different production techniques used within the industry
* How to develop your own production skills

FIGURE 2.1 *A media production team at work.*

How you will be assessed

This unit is assessed internally, through the completion of a number of projects, activities or assignments set for you in class. You will have to make sure that you submit sufficient evidence of knowledge, understanding and practical skill development to meet the unit assessment criteria in the Edexcel specifications. You can present your evidence as written reports, illustrated presentations to class or in some other format appropriate to the media.

At appropriate points in this unit, you will find more specific information on the work you need to submit and what you need to do to try to achieve marks in the top mark band.

FIGURE 2.2 *The researcher is carrying out primary research with a member of the public.*

2.1 Research methods and techniques

In order to undertake successful research, you need to have an understanding of the basic research methods and techniques that are employed by media companies, and by the agencies and organisations that undertake research on their behalf.

Primary and secondary research

One of the basic distinctions to be made is between **primary** and **secondary** research.

Primary research is original research that is carried out for a specific purpose and that involves the use of a range of different methods and techniques to obtain new data. Conducting a survey in the street, interviewing people over the phone and running a focus group are all examples of techniques used to undertake primary research.

Secondary research involves the use of data and information that have already been published or are already available within an organisation. Looking in books, journals and on the Internet for information that already exists are all examples of secondary research. Many media organisations also use data and information that have been gathered and analysed by another company to add to and support, sometimes even to replace, their own primary research.

Quantitative and qualitative research

Another important distinction is between research that produces **quantitative** and **qualitative** types of information and data.

As we saw in Unit 1, quantitative research produces data and information that is measurable and quantifiable.

FIGURE 2.3 *A researcher at work – using a range of secondary sources.*

The data can usually be represented numerically and are often presented in the form of tables, charts and diagrams.

Both primary and secondary research techniques can produce quantitative data – for example: ratings, circulation figures and market analysis, as well as aspects of the content analysis of a media product, such as the number of items or size of space available.

Qualitative research produces information about people's opinions, views and preferences about something. Again, both primary and secondary research techniques can produce qualitative data. These types of data are very important within the media industry – they are used to find out what individuals and groups think and feel about a particular product, such as an advertisement, film or television programme.

Depending on the nature of the research and the types of questions asked, it is not always possible to analyse the information resulting from qualitative research statistically, particularly if the responses are personal and subjective in nature.

Key terms

Primary research – original research to obtain new data, using such methods as interviews, questionnaires, focus groups and observation

Secondary research – research using pre-existing data and information that have already been gathered by other people or organisations – often available in books, journals or via the Internet

Quantitative research – research based on measurable and quantifiable facts and information, producing numerical and statistical data

Qualitative research – research that is based on opinions, attitudes and preferences rather than hard facts and figures

Learning activity 1

✓ Think carefully about the four key terms and, in your own words, give a definition of each one.

✓✓ Explain the purposes of each type of research and identify specific examples of media-related research that would require each of the different techniques.

✓✓✓ Assess the advantages and disadvantages of each method.

* When looking for examples of media-related research, remember that many media companies employ the services of external agencies and organisations that undertake research on their behalf.

To receive marks in the upper band you should demonstrate that you have a thorough understanding of the different types of research and their purposes and that you have assessed their strengths and limitations.

Audience segmentation

Segmenting the audience into different categories makes it easier for media producers to identify and target groups of people with the same needs and wants. Those undertaking research within, or on behalf of, media organisations therefore look for categories they can use to divide up the potential audience. There are four commonly used categories, as follows.

1. Age

One of the most significant and often used categories used within the media is that of age. Common divisions used by media researchers are fifteen or younger, sixteen–twenty-four, twenty-five–forty-four, forty-five–sixty-four and sixty-five and over, but individual pieces of research will use age divisions that are most appropriate for the task.

Research into the impact that advertising has on young children will need to sub-divide the fifteen or younger category into smaller divisions, while a company that is looking at the over fifty-five market may find it useful to compare the reactions to a particular product of a fifty-five–sixty-four and a sixty-five–seventy category, for example.

	TOTAL	AGE			
		16–24	25–44	45–64	65+
	%	%	%	%	%
Less than one hour	4	1	6	4	1
1–2	17	17	20	17	10
2–3	24	24	27	26	18
3–4	19	23	17	20	19
4–5	14	14	13	14	19
5–6	8	10	8	6	9
6–7	3	3	2	4	5
7+	10	7	6	9	19

Source: OFCOM, 2004

FIGURE 2.4 *Average number of hours a day spent watching television according to age (2003).*

Other more general age-related categories can also be used (such as pre-school children, school children, teenagers, pensioners). The regulatory system can also sometimes provide a framework, as in the different age categories used by the British Board of Film Classification (BBFC).

2. Gender

Gender is also a significant category for audience segmentation, as many media products may be targeted at a specific gender group. This is perhaps most clearly seen within the magazine market, which has specific products targeted at males and others targeted at females.

Of course, this does not mean that men do not read *OK!* magazine, or that women do not read *Four Four Two* magazine, and we should be careful of simply recirculating outdated gender stereotypes.

Learning activity 2

- ✓ Draw up a list of about twenty magazines and decide which ones are marketed primarily at men (or boys), which at women (or girls) and any where the gender of the targeted group is less clear.
- ✓✓ From looking at the magazines themselves, can you identify any characteristics or techniques that are commonly used to target men and women?
- ✓✓✓ Assess how successful you think these different techniques have been.
- * The magazine market is very diverse, and you will need to undertake some initial research into the different types of magazine that are available, and then make a careful choice of the ones that you are going to analyse further.

FIGURE 2.5 *BBFC age classifications.*

CASE STUDY

UK Bollywood

'Bollywood' is a term used to describe the Indian film industry, and is a play on the word 'Hollywood'. Bollywood is the largest and most prolific film industry in the world – in 2005 over 800 films Bollywood films were produced. Bollywood's cinema-going audience, in India, Pakistan and elsewhere, is also one of the biggest in the world.

Just like Hollywood, Bollywood has large production studios and huge stars, capable of making expensive, commercial movies.

Although the output from these studios is very diverse, the characteristics that are commonly associated with Bollywood films include epic romances that involve mythological and theological characters, and extensive use of song and dance sequences with elaborate costumes.

There is a strong UK market for Bollywood films, which is growing all the time. The Leicester-based organisation FilmPur has developed into a widely recognised gateway connecting the film industries in Britain and the Indian sub-continent. It provides Bollywood film producers who are looking to shoot within the UK and Europe with details and contacts for locations, crew and services, providing a 'one-stop-shop' for all their production requirements.

Further information can be found on the company's website: www.filmpur.com.

- What are the main conventions of a Bollywood film?
- Why do you think Bollywood films have become more popular in the UK in recent years?
- Can you think of any examples of other media products that have been influenced by Bollywood.

3. Culture and ethnicity

People's needs and wants as consumers will vary according to their culture, language and ethnic background, and a number of media products are available to meet this need. The media industry is now very much a global one and newspapers, magazines, radio and television programmes from all over the world are readily available to people living in Britain. However, there is also a growing production base in Britain for media products that target different cultures and ethnic groups.

4. Income and social class

The potential audience can also be segmented according to annual salary or type of job or social class. Establishing a person's disposable income can be important, particularly for advertisers who need to target the relevant income group as precisely as possible. It is no good advertising a top of the range sports car to households that have a low disposable income.

Most organisations involved with media research and production use the socio-economic

SOCIAL GRADE	SOCIAL STATUS	CHIEF INCOME EARNER'S OCCUPATION
A	Upper middle class	Higher managerial, administrative or professional
B	Middle class	Intermediate managerial, administrative or professional
C1	Lower middle class	Supervisory or clerical and junior managerial, administrative or professional
C2	Skilled working class	Skilled manual workers
D	Working class	Semi- and unskilled manual workers
E	Those at the lowest levels of subsistence	State pensioners or widows (no other earner), casual or lowest grade workers

Source: NRS

FIGURE 2.6 *Most commonly used categories for describing social class.*

TITLE	AB	ABC1	ABC1C2	C1	C2	DE
The Daily Telegraph	58	87	96	29	9	4
Guardian	60	90	94	30	4	5
The Independent	58	88	95	30	7	5
The Times	57	86	95	29	8	5
Daily Mail	29	64	85	35	21	15
Daily Express	28	58	83	31	25	17
The Sun	11	33	64	23	31	36
Daily Mirror	12	38	68	27	29	32
Daily Star	9	29	62	19	34	38

Source: NRS

FIGURE 2.7 *Socio-economic profile of readers of a selection of national newspapers by percentage of total readership (November 2005).*

groups A, B, C1, C2, D and E to identify and describe the different audience groupings according to income and social class (see Figure 2.6). Figure 2.7 shows how different newspapers fit their readership into the different groupings.

Learning activity 3

Look carefully at Figure 2.7, showing the socio-economic profile for the major national newspapers.

- ✓ What does the table tell you about the readership profiles of the newspapers?
- ✓✓ How are these profiles reflected in the design, style and news values of the newspapers?
- ✓✓✓ What changes could a newspaper make if it wanted to attract a different readership?
- * The Newspaper Marketing Agency website (www.nmauk.co.uk) has more detailed demographic information on these and other newspapers to help you with your activity.

Content analysis

Content analysis is another research method that is often used to analyse and compare media products. It involves the counting of distinct elements or features within a particular programme, magazine or newspaper and then comparing the results with similar information from other products.

For example, if you were researching the representation of teenagers in the media, you could conduct a simple content analysis of some selected popular media products such as a soap opera, a news programme and a daily newspaper to see how many times teenagers are featured, and then compare this to the amount of times that other groups of people are represented.

This will give you some very basic information about the under- or over-representation of teenagers within the different media. It might be useful also to try to categorise the different ways in which they are represented, to see if there are any particular patterns that emerge and any representations that could be seen as dominant.

Content analysis can also be used to look at the way media products have changed over time, by comparing a product from today with one from many years ago.

Care needs to be taken when drawing conclusions from the results of a content analysis. One area of concern is in deciding which category a particular example falls into. For example, a news report showing a group of teenagers drinking in a park might be seen by one researcher as a negative representation that highlights antisocial behaviour, but by another as a positive representation that shows the teenagers enjoying themselves.

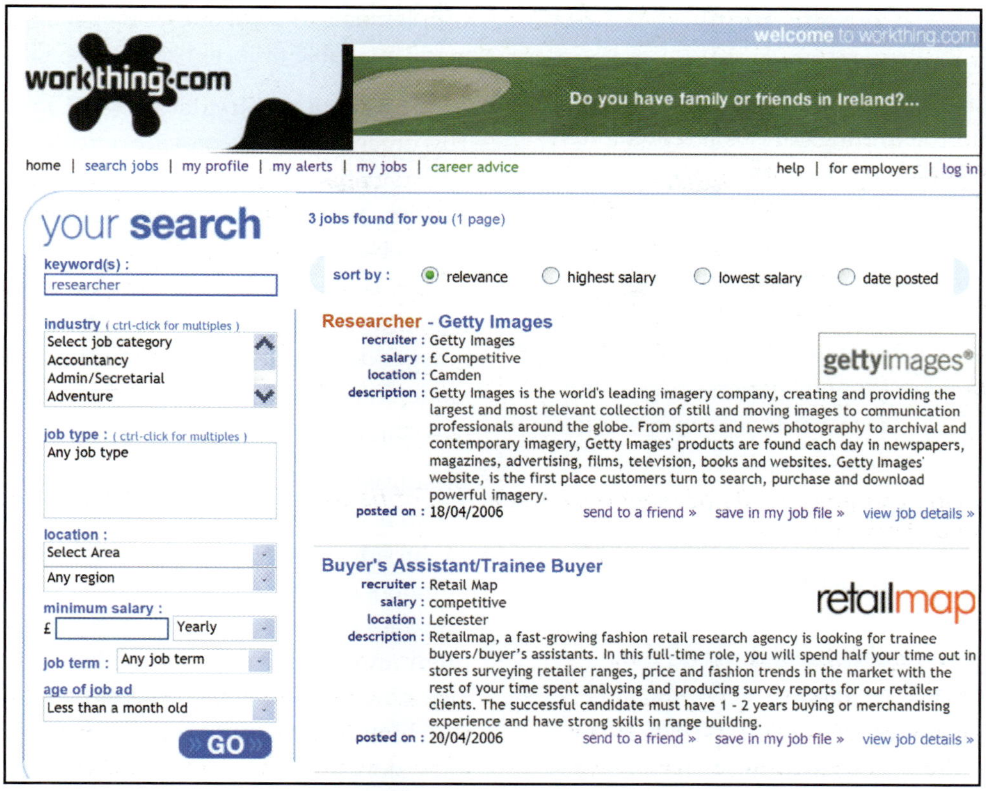

FIGURE 2.8 *Example of a job advert for a researcher from workthing.com.*

Another criticism of content analysis is that it concentrates too much on the product itself, and does not consider the different ways in which the audience might respond and react to the messages being communicated.

Learning activity 4

Decide on an area of study (e.g. representation of teenagers) and undertake your own content analysis of a selection of media products.

✓ Explain what your results show.

✓✓ What conclusions can you draw from your results?

✓✓ Assess the limitations of the methodology that you used and explain how you could improve it.

* Take care not to be over-ambitious with this activity. You should choose a very specific and well-defined area to study that includes only two or three media products. You should be very clear from the beginning what it is you are you looking at and what your methodology is.

2.2 The different purposes of research

Effective and successful media products are those that target the right audience and communicate to them in an effective way. As the media become more fragmented, so competition for a share of the audience becomes more intense, and knowing who your target audience are, and what makes them tick, becomes increasingly important.

This commercial driver is one of the main reasons why media producers undertake very detailed research into their target market or, more usually, commission other companies to undertake research on their behalf.

Think it over...

Why do you think media producers employ other companies and organisations to do research on their behalf? What are the advantages and disadvantages of this policy?

Media research organisations

There are various organisations whose main role is to undertake research on media audiences and products, and the findings of this research often becomes a commercial product in its own right that is sold to media companies.

Some of this information is also freely available in the public domain, and you can find examples by visiting the websites of the organisations listed below, as well as by looking in the media pages of newspapers such as the *Guardian* and *The Independent*, and in specialist magazines such as *Broadcast*.

National Readership Survey (NRS)

This non-profit-making organisation provides information to the industry on who reads each publication.

It provides a market breakdown of the readership of each newspaper and magazine according to such factors as gender, age, social class and many other demographic and lifestyle characteristics. This information is invaluable to companies and agencies that are planning, buying and selling advertising in the print medium, as the data allow them to target the right audience more effectively.

The NRS publishes data covering over two hundred and fifty newspapers, newspaper supplements and consumer magazines, which are made available to its subscribers via its website.

Audit Bureau of Circulation (ABC)

This organisation also provides circulation information to the newspaper and magazine industry and includes directories, leaflets, exhibitions and websites in its range of products researched.

It was launched in 1931 in response to demands from the advertising industry for independent verification of the circulation and readership claims made by the sales teams of newspapers and magazines.

Broadcasters' Audience Research Board (BARB)

BARB is used by the BBC and independent TV broadcasters to provide estimates of the numbers of people watching their programmes. The data produced include which channels and programmes are being watched at specific times, and a breakdown of the type of people who are watching a particular programme. BARB provides television audience data for all analogue and digital channels received within the UK. The information is obtained from panels of viewers from selected television owning households, representative of each ITV and BBC region. The data produced by the research represent the viewing behaviour of over twenty-five million households within the UK.

	AVERAGE WEEKLY VIEWING PER PERSON		SHARE OF TOTAL VIEWING	
	Jan. (hrs: mins)	Dec. (hrs: mins)	Jan. (%)	Dec. (%)
All TV	27:44	27:50	100.0	100.0
BBC ONE	6:09	6:22	22.2	22.9
BBC TWO	2:35	2:42	9.3	9.7
Total BBC ONE/BBC TWO	8:44	9:04	31.5	32.6
ITV	5:40	6:10	20.5	22.1
C4/S4C	3:03	2:24	11.0	8.6
five	1:37	1:41	5.8	6.1
Total/terrestrial TV	10:20	10:15	37.3	36.8
Other viewing	8:40	8:31	31.3	30.6

Source: BARB

FIGURE 2.9 *Share of viewing time of the different TV channels in December 2005 and January 2006.*

CASE STUDY

PQ Magazine

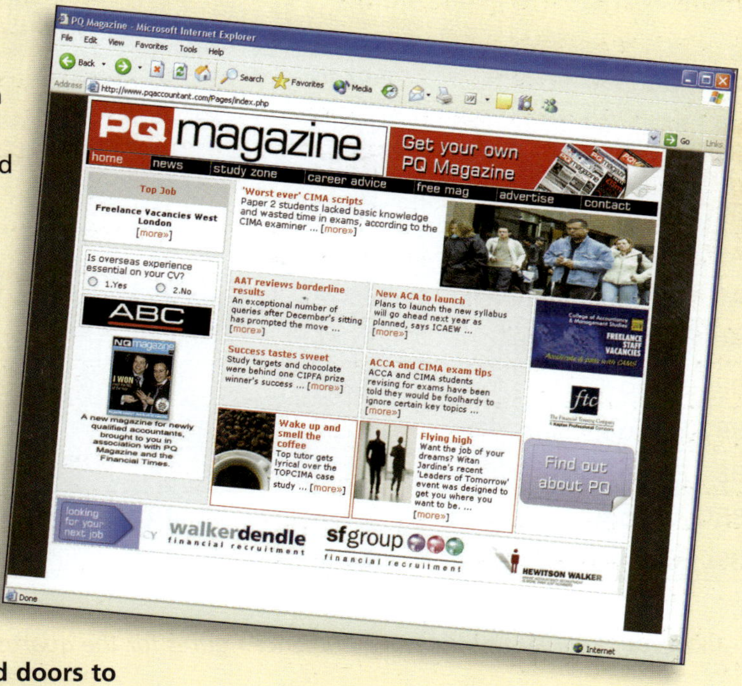

PQ Magazine is a business-to-business title published by PQ Publishing, which was launched in January 2003 as a monthly journal aimed at part-qualified accountants.

Since its launch, *PQ Magazine*'s advertising sales team was consistently being asked for ABC certification by prospective advertising clients, to provide them with reassurance in their advertising decisions. As a new title, *PQ Magazine* felt it wasn't able to have its circulation figures audited by ABC immediately, but the process of achieving certification was high on its agenda.

'ABC certification is vital to our business and our advertisers. It opened doors to clients and shows we are a major player.'

As it does for many business-to-business magazines, ABC certification provides publishers with an independent stamp of approval that verifies their circulation claims. It proves that their figures are robust and therefore have the capacity to deliver return on investment for advertisers. In addition, ABC verification offers publishers further value by ensuring that their systems are efficient and comply with industry agreed standards. After completing its first year, *PQ Magazine* committed to having its circulation figures audited by ABC.

'Our perceptions of ABC were quite stuffy and inflexible but the reality was very different. The ABC Account Manager put our minds at rest that not only could we achieve ABC verification but that we were ready to do so.'

Although *PQ Magazine* feared the audit process was going to be difficult to negotiate, it soon found ABC was always on hand to lead the way. ABC account managers are experts in the audit process, enabling them to provide solutions to any perceived difficulties or issues. They worked with *PQ Magazine* beforehand to ensure potential difficulties were highlighted and could be worked through prior to the audit, and maintained this support throughout the process.

Much of *PQ Magazine*'s circulation is controlled free distribution, and part of the process involved setting up its reporting methods to provide the information needed to ensure all copies met with the terms of the controlled circulation. With the ABC account manager's help, *PQ Magazine* devised new reporting forms which ensured all relevant information for the audit were collected, to speed up the process even further.

'We knew we had first class editorial but now we could also prove our circulation too. Having ABC visit clients alongside us is a great option.'

Having an ABC certificate aids the promotion of magazines. It identifies to prospects and those in the market that the publisher has invested in good business practices and has been willing to open its business up to the scrutiny of an audit adhering to the rules agreed by the media industry.

- Why is it important for a newspaper of magazine to have its circulation figures checked and authorised?
- Do you think that the growth of online versions of newspapers and magazines is a factor that needs to be taken into account when looking at a publication's circulation figures?

	AUDIENCE (000s)	% OF POPULATION	AVERAGE HOURS	SHARE OF LISTENING %
All radio	44,439	90	23.9	100.0
All BBC	32,973	67	17.7	55.1
All BBC network radio	28,802	58	16.2	44.0
BBC local/regional	10,435	21	11.3	11.1
All commercial	30,888	63	14.7	42.8
All national commercial	12,828	26	8.3	10.1
All local commercial	25,064	51	13.8	32.7
BBC Radio 1	10,294	21	9.5	9.2
BBC Radio 2	13,252	27	12.8	16.0
BBC Radio 3	1,973	4	6.4	1.2
BBC Radio 4	9,318	19	13.4	11.8
BBC Radio FIVE LIVE	5,721	12	7.8	4.2

Source: RAJAR

FIGURE 2.10 *Summary of the radio audience figures for the quarter ending December 2005.*

The **Radio Joint Audience Research Limited** (RAJAR) was established in 1992 to operate a single audience measurement system for the radio industry, including all BBC, UK licensed and other commercial stations. The company is owned by the Commercial Radio Companies Association (CRCA) and by the British Broadcasting Corporation (BBC).

In addition to these organisations, there are a growing number of commercial agencies that offer research and analysis services to media producers, advertisers and regulators.

Learning activity 5

- ✓ Find out the names of at least three commercial companies that offer a research service to other media companies.
- ✓✓ What range of services does each company offer to media companies?
- ✓✓✓ Describe the different ways in which they market themselves and assess the advantages and limitations of these methods.
- * A carefully worded Internet search will provide you with a current list of UK-based companies. Choose from this list by looking at their website for more information about the services that they offer.

Advertising

Advertising is an important source of income for many of the media products that we watch, listen to, read and interact with. You only have to look at a popular lifestyle magazine such as *Marie Claire* to see the amount of pages that are dedicated to advertising, and each of these pages is a valuable source of income for the publishers. Turn on any commercial television station or tune into any commercial radio station and you will soon notice the amount of advertising space that is available.

Think it over...

Why do you think advertising has become such an important part of the media products that we consume? Do you think advertising is becoming more or less effective over time?

Advertisers are attracted to media products such as newspapers, magazines, broadcast programmes and websites because they deliver a ready-made audience to them. The popular programme *Coronation Street* is watched by around twelve million people, and this is clearly of interest to companies such as Cadbury's, which is its current sponsor.

FIGURE 2.11 *An example of advertising in the print media.*

Learning activity 6

✓ Undertake a small research project to identify the types of products and services that are advertised within specific programmes or publications.

✓✓ Extend your research to find out the cost of buying advertising time or space within each product.

✓✓✓ What do these adverts tell you about the anticipated audience for the programme or publication concerned? Explain to what extent these adverts actually work and get the right message across.

* As with your previous research activity, you need to plan carefully and make sure that your project is well defined and that you have a very clear idea of the scope and scale of the research – what you are looking for and where you are going to look.

Predicting accurately how many viewers or listeners a particular programme is likely to attract, and after it has been broadcast, knowing how many actually did, is clearly very important information to the companies who are buying advertising space and time within the programmes. The same goes for magazines, newspapers, comics, websites and other commercial media products that rely on advertising revenue.

Predicting and then verifying circulation, readership and rating figures is clearly the major purpose of much media research. However, advertisers are not only interested in the size of the target audience but, perhaps more importantly, the demographic make-up of that audience. The advertising agency charged with promoting Club 18–30 style holidays would probably not choose to advertise within a religious broadcast targeted at the over-thirty-five age group.

Finding out detailed, demographic information about the audience is another important purpose of the media research that is regularly carried out.

If a media organisation is planning the launch of a new product, then they may also require information on how similar products already in the market compare with each other, how successful they are and what the target audience thinks about these products. So investigating and comparing existing media products is another important purpose of media research.

Think it over...

As the BBC gets a fixed amount of money from the licence fee, why would it need to undertake research for its programmes?

It is not only commercial media organisations that undertake and commission media research. The BBC derives the bulk of its income from the licence fee, and does not have any advertising revenue to support its terrestrial broadcasting services. However, it is still in competition with commercial broadcasters and therefore needs research data to demonstrate its continued popularity, to show that it is providing a service to the public and to support the political argument for its continued status as a public service broadcaster in an increasingly competitive and market-driven industry.

Learning activity 7

- ✓ Research and compare the latest viewing and listening figures for a range of commercial and BBC programmes.
- ✓✓ Explain what the figures tell you about the different programmes.
- ✓✓✓ With reference to your results, assess the future of the BBC in an increasingly competitive market.
- * The future of the BBC is always a hot topic of conversation and you should be able to find a range of different viewpoints in the newspapers and on the Internet. Think carefully about the different points of view and try to understand the different ideas and positions about what the role of the BBC is and how it should operate.

Researching content

When planning a new media product, the company making the programme, film, magazine, website or game will also need to undertake a lot of research to provide content and gather materials for the new product. Some of this research will be generic, but much of it will depend on the type of product being planned.

For example, a newspaper journalist asked to write an article about a new piece of government legislation and its impact on people might have to do some very quick primary and secondary research to be able to write the copy. He or she might use secondary research to find out more specific information about the legislation and the background issues, as well as conducting some primary research in the form of interviews with politicians and sample members of the population to try to understand the potential impact. The information gained would then be used to inform the writing, with some of the quotes used in the article itself. Some form of picture research would probably also be undertaken to find a suitable image to accompany the article.

A documentary film maker will also undertake both primary and secondary research, but may have a little more time to do so. As well as researching for the content of the documentary, they may also have to undertake research into the cost of hiring equipment and personnel to shoot the documentary as well as the post-production and distribution services that they might need.

They will almost certainly also have to undertake some location research (a recce) to identify suitable venues for filming to take place, to assist in the planning of specific shots, and to try to assess any problems or health and safety issues that the crew might face.

Think it over...

What sort of problems might a crew face when out on location, and how might a recce help to overcome some of these?

The amount of information that is gathered can often be very large, particularly if the production is a complex one that involves many different aspects – it is important that all of the information is carefully logged, organised and stored to ensure it is secure, while also allowing easy access and cross-referencing.

CASE STUDY

Careers in research

There are hundreds of market research agencies in the UK, from large international companies to smaller consultancies. The largest market research agencies now commonly take on graduates every year, some have year-round recruitment procedures, but places are much sought after so you have to make sure you are right for the job. Get some work experience in a firm before you apply – as always it will make you look really keen!

As a researcher in an agency, you will oversee a number of client accounts, working on a variety of projects in, quite possibly, a range of different industries. Most people in the agency will be pursuing the same career path as you and you may have the opportunity to move between different research sectors, giving you a broad experience of research techniques.

Virtually every company in the UK uses market research. As a result, many of these companies, particularly the larger ones, will employ their own researchers, usually one or two.

In this role, you will be expected to keep the company in touch with its customers and informed of its investment and marketing decisions. You will commission researchers in external agencies to work on behalf of your company, as well as organising internal research among staff and customers. You will gain a close knowledge of your company's overall way of working and play a key role in shaping its future development.

Day-to-day role

You'll start off as a research executive, overseeing the day-to-day smooth running of specific projects, from the commissioning stages right through to the final presentation to the client.

Your role is likely to include designing the best way to fulfil a client's need; managing the budget; advising on questionnaire design; briefing interviewers (the people who hold the clipboards); monitoring the conduct of the research process; checking and analysing the data; and writing a results and recommendation paper for your client, which you may also have to present to them.

The type of research you are involved in will determine the specific tasks you undertake, but your days will definitely be full and varied.

Career path

Market research is far from a desk-bound career. As you progress, you'll be expected to have increasing levels of client contact. Depending on your clients, this could involve a fair amount of national and international travel. You'll also have to make presentations to clients, meet interviewers and respondents, and visit appropriate research venues.

Career progression in market research can be very rapid! As a general rule, you can expect to be a research executive for 18 months, after which time you will become a senior research executive. From then on, most companies base promotion on merit, so you can progress as fast as the quality of your work and opportunities permit. It wouldn't be unusual for you to be holding responsibility for accounts and managing a team by the time you are thirty.

Once you've gained a range of experience, you could find yourself making the brave move of going it alone and setting up your own agency. This is a popular route in this industry and will allow you to pick and choose the projects you work on and the hours you put in. Something to bear in mind during the long months of summer!

Excerpt taken from the article 'Researching the markets – Becoming a Market Researcher' published in the Channel 4 website magazine Frontline.

- What skills do you need to be a successful researcher?
- What sort of tasks does a researcher undertake?
- What is it about the role of a researcher that makes it such a good introduction to working in the media?

Some radio and television productions employ researchers as part of the pre-production team. The role of a researcher on a television programme, such as the talk show *Trisha*, is to find out background information about the themes that are going to be covered in a particular show, and to contact and interview potential guests to find out what their stories are and if they would be suitable for the show. The reality TV programme *Big Brother* employed a team of researchers and research assistants to sift through and interview potential housemates.

Researchers are also employed on radio programmes such as *Today* on BBC Radio 4 and *Newsbeat* on BBC Radio 1 to find out information about the stories of the day, make contact with potential sources of information and arrange interviews.

Remember

If you continue your media studies through to A2 level, you will study the area of research in more detail in Unit 4.

Did you know?

The Channel 4 presenter Mark Durden-Smith was a researcher for programmes presented by both Clive James and Clive Anderson before moving on to become a sports presenter with Sky One.

FIGURE 2.12 *Mark Durden-Smith*

Undertaking your own research

In the first part of this unit we looked at the different types of research that are used within the media industry and some of the purposes for that research. In this second section, you will learn how to apply this knowledge of different research techniques to your own research.

UNIT ASSESSMENT

To successfully complete this part of the unit you will need to need to carry out two distinct pieces of research.

1. Gather information for the content of a proposed media production.
2. Produce an investigation into an existing media product.

You will need to undertake both primary and secondary research when conducting these two tasks, and obtain data that are both quantitative and qualitative in nature.

It is important that you record and explain your methods of research and the processes that you carried out as clearly and as thoroughly as you can.

Through your work in section 2.2 you will be generating evidence to meet assessment criteria (a) and (b). To achieve marks in the highest mark band, you will need to:

- demonstrate a thorough understanding of the different types of research technique, and their purposes, strengths and limitations
- gather a substantial amount of highly focused data using a wide range of techniques and procedures
- show the results and conclusions of your research in a thorough and well-presented way.

Your evidence is likely to be presented in the form of one or more research files, and will probably include written material, numerical data, tables, charts and diagrams.

- More detailed information about the unit assessment can be found on page 99.

Undertaking primary research

When planning your primary research it is important to think carefully about what you are trying to find out, and that you choose an appropriate sample, an appropriate research technique and are aware of the size, scope and time scale of the task ahead.

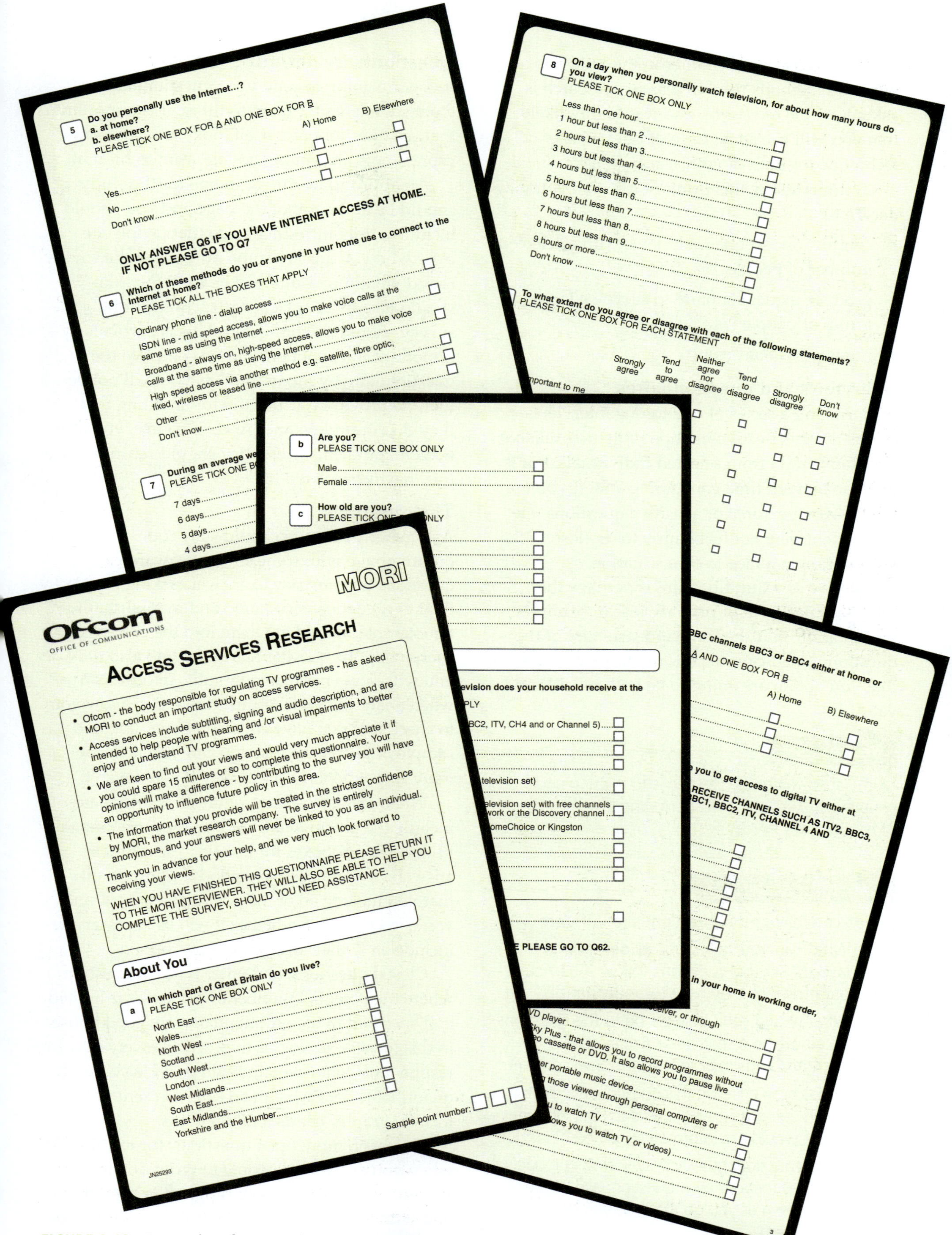

FIGURE 2.13 *Example of a questionnaire used by OFCOM/MORI.*

As you discovered earlier in the unit, one of the main methods used in primary research is asking people questions, and it is highly likely that you will use some form of questioning technique for both of your research tasks.

In undertaking this primary research you may decide to:

* conduct one-to-one interviews with a selected number of people
* produce a questionnaire to survey a larger group of people
* organise a focus group.

Interviews and questionnaires

Undertaking a series of one-to-one interviews can be a very effective method of getting reliable, qualitative data from selected individuals, but it can also be very time-consuming and, if you are asking very personal or sensitive questions, the respondent may not feel happy to disclose such information in a face-to-face situation.

The use of a questionnaire is perhaps the most popular form of primary research, but its presentation, and the form and structure of the questions, need careful consideration if the results that you obtain are going to be both reliable and valid.

Remember

Time spent planning, testing and revising your survey will be time well spent, and should improve the effectiveness of your research project.

Learning activity 8

Look carefully at the questionnaire in Figure 2.13.

- ✓ What can you say about its design and layout? Do the questions follow a particular pattern? Are they easy to understand?
- ✓✓ What would your answers be to the questions asked by the researchers? Explain the strengths and limitations of the questions set.
- ✓✓✓ Assess how effective this questionnaire is in encouraging the respondents to reply. To what extent would the information gained be useful?
- * As you are doing this activity you will probably get ideas for your own questionnaire. Write these down as you go along so you don't forget them.

Questionnaire design

If you are going to send your questionnaire to the respondents for them to fill in, it is important that the questionnaire itself looks attractive and professional and makes people want to fill it in.

An appropriate title or theme for the study should be at the top of the page and you should include a brief introduction so that people are clear who you are, what the purpose of the survey is and what the results will be used for. You should also include clear instructions for how the survey should be completed. This is particularly important if respondents are to complete the questionnaire by themselves, as you will not be there to provide clarification for anything that they do not understand. And, of course, you also need to tell them where they should return it once they have completed it.

The questions

As a general rule you should start your questionnaire with some straightforward closed questions that are easy to answer. Asking people their age, gender, occupation and marital status, for example, should get them into the process of completing the questionnaire, and will also provide you with some basic demographic information when analysing your results. It will also allow you to check that you have covered a representative sample of people, so that you can include some more respondents in the survey if you haven't.

When using closed questions, it is often easier to include the potential answers on the questionnaire itself, with tick boxes for people to select their answers. If you use this method it is important that you include all of the potential answers, and you need to decide whether it will be necessary to include an 'Other' or 'Don't know' option.

Closed questions, and other types of question where the potential number of responses is limited and specified in the questionnaire, are good to use in this form of survey, as they are relatively easy for respondents to answer and will provide you with quantifiable data which you can represent in the form of graphs, charts and diagrams.

However, more open questions, for example when you are asking people to write down a personal response to something, often provide you with qualitative information that gives a more meaningful insight.

Key terms

Open questions – these allow the person answering to give his or her own view of the subject; questions usually start with words such as:

- What
- Why
- When
- How
- Who

Closed questions – these are more limited in terms of the potential responses possible; they are often answered by yes/no, or an answer picked from a range of given options; questions often start with words like:

- Do you
- Which
- How many
- How often
- Have you

As a general rule, your questionnaire should contain a mix of open and closed questions, and require simple tick box responses as well as one or two more in-depth, written responses.

For some questions you might want to gauge the extent to which the respondents agree or disagree with a particular statement, or the degree of their feelings on a subject. Here you can use a rating system or a response scale of some kind:

* **Likert scale** asks the respondent how strongly they agree or disagree with a series of statements.
* **Rank order scale** asks the respondent to indicate the order of preference from a list of given answers, usually through the use of numbers.
* **Semantic differential scale** uses a sliding scale between two opposing words and asks respondents to indicate where on the scale their opinion lies.

Examples of the use of all three types of scale are given in Figures 2.14 to 2.16.

	STRONGLY AGREE	AGREE	NEITHER AGREE NOR DISAGREE	DISAGREE	STRONGLY DISAGREE
The magazine is informative		✓			
The magazine is good value for money				✓	
The front cover is attractive	✓				

FIGURE 2.14 *Example of a Likert scale.*

Where do you get your news from? Rank the following sources of news in their order of importance to you, with 1 being the most important and 5 being the least important.

Television	1	Internet	3
Radio	4	Local newspaper	5
National newspaper	2		

FIGURE 2.15 *Example of a rank order scale.*

Looks attractive	........X..	Looks unattractive
Healthy	..............................X....................	Unhealthy
Good value	.....X..	Poor value
Tasty	........................X........................	Tasteless

FIGURE 2.16 *Example of a semantic differential scale.*

FIGURE 2.17 *Making your questionnaire enjoyable to fill in will ensure that more respondents take part in your survey.*

You might also want to group questions on different topics together in sections, perhaps with headings. This can make the questionnaire look more attractive and appealing and may also give people a sense of achievement when they have completed a section, so the questionnaire does not seem so long.

Think it over...

If you were completing a questionnaire for somebody else, what are the features that would encourage you to answer truthfully, and what would put you off?

What is perhaps most important in constructing your questionnaire is the form and structure of the questions that you are asking. You need to make sure that people will be able to understand and respond to the questions that you are asking, and that the responses will provide you with the information that you require.

Avoid ambiguity and keep the language as simple as possible. Questions that are too vague or too complex are unlikely to provide you with useful answers, if they are answered at all. You should also try to avoid asking leading questions that suggest a response to the respondent, or the use of emotive language that, again, might prejudice the response.

Presenting your questionnaire

There are four main ways in which you can present your questionnaire to your sample audience. You can:

* stop and ask people the questions face to face
* telephone them
* post or e-mail the questionnaire to them
* include the questionnaires in a magazine or newsletter and ask respondents to post them back or hand them in.

The first three ways listed will allow you to identify and select specific respondents, so you can target your questionnaire at a selected audience, or make sure that you cover a representative range of people according to age, gender, culture and other demographics.

Think it over...

What do you think the advantages and disadvantages are of the different ways of presenting your questionnaire?

YOUR DETAILS

1. Are you?
- Male ☐
- Female ☐

2. How old are you?
- 25 or under ☐
- 26 to 34 ☐
- 35 to 44 ☐
- 45 to 54 ☐
- 55 or over ☐

3. Do you get your own personal copy of The Bookseller?
- Yes, I pay for it personally ☐
- Yes, the company pays for my personal copy ☐
- No, I share a copy with colleagues ☐
- No, I do not receive The Bookseller ☐

4. How many people do you share your copy with?
- 0 ☐
- 1-3 ☐
- 4-6 ☐
- 7-10 ☐
- 11 or more ☐

5. How do the copies get shared around the team?
- I get it first ☐
- Strict distribution list ☐
- Unpredictable distribution list ☐
- Put in the same place each week ☐
- Pick it up off someone's desk ☐
- I have to ask around ☐

Name ______________________

Job title ______________________

Company ______________________

Address ______________________

____

____

Email ______________________

Telephone number ______________________

FIGURE 2.18 *Example of a questionnaire in* The Bookseller *magazine.*

Asking people face to face or via the telephone can be very time-consuming, particularly if you are covering a large sample of people, but it does allow you to explain any questions that they might not understand or need further clarification on. If you use either of these methods you will also need to think carefully about how you are going to record their responses. Using a tally chart or data recorder might be more efficient than filling out an individual questionnaire sheet for each respondent.

If you post or e-mail the questionnaire, or include it within a publication of some sort, people can complete the questionnaire in their own time and in their own environment – this means that some people may be more willing to give you confidential information, though of course you have little control over how many people actually complete the questionnaire or return it to you!

Pre-testing

Pre-testing your questionnaire on a small sample of your audience before you start conducting your full survey is a very good idea, as it will allow you to identify any potential problems with specific questions or the design and layout of the questionnaire itself, in good time for you to make any changes. You may also be able to identify responses that fall under the 'Other' option which it might be better to include among the specified options.

Focus groups

Focus groups are pre-selected panels of people who are chosen to represent the target audience. They tend to be used by marketing and advertising agencies to test the likely response of the target audience towards the product that is being advertised as well as to the advertisement itself.

Film studios also use focus groups in preview screenings of major films prior to release, so that they can try to ensure that the audience reaction is the desired one. There are many examples of studio executives changing the ending of a film, often against the wishes of the director, because the audience in the preview screening didn't like it.

Did you know?

The studio that commissioned Ridley Scott to direct the science fiction film *Blade Runner* (1982) didn't think that the audience would understand parts of the story and they didn't like the unresolved ending.

Against the wishes of the director, they added additional voiceovers to explain certain scenes, removed the now famous 'unicorn scene' and added a happy ending.

Ridley Scott later released a 'director's cut' version with the additional voiceovers removed, the unicorn scene reinstated and the original ending. This version is regarded as the better one by many people.

FIGURE 2.19 *The ambiguity of Ridley Scott's original version of* Blade Runner *resulted in the studio making additions against the director's wishes.*

If you are going to use a focus group as part of your research you will need to think carefully about who you invite to be in the group, where you will hold it, how you are going to manage the discussion and what you will use to record what is said.

Undertaking secondary research

There is a wealth of information and research data already available in books, journals and on the Internet, and you will need to undertake some form of secondary research to supplement the findings from your primary research. It is worth noting that simply collecting pages of information from the Internet does not in itself constitute secondary research. Any information that you print off from the Internet, or photocopy from books and journals, needs to be read and understood, perhaps annotated to explain how you have used this information to inform and support your primary research.

When you are considering using a piece of secondary research it is important that you clearly understand what the original purpose of the research was, who commissioned it and when it was conducted. Not every piece of research that you may come across will be reliable or valid. For example, while we were researching the effects of advertising on young people, we discovered a piece of research that concludes that there is no evidence to show that cigarette advertising encourages young people to smoke. Always consider:

* when the research was published – this smoking research is very old (from the 1960s)
* where the research took place – this study was carried out in the USA, not the UK

* who commissioned/published the research – in this case the study was sponsored by a leading cigarette manufacturer!

Remember

It is important that you clearly reference any work that you use and take account of any copyright issues that may apply.

UNIT ASSESSMENT

Look again at the unit assessment information on page 92. You now need to plan and undertake **two** distinct research projects to show evidence of your knowledge and understanding of a range of research methods and techniques, and your skill in applying them and presenting your results.

1. In your first research project, you will need to gather information for the content of a proposed media production. There is clearly potential to link this project with the work that you will undertake in Unit 3, and you may find that this a very good way to structure and focus this research project.

   To complete the assessment for this unit you do not have to do a complete research project, and you may prefer to demonstrate the necessary skills, knowledge and understanding by the completion of a series of smaller exercises.

   Discuss with your teacher what is the best approach for you.

2. For the second research project you will need to undertake an investigation into an existing media product, and here there is potential to link to the work you did in Unit 1. In Unit 1 you investigated a particular media company or organisation – you could extend your investigation to include researching one of the media products produced by the company or organisation you are studying.

* To achieve marks in the highest mark band, you will need to:
  - demonstrate a thorough understanding of the different types of research technique, and their purposes, strength and limitations
  - gather a substantial amount of highly focused data using a wide range of techniques and procedures
  - show the results and conclusions of your research in a thorough and well-presented way.

2.3 The production technology available

One of the defining aspects of media production is that it involves some form of technology. Having an up-to-date knowledge and understanding of the different forms of technology available is important for all people working within the media industry. In this unit you will work primarily in one of the four main areas of media:

* audio
* moving image
* print
* interactive media.

Whichever medium you choose to work in, you will need to find out about the range of production equipment that is available. You will also need to spend time using this equipment. It is important that you have practical, hands-on experience of using a range of relevant equipment so that you develop a clear understanding of what the equipment can do, what its strengths and limitations are and how you would best use the equipment in different situations and for different purposes.

FIGURE 2.20 *Students using video production equipment.*

UNIT ASSESSMENT

For section 2.3 of this unit it is important that you include clear evidence of your understanding of the relevant production technologies available within your chosen media form.

The Unit 2 assessment grid in the Edexcel specification shows that, to achieve marks in the highest mark band, you will need to show a thorough understanding of the production technology and equipment available for your chosen media form, and an ability to assess the relative advantages and disadvantages of different versions.

This evidence can be presented in written form, as presentations to the class, or in some other format appropriate to studying the media.

You may also want to use the evidence in your portfolio, and this will be discussed in more detail in section 2.4.

Digital technology

Before looking at the four main forms of media production in turn, it is worth noting the importance of digital technology within the industry. The widespread availability and use of high-quality, digital technology has had a far-reaching effect on nearly all aspects of media production, and no study of media production technology would be complete without reference to this growth.

Think it over...

Think of the different ways in which digital technology has had an effect on your own life.

The increased use of digital, rather than analogue, data has put the computer at the heart of most media production processes, allowing people to control, manipulate and edit digital information that can then be used in a variety of different ways. This shift has had a profound effect on the skills needed by the people working in production within the industry, as well as on the training and skill development that is now required.

FIGURE 2.21 *Some examples of digital consumer products.*

It has also led to an improvement in the quality of the material that can be produced and in the necessary equipment being far cheaper to buy than was previously the case. For example, at the time of writing, for around £2000 you could buy a mid-range digital video camera that is lightweight and highly portable and will give you recordings of a quality that would not look out of place in a corporate video, or as location footage in a news programme or a documentary.

Another impact of the rise of digital technology is that audiences now expect more control and greater access to media material. This means, for example, that television producers need to think beyond just making a show for broadcast. Now they also have to look at ways of offering more content through digital TV, mobile phones and online services.

Digital content is easily distributed and transferred via the Internet, and this has had a huge impact on the music industry. The growth of peer-to-peer file sharing software has forced music companies to allow the legitimate online purchase of music. Indeed, some music is now only available as downloads.

In the print industry, journalists are now able to report from further afield, more quickly and in more depth thanks to mobile technologies. The use of digital print technology means that newspapers can be produced later in the day, with more lively content and with more pages and they can be distributed faster.

FIGURE 2.22 *Film clips are now available via mobile phones.*

FIGURE 2.23 *David Bowie playing live with Arcade Fire, available via Internet download only.*

Most newspapers now have an online version that readers can access via the Internet, and this has led to the introduction of interactive features and the addition of video and audio elements to the news pages.

Learning activity 9

✓ Compare the online version of a newspaper like *The Times* with the printed version. Consider such things as:

- layout
- use of pictures
- length of news items
- range of items covered
- additional features
- how current the stories are
- how readable each version is.

✓✓ Identify how many other newspapers and magazines have an online version.

- Are they all free or are some subscription only?
- Are some online versions 'teasers' for the printed versions?

✓✓✓ Assess the advantages and disadvantages of the online and print versions.

Have the most recent printed copy of the newspaper next to you when looking at the online version in order to compare the two versions.

The growth of blogging (people posting their own reports and views on a particular topic or event on the Internet) is another feature of digital technology. Blogging is seen by many as an important avenue for free speech and a way of breaking down many of the existing barriers and restrictions that media organisations and regulators have developed to try and restrict and control access to the media.

Digital technology has also had a big impact in the film industry, with the development and use of ever more sophisticated computer-generated images (CGI) in feature films such as *The Lord of the Rings* trilogy and *King Kong*.

FIGURE 2.24 *The use of CGI in the film industry can produce some very convincing characters.*

Did you know?

The actor Andy Serkis provided the physical foundations for the character Gollum in *The Lord of the Rings* trilogy and also for King Kong in the film of the same name. He did this by performing in a motion capture suit that provided a digital template from which the animators could then create the computer-generated characters.

Traditional versus digital

When investigating the technology that is available within a particular area of the industry, you might need to compare traditional equipment with the more recent equipment that is based on digital technology.

Remember

The pace of developments in technology is very rapid and you will need to decide, in conjunction with your tutor, how much you need to know about the older technologies and the more traditional methods of production.

My first experience of 'crash editing' video tape involved the use of two reel-to-reel tape machines and a chinagraph pencil. I used the chinagraph pencil to physically mark the video tape, so that when I rewound the reel-to-reel machines and then played the tape, I could see when to press the edit button as the correct pieces of video tape reached the play and recording heads. Fortunately, the advances in digital editing technology mean that we no longer have to devote a section to the sharpening of chinagraphic pencils!

Remember

You do not have to study all of the different areas of media production – you should choose the area that interests you the most and in which you can gain access to the necessary technology. You will need to discuss the area that you are going to work in with your teacher.

Audio technology

When considering the technology that is available for audio production, a basic distinction can be made between studio-based equipment and equipment that is primarily used on location.

Equipment that is used in a studio can be larger and heavier than would be possible on location. This ensures a level of quality that is not compromised by portability requirements. Whatever the set-up of the studio and the equipment available, it is important to remember that it is what you do with the equipment that is important, rather than the quality of the equipment itself.

Did you know?

Most of Daniel Bedingfield's debut album *Gotta Get Thru This* was recorded in his bedroom using a computer and a single microphone.

Recording media

If you are still using analogue technology, then you will use a portable **cassette tape recorder** to record your material on location, though digital technology is now used for most, if not all, of the professional sound recording in this country.

Minidisc recorders make compressed digital recordings on 2.5 inch disks that are housed in a protective cartridge. Minidisc recorders are highly portable, being very small and light, and are capable of producing high-quality recordings. However, their small size can also make them rather difficult and fiddly to operate.

A recent innovation in minidisc recorders is the **Hi-MD** recorder. These use larger capacity disks that can record up to an hour of audio in an uncompressed format, and also have a USB interface which can be used to upload recordings directly onto a computer.

Digital audio tape (DAT) recorders provide an alternative to minidisc technology and make digital recordings on 6 mm tape cartridges. They can produce very high-quality digital recordings, though the complexity of the rotating head and tape transport mechanism mean that they are relatively fragile.

A number of professional and semi-professional **solid-state recorders** are now available that record digital information either onto memory cards, such as compact flash cards, or onto high-capacity disk drives inside the recorder itself.

Microphones

Once you have decided on the type of recorder that you are going to use, you must then select the appropriate microphones to use. This is an equally important choice as there is little point in selecting a high-quality recorder if you then choose a poor-quality microphone to go with it.

Key terms

Transducers – devices that convert energy from one form to another

Microphone – a type of transducer that converts acoustic energy (in the form of sound waves) into electrical energy (in the form of an audio signal)

Diaphragm – a thin piece of material (such as paper, plastic or metal) inside a microphone which vibrates when it is struck by a sound wave

Loudspeaker – a type of transducer that converts the energy back into acoustic energy

The two most common types of microphone are dynamic and condenser microphones.

Dynamic microphones are versatile and ideal for general use, as they are relatively sturdy and resilient to rough handling. They do not require an additional power source and are well suited to coping with high volume levels, including musical instruments and amplifiers.

Condenser microphones require power from a battery or from an external source. The audio signal produced is stronger than that produced from a dynamic microphone. Condenser microphones also tend to be more sensitive than dynamic types, and this makes them particularly well suited to capturing quieter, subtler sounds. This greater sensitivity does mean that they can sometimes distort the sound when handling loud volumes.

The directions that a microphone will pick sound up from is an important characteristic that you will need to consider. This characteristic is known as **directionality**. Some microphones pick up sound equally from all directions, others pick up sound only from one direction or a particular combination of directions. There are three main categories of directionality.

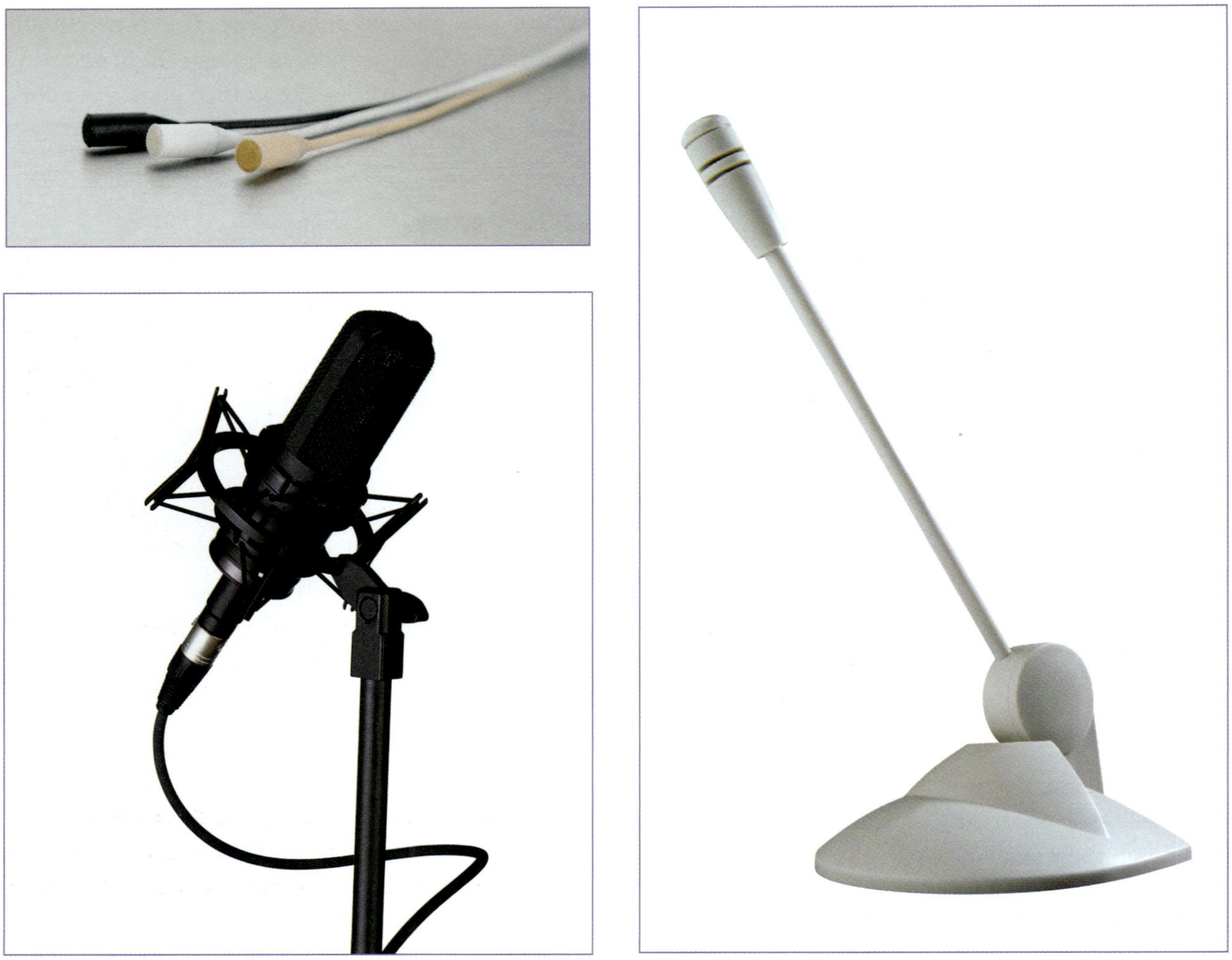

FIGURE 2.25 *Some of the different microphones available.*

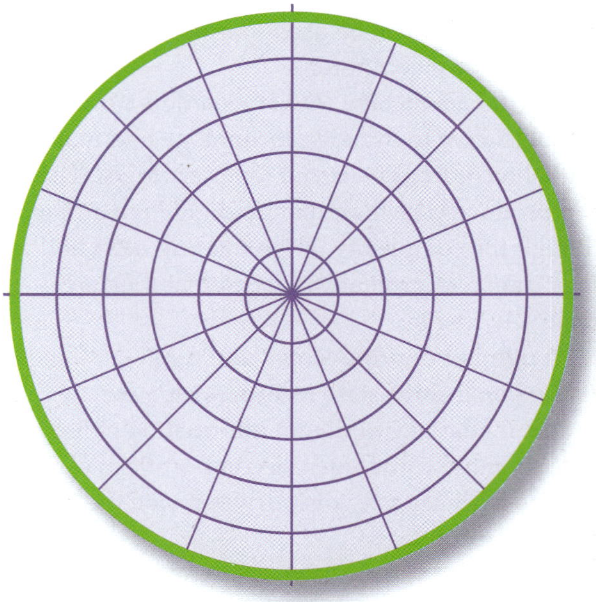

FIGURE 2.26 *Diagram showing the pick-up area of an omnidirectional microphone.*

Omnidirectional microphones pick up sound evenly from all directions and are used when it is not necessary to target a specific sound source – when recording ambient or background noise, for example. They can also be used when the microphone position must remain fixed while the sound source is moving.

Unidirectional microphones pick up sound predominantly from one direction and allow a specific sound source to be targeted. A very popular and versatile unidirectional microphone is a **cardioid.** Here the sound is picked up mostly from the front, but also a little from the sides as well so that some background sound is present.

FIGURE 2.27 *Diagram showing the pick-up area of a cardioid microphone.*

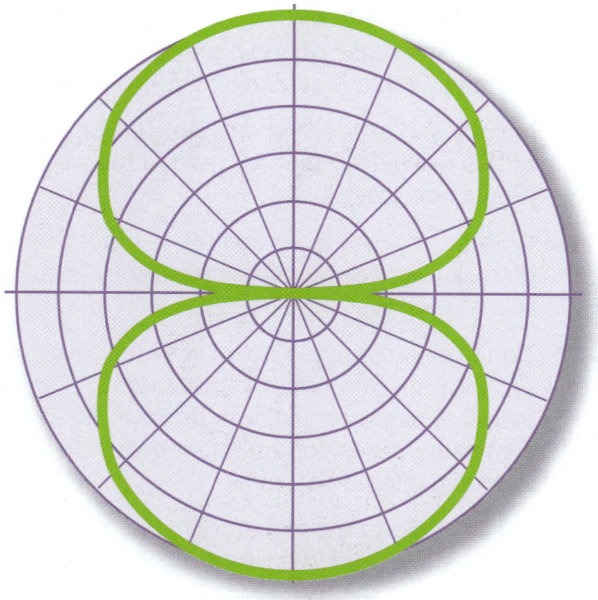

FIGURE 2.28 *Diagram showing the pick-up area of a bidirectional microphone.*

A **hypercardioid** is a version of a cardoid microphone that is more directional and eliminates most sound from the sides and rear. Due to the long, thin design of the hypercardioids, they are often referred to as rifle microphones.

Bidirectional microphones pick up sound from two opposite directions and are very useful when recording an interview.

Two other factors to consider when choosing a microphone are the level of **impedence** and its **frequency**.

Impedence refers to the amount of opposition the microphone has to an audio signal and, as a general rule, the lower the level of impedence the better. The **frequency** of the microphone refers to the way it responds to different frequencies of sound, and each microphone will have its own frequency response pattern.

Condenser microphones generally have a flatter frequency response pattern than dynamic microphones, and this usually means that they are better at producing a more accurate recording of the original sound source.

When using a hand-held microphone, it is important to handle it carefully so that it doesn't pick up any unwanted sounds from being tapped or knocked. If the setting allows it, you may want to use a microphone stand to secure the microphone or use a clip microphone that attaches to a person's clothing.

Remember

When choosing the right microphone you need to decide between a **dynamic** or a **condenser** microphone, and consider the **directionality**, the **impedence** and the **frequency** so that you can get the best-quality recording for the particular type of sound and the setting.

Editing

In the days of analogue recording, the editing process involved either physically cutting and splicing audio tape or transferring the sound signal electronically from one piece of tape to the master tape. Today it is the computer that is at the heart of most audio editing and there are a range of different audio editing software packages available that allow digital audio recordings to be edited and manipulated to suit the required purpose.

Learning activity 10

✓ Identify the range of audio production technology that is available to you.

✓✓ Identify and explain the different versions of this technology that are used in the production process.

✓✓✓ Explain the advantages and the disadvantages of the different versions and forms used.

* Don't get too bogged down with the technical specifications of the various pieces of hardware that you discover. Try to summarise the important differences in a clear and concise manner.

To achieve marks in the higher mark band you must be able to demonstrate a thorough understanding of the technology available to you and explain what the advantages and limitations of it are. You should also be able to compare it with the different versions and other forms that are used within the industry.

Moving image technology

Unless you are a student in a specialist centre that teaches film production or television broadcasting, the chances are that you will probably be using video recording technology if you choose to work within a moving image medium.

Recording formats

One of the first decisions to make is about the recording format that you will use, and this will be dependent on the technology that is available to you.

Did you know?

Although **VHS** tapes won the battle for the domestic market over their rival format **Betamax**, they lost out at the professional end of the market where **Betacam** was generally preferred to **S-VHS** and went on to become the industry standard.

Betacam was a success in the professional market because of its quality and reliability, whereas the consumer market was won over by the longer recording times of VHS tapes and the wide availability of pre-recorded films in the VHS format.

VHS, and the more compact VHS-C, were popular consumer formats up to the 1990s and are still used for production today in some schools and colleges, though they are now being replaced by digital formats such as MiniDV and Digital8.

If you are producing video as part of a multimedia product, or for streaming on the Internet, then a number of different file formats are available to create video streams. These include: Windows Media, RealMedia, QuickTime, MPEG and Macromedia Flash.

Camcorders

When recording video images, you are most likely to use a single unit consisting of a video camera

FIGURE 2.29 *Some of the different video tape formats.*

and recorder, though it is still possible that you may use a separate camera connected via a lead to a separate video tape recorder.

The term **camcorder** is derived from the words **cam**era + re**corder**. Most people think of a video camera and camcorder as being the same thing, but technically a camera is only a device that takes light from the lens and converts it into an image. The recorder is a separate device, often known as a 'camera back' that records this image in a suitable format. In professional equipment, the camera and recorder are combined to make a single unit.

Producing good-quality recording often requires the use of a **tripod** to ensure that the camera remains steady and can be moved in a slow and smooth fashion. A tripod consists of a head and a set of legs. Usually these are separate components, although cheaper tripods often have them already attached together.

Tripod legs are usually adjustable in terms of height and stance, and are available in various different weights and levels of sturdiness. The head is the part that supports the camera and provides the movement. The quality of the head determines how smoothly you will be able to perform camera movements such as tilting and panning.

Cameras can also be mounted on stabilising brackets and harnesses that support the weight of the camera and allow the operator to move the camera while filming.

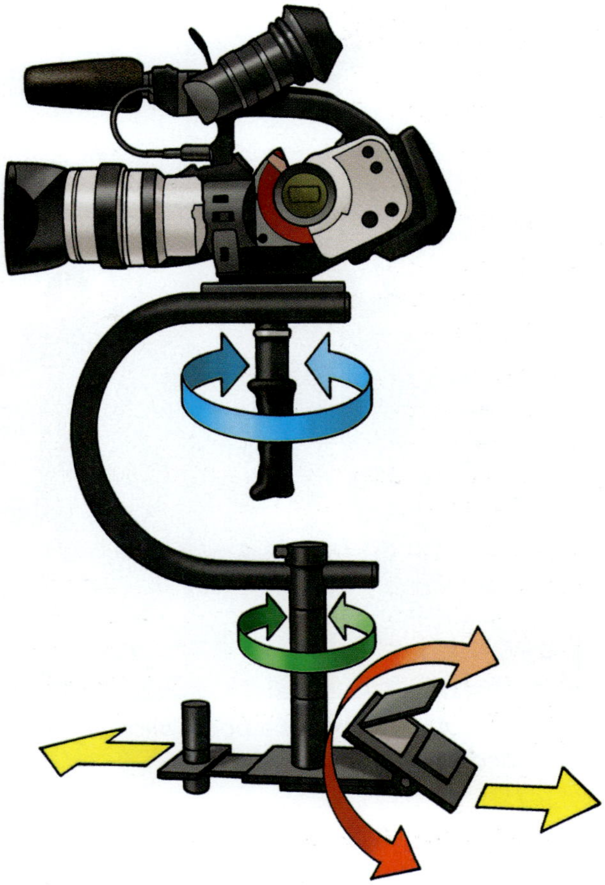

FIGURE 2.31 *An example of a camera stabilisation system.*

There are many different types of stabilisation device and system available, with Steadicam and Glidecam being two of the more popular.

FIGURE 2.30 *An example of a professional camcorder.*

Did you know?

Stanley Kubrick's 1980 film ***The Shining*** was one of the first feature films to successfully use a steadicam. One of the most memorable scenes in which a steadicam was used was the sequence when the main character (played by Jack Nicholson) is chasing his son through a hedge maze.

In this sequence the camera sometimes follows the son, at others it leads Jack and in others we get a point-of-view shot from Jack's perspective. The camera appears to glide through the maze and adds to the sense of tension and the thrill and fear of the chase.

FIGURE 2.32 *An example of a boom microphone being used in a production shoot.*

Did you know?

There are many famous examples of boom microphones appearing by accident in films. One such example is in the 1987 film *Wall Street*, where Michael Douglas is walking around in Charlie Sheen's apartment. It is dark outside, and the reflection of the boom microphone is clearly visible in the window following him around.

Sound

Sound is an integral part of any video production and much of the technology already discussed within the section on audio technology above is equally applicable to moving image production.

Many camcorders have a built-in microphone, but for greater control over the sound production a separate microphone is often used.

A **boom** microphone is very popular in film and television production. This is a directional microphone that is mounted on a boom arm and positioned just out of camera frame. Booms have the advantage of freeing up those in the shot from having to worry about holding a microphone, and means that they can move freely without disturbing the sound.

As with any audio recording, the distance between the microphone and the subject must be carefully controlled, and you have the added complication of ensuring that you do not see the boom microphone, or its shadow, in the shot.

Lighting

Lighting is a fundamental part of all moving image productions and poor lighting will have a detrimental effect on the quality of the finished product. If you are shooting in a studio, then a range of lights should be available to you. These will include both **spot** and **floodlight**s, and they may be mounted on a lighting rig attached to the ceiling, or on floor-mounted stands.

Key terms

Spotlight – a strong, focused beam of light targeted at a specific subject

Floodlight – a broad beam of light that is less directional and less intense than a spotlight

The level of both types of light can be controlled using a lighting console or **dimmer board** and these can be pre-programmed to run a set sequence of lighting effects.

If shooting out on location, then you will need to take lightweight, portable lights that are mounted on adjustable tripods. Movable flaps on the lights are called **barn doors**, and can be used to control the direction of the light and restrict the width of the beam. They can also be used to hold coloured filters, called **gels**, in place.

Camera-mounted lights are available and are useful for documentary and news-gathering work, but the light produced is quite harsh and is really only designed to illuminate the scene enough to allow the camera to operate.

Reflector boards are often used on location and in studio settings to provide a secondary light source and to act as a fill light (see key terms below). The board is lightweight and flexible, and can normally be folded up so that it can be easily carried.

FIGURE 2.33 *A lighting set-up for TV production.*

Key terms

3-point lighting – the standard form of lighting used in moving image production; it involves the use of three types of light:

- *Key light* – the primary light that is placed to one side of the subject so that one side is well lit and the other side has some shadow – normally a strong light
- *Fill light* – the secondary light that is placed on the opposite side to the key light – it is used to partially fill in the shadows created by the key light and is usually softer and less bright than the key
- *Back light* – a light placed behind the subject to light them from the rear and make the subject distinct from the background

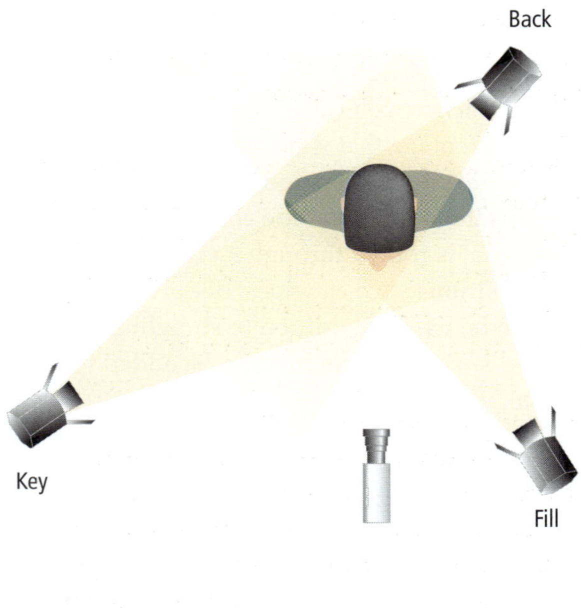

FIGURE 2.34 *A 3-point lighting set-up.*

Editing

Once the video recording has been completed, the post-production stage begins, where the video footage is edited together to make the final product.

> **Key terms**
>
> *Linear editing* – a process in which the recorded footage is copied from one tape onto a master tape in the order required for the completed product
>
> *Nonlinear editing* – a method that uses a computer and editing software to edit the footage

Linear editing was the original method of editing footage recorded on video tapes, before computerised editing became available in the 1990s. Again, the equipment that you have available to you will determine the form of editing that you use.

In linear editing, the video footage is selectively transferred from one tape to another via at least two video machines connected together. The resulting master tape becomes the edited version. This method of editing takes its name from the fact that it is mainly done in a linear fashion; that is, starting with the first shot and working through to the last shot.

With practice, you can go back and insert additional footage that is not in sequence using an **insert editing** function on the recorder, which maintains the integrity of the control track. If the video signal is routed through a **vision mixer**, then **transitions** such as wipes, dissolves and fades can be used in addition to straightforward cuts, and **special effects** can also be added to the material.

With nonlinear editing, the recorded footage is captured onto a computer hard drive and then edited using specialised software. Once the editing is complete, the finished product is recorded back to tape, or transferred to disk or distributed directly via the Internet.

There are a number of different editing software packages available, depending on whether you are using a Mac or PC platform, including *AVID Xpress, Adobe Premiere* and Apple's *Final Cut Pro*. Once you have mastered the software, you will be able to edit the footage very carefully and precisely and there are many different ways in which the original material can be changed, enhanced and manipulated.

> **Learning activity 11**
>
> ✓ Identify the range of moving image production technology that is available to you.
>
> ✓✓ Identify and explain the different versions of this technology that are used in the production process.
>
> ✓✓✓ Explain the advantages and the disadvantages of the different versions and forms used.
>
> * Try to contact some independent video production companies to find out what equipment and software they are currently using.
>
> To achieve marks in the higher mark band you must be able to demonstrate a thorough understanding of the technology available to you and explain what the advantages and limitations of it are. You should also be able to compare it with the different versions and other forms that are used within the industry.

Print technology

Digital technology has had a particularly large impact on the print industry. The biggest change has perhaps been to the **pre-press** stages, with the introduction of ever more sophisticated computer-based programs to replace the traditional labour-intensive methods of cut and paste.

> **Think it over...**
>
> Think about the changes that digital technology has brought to both the **production** and the **distribution** of news. Think about all the different ways in which you as a consumer can now get information about what is going on in the world around you.

Key terms

Pre-press – the generic term for all of the design and preparatory work that takes place to get a product ready for print

Press – the term for the actual printing process

Post-press or *print finishing* – the processes such as cutting, trimming, folding and binding that take place on the printed material before a product can be distributed

Pre-press software

Pre-press includes all of the design work and collation of material needed to get a product ready for print. The increased use of computers and desktop publishing software means that a pre-press designer today needs to be familiar with a number of the different software programs that are used to manipulate, control and combine text, image and layout features.

Logos and **graphics** tend to be produced using **vector-based** programs such as *Adobe Illustrator*, *Macromedia FreeHand* or *Corel Draw*. A vector is a mathematical line or curve which can be filled with colour or gradients. When vectors are combined they can produce high-quality graphical images which can be scaled to any size.

Digital **photographic images** are made up of **pixels**, which are small coloured squares that overlap to produce literally millions of colours. Pixel-based images are also called **bitmap** images, and include greyscale and multitone images as well as full colour ones. *Adobe Photoshop* is the main pixel-based programme used within the print industry to control and manipulate digital images.

Pixel-based images have to be taken or scanned in at the correct resolution, as programs such as *Photoshop* are resolution dependent. If the images are at a low resolution they will be of poor quality when printed. For a typical printing job, the pre-press designer will require a resolution of about 300-350 dpi (dots per inch).

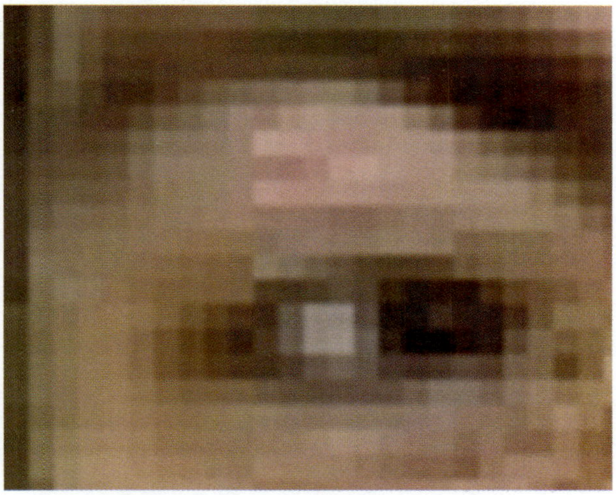

FIGURE 2.36 *You can clearly see the pixels in this magnified digital photo.*

FIGURE 2.35 *A logo that has been produced using vector-based software.*

Key terms

Vector-based programs – used to produce **logos** and **graphics**

Pixel-based programs – used to control and manipulate **photographic** images

There are two main page layout programs used by pre-press designers: *Adobe InDesign* and *QuarkXpress*. The two programs have similar features and can handle image and graphic files from both pixel-based and vector-based programs. They can also allow type to be added directly into the page layout, or imported from programs such as *Microsoft Word* or *Excel*.

Theory into practice

Before the final proof is sent to print, a pre-press designer will often run the finished design through some additional software to ensure that there are no problems or conflicts with the various files.

Pre-flight software, such as *FlightCheck* produced by Markzware, and **post-flight** software, such as *PitStop* produced by Enfocus, both analyse the digital files that have been designed on a computer to ensure that they are fit and ready for their intended purpose, before they are sent to print. The software highlights potential problems linked to poor image resolution, colour matching and fonts, and suggests corrective action that can be taken. (The terms 'pre-flight' and 'post-flight' come from the checklist that pilots go through prior to take off.)

Think it over...

Why do you think pre- and post-flighting software has become so popular within the print industry?

Cameras

As with the equipment for other media forms, when looking at cameras for producing still images you have a choice between traditional and digital technology.

FIGURE 2.37 *A photographer using a traditional SLR camera.*

Think it over...

What are the main differences between traditional and digital photography? Digital photography has many advantages, but are there any disadvantages?

Traditional **SLR** (single lens reflex) cameras allow you to shoot with different types of film stock, including colour and black and white negative film in various sizes and formats (35 mm, medium format) and positive slide film, again in various sizes.

Once you have taken your images, the film is subjected to a series of chemical processes to realise and stabilise the image on the film itself, and then to transfer, develop and fix the image onto photographic paper or other photosensitive material. This processing of film stock and the developing and fixing of the images onto paper can be done by hand in a dark room or automatically using equipment that is still commonly seen in high street processing stores.

The growing popularity of **digital photography** has meant that there has been a sharp fall in the amount of film that is processed as more and more people are taking digital photographs and transferring these directly to their computer. The digital images can, of course, be printed onto paper, and this is a relatively simple process using a computer printer and does not require any chemical processing.

The quality of digital images has increased dramatically in recent years and many professional photographers now shoot almost exclusively using digital cameras. Many of the leading manufacturers of SLR cameras are now making professional standard digital camera bodies to which different lenses can be attached to cope with the demands of different shoots.

Did you know?

The first digital cameras that the *Guardian* newspaper bought for its photographers cost over £11,000 each. The latest model being bought by the paper costs around £4500. Not only has the price dropped considerably but the quality has much improved and is now as good – if not better than – traditional film. Digital cameras have the additional advantage that the images are instantly available.

FIGURE 2.38 *A professional digital camera.*

Lenses

Most domestic cameras come with a fixed lens, but all professional cameras have detachable lenses so that different types of lens can be attached to the camera body for taking different types of photograph.

Photographers use different lenses to achieve different views and effects. Lenses are distinguished by their focal length and by the type of view that can be obtained.

Key terms

Focal length – the distance from the lens to the point behind the lens where the light entering it will converge; the focal length defines the angle of view and how magnified an object appears

A **standard** 50 mm lens for SLR cameras using 35 mm film displays the image at approximately the same magnification as the human eye. Lenses with a longer focal length produce images of a higher magnification, while those will a shorter focal length produce images with a lower magnification, and so allow you to fit more of the image into the frame.

A **zoom** lens has a variable focal length that is easily adjusted by a simple twisting or sliding movement.

There are hundreds of individual lenses available with different settings, and they are often grouped together by the sort of images that they can produce.

Wide-angle lenses allow more into the frame than a standard lens and are often used for landscape photography. A **fisheye** lens is an extreme version of a wide-angle lens and will take in a 180-degree panoramic view, with no attempt to compensate for the distortion involved in reproducing this view onto a flat panel.

A **telephoto** lens magnifies distant objects so that they appear a lot closer than they really are. They also have a small depth of field, which means that unsightly background objects can easily be left out of focus. Telephoto lenses can be very large, and are often used by the paparazzi to capture shots of celebrities from a long distance without them, or their minders, knowing.

FIGURE 2.39 *An image taken using a fisheye lens.*

In contrast, **macro** lenses are designed to take very close-up shots that are highly magnified, and are often used to shoot insect and plant life.

Lighting

The requirements for any additional lighting needed will depend on the location, the type of film or digital camera being used and the type of images that are needed.

The use of **flash** lighting is perhaps the simplest method, particularly if on location, but in a studio there is the potential to use a more sophisticated set-up involving **floodlights**, **fillers** and **spotlights** to achieve the required results.

Filters or 'gels' can be used with the different forms of lighting to produce different colours and effects. **Scrims**, which are thin pieces of material placed in front of a light, can be used to soften and tone down a particular light source.

Reflectors can also be used with both natural and artificial light to bounce and redirect the light. They are often used to soften shadows or to add a warmer colour to a person's face.

Scanners

The increased use of computer-based desktop publishing methods has meant that already existing images, graphics and artwork need to be converted into a digital format. We use **scanners** to do this and they are now common pieces of equipment in the home, education and office environment. A scanner should be readily available for you to use in your own production work.

Remember

You can obtain a digital photographic image by taking an original photograph with a digital camera, or you can scan an existing printed photograph into a computer to produce a digital version.

Printers

Traditional methods of printing such as **offset litho**, **screen** and **gravure** are still very much a part of the print industry, but **digital printing**, already common place in the domestic and office environments, is now becoming increasingly popular commercially. This is because digital printers such as **inkjet** and **laser** are now capable of high-quality colour printing using variable data, and they are also cost effective for shorter print runs.

Key terms

Variable data – the different information that can be sent to a printer when printing the same job: for example, digital printers can rapidly print personalised and individually addressed letters from a generic template – the result has been the widespread use of personalised promotional material that has specific elements targeted at individual recipients

Of the more traditional methods, **offset litho** printing is still one of the main commercial printing processes, used to produce newspapers, magazines, books, brochures and flyers. **Sheet-fed litho** presses print on individual sheets of paper or board and are used for high-quality jobs. **Web litho** presses are fed by a large roll of paper and are therefore quicker and cheaper for producing large print runs, for example of a magazine or newspaper. However, quality can sometimes be compromised by this speed.

Although it is the most widely used form of printing, and can achieve very good results, offset litho is perhaps the most complicated of all the print processes. The person running an offset litho printer has to control very precisely the flow of ink and the balance between ink and water, and maintain optimum temperature and humidity levels within the press hall to maintain the high-quality results.

Gravure is a printing process that uses a copper-coated cylinder onto which a reverse image of the print product is engraved. The cylinder prints directly onto the substrate (the material, such as paper, onto which the printing takes place), with a softer roller applying pressure to the substrate.

The gravure process is used for printing large-quantity runs such as free catalogues and brochures where the set-up costs are high, but the unit cost is relatively low.

Screen printing is the process of forcing ink through a taut mesh that is stretched over a screen. In this process, each colour is laid down individually onto the substrate, giving the printer greater control over how the finished product will look. It has many applications, including T-shirt and other fabric printing and a range of promotional materials.

FIGURE 2.40 *An offset litho press.*

Key terms

Offset litho – one of the main commercial print processes, used to produce media products such as newspapers, magazines and books

Gravure – a print process used for large-quantity runs where the set-up costs are high, but the unit cost is low, including the large-scale printing of free catalogues and brochures

Screen printing – a print process that allows for greater control over the application of each individual colour and is used for a range of promotional materials

Digital printing – a form of printing that is now capable of producing high-quality colour work using variable data; cost effective for shorter print runs

Print finishing

Many of the processes associated with print finishing, such as cutting, trimming, folding, creasing, collating and binding, are now automated, though traditional handcraft skills are still to be found in some parts of the industry.

Commercial printers will either finish their print products themselves using **guillotines**, **folding machines** and **binders**, or outsource the finishing process to a dedicated print finishing company.

Think it over...

Think of the range of different media products produced by the print industry.

What sort of print-finishing processes can you identify in these products?

Interactive media technology

Of all of the main media forms that you will study, it is perhaps inevitable that it is within the area of interactive media that the speed of technological change and development is the fastest. Interactive media products include websites, computer games, CD-ROMs, DVD-ROMs and online newspapers. New ideas and innovations are constantly being developed as the technology advances to allow greater levels of interaction and integration of different media.

Think it over...

What effect has the growth of web pages, computer games and CD-ROMs had on the consumers of media products?

Advances in digital compression technology mean that increasingly sophisticated sound, graphical and video elements can be incorporated into interactive media products.

Remember

Much of the equipment and software already discussed in the sections on audio, print and moving image technology in this unit are of relevance to the interactive media production team.

The relevant sections looking at production skills and techniques within the different media forms in section 2.4 will also be of interest to those working in interactive media.

Learning activity 12

- ✓ Identify the range of print production technology that is available to you.
- ✓✓ Identify and explain the different versions of this technology that are used in the production process.
- ✓✓✓ Explain the advantages and the disadvantages of the different versions and forms used.
- * Don't worry if your school or college does not have a large range of print production technology available for you to use. You will still be able to research the technology used in professional media production and compare it to what is available to you.

To achieve marks in the higher mark band you must be able to demonstrate a thorough understanding of the technology available to you and explain what the advantages and limitations of it are. You should also be able to compare it with the different versions and other forms that are used within the industry.

FIGURE 2.41 *Some examples from the wide range of interactive media products available.*

Interactive media design software

Many of the design packages that we discussed in the print technology section of this unit are used to help design and produce the various elements that go to make up an interactive media product, as well as more specialised web authoring software. Most of these programs are now available in versions for both Apple Mac and PC platforms.

Some of the most popular programs include:

- *Adobe Photoshop* for creating pixel-based images and graphics and for manipulating and editing photographic images
- *Adobe Illustrator* for creating vector images and illustrations
- *Macromedia Sound Edit Pro* for sound file manipulation and editing
- *Adobe Premiere* for video manipulation and editing
- *Macromedia Fireworks* – similar to *Photoshop*, but a vector-based tool that can be integrated with *Dreamweaver*
- *Macromedia Flash* for creating animated and interactive vector-based websites
- *3D Studio Max* for 3D animations
- *Macromedia Director* – one of the leading multimedia authoring tools
- *Macromedia Dreamweaver* for web publishing.

HTML (hypertext markup language) is the hidden coding behind any web page, and tells the browser what to display on the user's screen. You can produce websites and other online interactive media products by programming in HTML script, though it is more common to use a **WYSIWYG** design and authoring program, such as one of the ones mentioned above (*Dreamweaver* for example).

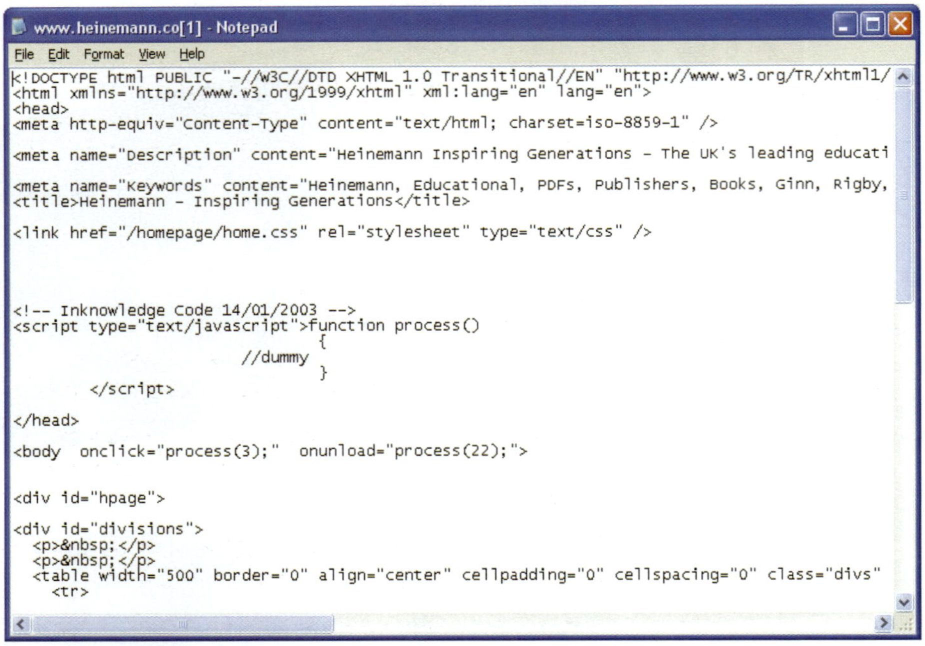

FIGURE 2.42 *An example of the HTML used to generate a web page.*

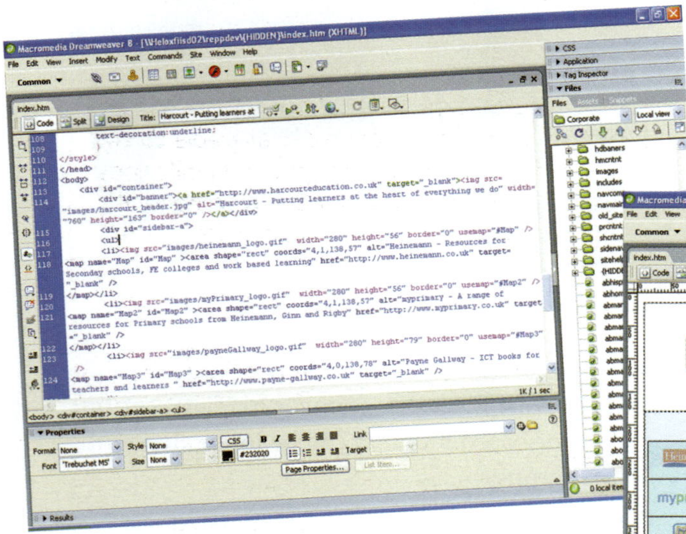

FIGURE 2.43 *When using a WYSIWYG web design application, you can switch between the design view and the HTML, as well as previewing the resulting web page.*

Key terms

WYSIWYG – an acronym that stands for "what you see is what you get" - it refers to the fact that when you use the appropriate software to edit the file on the screen, this is what it will look like when published as a web page; WYSIWYG programs allow you to design and produce websites with little practical knowledge of HTML code

File types

Interactive media production is mainly concerned with the creation and manipulation of different types of digital file, and then combining and integrating these files into a coherent form to produce a web page or interactive computer game or product.

Remember

In the section on print technology above, we discussed the difference between vector- and pixel-based or bitmap images. Each of these two types of data can be saved in a wide variety of file formats.

The most common file formats for saving graphical files are:

* EPS (used for both vector and bitmap images)
* GIF (mainly used for bitmap Internet graphics)
* JPEG (also used for bitmap Internet graphics)
* PDF (a versatile file format that can contain most types of data)
* PICT (mainly used for Mac computers)
* TIFF (the most popular bitmap file format).

Video file formats used for web publishing include AVI, MPEG and QuickTime. ASF, RMFF and WMV support both video and audio data.

Think it over...

PDF stands for portable document format. Try to find out what the other file format initials mentioned above stand for. Are there any other file formats that you can find? What are they used for?

Learning activity 13

- ✓ Identify the range of interactive media production technology that is available to you.
- ✓✓ Identify and explain the different versions of this technology that are used in the production process.
- ✓✓✓ Explain the advantages and the disadvantages of the different versions and forms used.
- * The websites of the various software producers will give you information about the latest versions of software that are available to professional interactive media producers.

To achieve marks in the higher mark band you must be able to demonstrate a thorough understanding of the technology available to you and explain what the advantages and limitations of it are. You should also be able to compare it with the different versions and other forms that are used within the industry.

UNIT ASSESSMENT

Having decided on your chosen media form and having read the relevant sections above, you are now ready to undertake additional research into the production technology, equipment and software that is available and to present your findings.

To achieve marks in the highest mark band, you will need to show a thorough understanding of the production technology and equipment available, for your chosen media form, and be able to assess the relative advantages and disadvantages of different versions.

The rate of change within the media industry can be very rapid and you will need to ensure that your research is current enough to include the latest developments.

Most of the equipment manufacturers have websites with up-to-date information on the latest technology, and there are also a number of trade magazines and publications that have specific sections on equipment and technology.

Also look out for trade shows and exhibitions where manufacturers showcase their latest products.

You could also explore any links with the industry that your school or college has, so that you can gain a better understanding of the current vocational demands and expectations.

Once your research has been completed, you need to present your findings in an appropriate form. You could choose to produce a written report, or a presentation to the class with accompanying slides and handouts, or some other format appropriate to studying the media.

This evidence will be assessed and marked by your teacher and you will need to keep the evidence safe so that the external moderator can also look at it if required at the end of the course.

2.4 Production techniques and skills

Having demonstrated your knowledge of the production technology available, you also need to demonstrate your ability to use this technology effectively in a media production context. Some of the work that you do may be as part of a team and it is important that you record and document the work that you do yourself within the team.

Remember

For this unit you do not have to produce finished media products, though of course you can if you wish, but you do need to produce a portfolio of practical work that shows evidence of your skill development.

Portfolios

A portfolio is a carefully selected sample of your work that showcases your abilities as well as providing evidence of the developmental processes that you have gone through.

For this unit, your portfolio will contain practical examples of your production work, together with supporting documentation such as planning sheets, treatments, storyboards, scripts and layout designs that you have developed, as well as assessment records, witness statements and observation sheets and your own commentary and assessment of your skill development.

If your chosen medium is audio, then an important part of your portfolio will probably be in the form of an audio tape, DAT tape, minidisc or CD that contains examples of your production work. This might include examples of audio recordings that you have made using different microphones in different situations, extracts from a news programme, drama or comedy show that you have written and recorded, and samples of work that you have edited.

If your chosen medium is video, then your portfolio will probably be in the form of a video tape or DVD that contains examples of your production work to date. This might include examples of you using the camera in a variety of different locations and employing a range of different techniques, examples of different sound recording and lighting set-ups, together with material that you have edited and manipulated in post-production.

UNIT ASSESSMENT

As well as collecting clear evidence of your understanding of the relevant production technology available within your chosen media form, it is equally important that you record and document your progress in developing relevant technical and operational skills.

This evidence will probably include a portfolio of experimental and (possibly) finished material with an accompanying commentary that explains what you were trying to achieve, how it fits in with your skill development and what you have learnt through the developmental process.

You will also need to include an initial assessment of your skills at the beginning of the course, together with assessments throughout your studies that document the development of your skills.

The assessment grid for this unit specifies that, to achieve marks in the highest mark band, you will need to show an ability to operate the equipment that you use with confidence and proficiency, and in a context in which you show increasing independence.

You also need to have made extensive progress in improving your skill levels throughout the duration of the course, and to have developed skills in a substantial range of techniques, using them with confidence and creativity.

You do not have to produce a finished media product, but you do need to demonstrate confidence and proficiency in operating the equipment and show progress in developing a range of relevant skills.

If print is your chosen medium, then your portfolio could include layouts, drafts and mock-ups of the print products that you are working on such as flyers, posters and magazines, together with examples of copy and images that you have developed.

These images might include your own photographs, if you have included photography as one of your chosen areas to study, as well as examples of images that you have manipulated using creative software packages such as *Photoshop* or *InDesign*.

Examples of manipulated digital images could also form part of a multimedia portfolio, presented on disk or on a CD-ROM or DVD-ROM. This could also include examples of web pages, computer graphics and animations and gaming sequences that you have designed and produced.

FIGURE 2.44 *Planning what are going to do for your portfolio is an important stage in your work for this unit.*

Theory into practice

Think carefully about your chosen medium and the sort of work that you will be undertaking. What do you plan to include in your portfolio and how can you present your work in the best way possible?

FIGURE 2.45 *An example of a portfolio of print work.*

Initial skills audit

An important first step in showing evidence of your progress, is to assess your skill level at the start of the course. This will help you to decide which skills you need to develop further and to plan how you will go about doing this. You can then monitor your skill development and, towards the end of the course, show clear evidence of how your skills have improved.

Learning activity 14

Carry out an initial skills audit.

✓ Write a list of all the equipment that you already have experience of using and the media production skills and techniques you already have.

✓✓ Try to assess the level of your knowledge, understanding and skill for each item on your list. Identify the gaps in your knowledge and skills.

✓✓✓ Draw up an action plan to further develop your existing skills, and to fill any gaps that you have identified.

* Try to use SMART targets in your action plan. This means they need to be **S**pecific, **M**easurable, **A**chievable and **R**ealistic, and within an appropriate **T**imescale.

You might wish to use a SWOT analysis when doing your initial skills audit. Here you identify the *strengths* that you already have and then identify the *weaknesses* that you will need to improve. You can then identify the *opportunities* that are available to you (resources, workshops, support) and any *threats* (barriers) that might get in your way.

Group work

Much media production is undertaken by teams of people rather than individuals. You only have to look at the credits for a film, television programme or computer game to see the number of people who are involved in the production process, all of them undertaking different roles. A little bit of background research will also reveal the nature of the teams that produce radio programmes, newspapers and magazines.

Learning activity 15

✓ Choose a media product and research the different roles and activities that were involved in its production.

✓✓ Can you group the roles into different categories? The categories of **pre-production**, **production** and **post-production** might be a useful starting point.

✓✓✓ Try to find out more information about some of the key roles identified. What do people do in these roles? What equipment do they use? What skills do they require?

* The websites of the Sector Skills Councils will provide you with more information about job roles and occupational skills. The Sector Skills Council that represents the audio-visual industries is Skillset (www.skillset.org). The multimedia industries are represented by E-skills (www.e-skills.com), and the print industry is represented by Proskills (www.proskills.co.uk).

Remember

It is likely that you will work in groups when developing your practical skills for this unit, but it is important that you document and evidence your own skill development within the production process.

As well as producing a self-assessment of your skill development, it is important that your assessors complete witness statements, checklists and other observational documents to authenticate your work and provide evidence that you have reached the appropriate level of performance.

Witness Statement

Candidate Name: Shona Edwards

Unit Number and Title: Unit 2: Skills for Media Production

Activity: Digital Photography workshop
Having already taken a set of digital photographs, students were required to transfer selected images to a PC or Mac, to save them in an appropriate folder and then to open them using an appropriate software program.

Assessment criteria:
c) understanding of and ability to operate the technology of production
d) progress in developing technical skills

Observations: Shona demonstrated a competent understanding of the production equipment and technology throughout the workshop and was able to select and operate the hardware and software with only very limited guidance from her tutor.

Shona took an active role in her group's discussion as to which images to transfer and these decisions were based on a thorough analysis of the technical and aesthetic merits of each photograph, and were clearly informed by knowledge and understanding gained in previous theory sessions.

Shona was able to save the selected images in her personal folder and access and use *Photoshop* with competence. It was clear from this session that she has improved her skills in using this software in line with her skills development action plan.

Assessment Summary: Evidence shows Shona working towards the top of Band 2 for Assessment criteria (c): ...competent understanding...operate [equipment] competently...require only limited support and guidance.

Also working towards the top of Band 2 for Assessment criteria (d): ...made recognisable progress in improving skills levels...in a range of techniques.

Supporting evidence:
- File of saved digital photographs
- Initial skills audit and skills development action plan
- Student commentary

Assessor Signature	Ms Terezia Zimsek	**Date**	16/11/06
Verifier Signature	Mr Paul Baylis	**Date**	16/11/06
Comments	I observed the student undertaking this exercise and I agree with the observations and assessments made by Ms Zimsek.		

FIGURE 2.46 *An example of a witness statement.*

Health and safety

Whichever media form you are working in, an awareness of health and safety is of utmost importance. In all aspects of production, you need to consider the safety of yourself and your team members, as well as members of the general public – that includes anyone you ask to be involved in the production and anyone who happens to be in the vicinity when you are working on your media product. Find out what the relevant health and safety regulations are and apply them to your own work.

If recording or photographing on location, you should make sure you do not cause an obstruction or cause other people to have to step out into traffic to get round you. You must always have a clear escape route available if there should be a fire, wherever you are working. You must always take care, too, with electrical equipment – because of the risk of fire and electric shock. All electrical equipment must be safety checked and used in the correct manner and in an appropriate environment.

Studios have a lot of mains-powered equipment including computers. No liquids should be taken near these items – no matter how thirsty you are – and you mustn't be tempted to tamper with them. Care also needs to be taken when connecting and disconnecting cables, wires and plugs. As well as the risk of electric shock, there is always the possibility that you may damage the equipment by pulling or forcing a connection.

FIGURE 2.47 *Care needs to be taken when on location.*

Transport and storage of equipment is also a factor that needs careful consideration. Advances in digital technology have resulted in most equipment being lighter than was previously the case, but you still need to take care when you are lifting and carrying equipment to ensure that you do not injure yourself. Find out the proper way to lift heavy items and get into the habit of lifting in the correct way.

You also need to ensure that the equipment is not damaged when it is being handled and transported, and that it is safe and secure when not in use.

Pre-production

Remember

In the early parts of this unit we looked at the importance of thorough research and effective planning to the production process. You need to ensure that all stages of the pre-production process have been successfully undertaken before embarking on the practical production work itself.

Once you have completed your research into the medium, the audience and the subject matter, you will need to get yourself organised for the production stage. The allocation of tasks and roles is an important aspect of this so that everybody knows what they are doing and can contribute in an effective manner.

FIGURE 2.48 *Getting organised at the beginning will save you a lot of work later on.*

Theory into practice

You may well be involved in a number of different productions in order to make sure that you cover all of the necessary skill areas, so being organised from the start is crucial.

You will need to have a clear idea of the aim of your finished product. For example, if you are working on a video production, then you will need to have a treatment, storyboard and script, from which you can produce a shooting script.

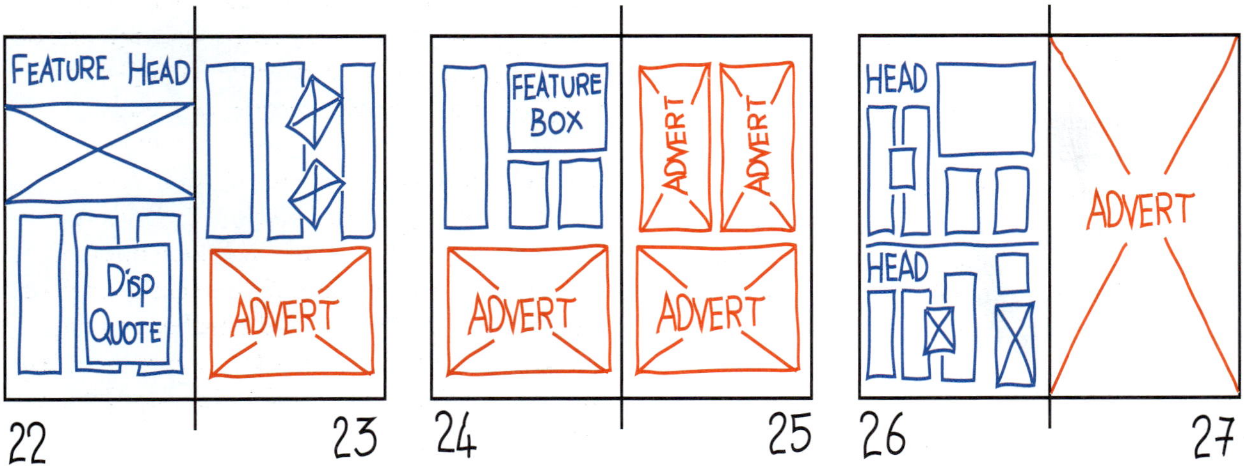

FIGURE 2.49 *An example of thumbnails used to draft page layouts.*

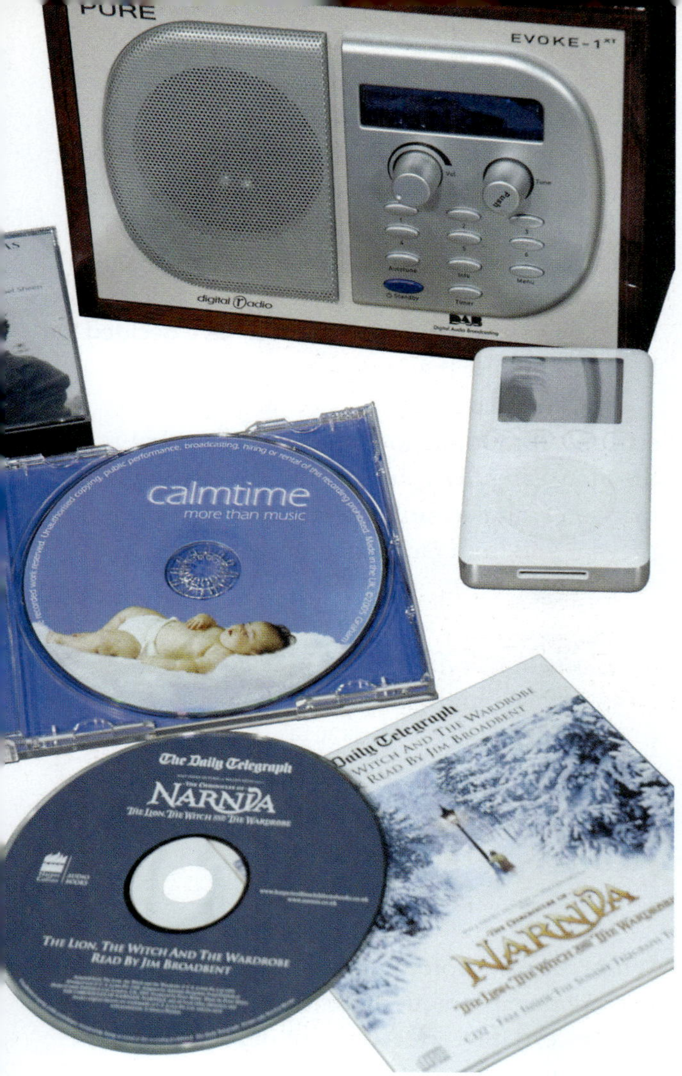

FIGURE 2.50 *A range of audio products.*

If you are working in print, you will have a series of draft layouts and thumbnails of the proposed product, and perhaps sketches and drafts of the images and copy that you are planning to use.

> **Remember**
>
> Spending time planning and preparing the groundwork for your media production can save you time in the production process itself, and can prevent you making costly mistakes.

Let's now consider each of the four main media forms in turn.

Audio production

Most audio production is in the form of radio programming, and the radio industry is perhaps the most obvious place to research and investigate the types of audio product that you could produce yourself. Outside the radio industry, an audio product could refer to a talking book, a newsletter for the blind, in-store entertainment, a workout CD or a self-help CD for relaxation or meditation.

Whatever the type of product you choose to make, you should aim for a professionally produced audio product that is of a competent technical standard.

You will need to consider where your recording will take place. Recording on location and in the studio are different in many respects. Usually, when you are recording on location, you will use lightweight portable recording equipment, whereas in a studio, you will use equipment that is often larger and heavier. The studio will often be set up more or less ready for your recording needs, whereas on location you must make sure you have the correct equipment with you, and adequate access to mains power or a plentiful supply of charged batteries.

For audio productions, it is not usually necessary to carry out a recce as there are far fewer factors to consider than for TV and film. If there is some noise that will disturb your recording, or if the accoustics produce too much echo, you can fairly easily move to another room or location. Moving to and from a different location shouldn't prove too much of a problem, especially if you are using lightweight equipment.

You will still need to consider the logistics involved and plan the recording carefully. If you are planning an interview, you will need to arrange a convenient meeting point, and find out if there is somewhere you can record without being disturbed by unwanted noise or other people. You will also need to check on your interviewee's availability and whether you will need to obtain permission before you are allowed to record on the premises – for example, if it is a factory or a shop.

Think it over...

The atmosphere you are trying to create for your product will need some thought, in order to make your recording sound more interesting and memorable – the atmosphere you create will add 'colour' to your piece and make it come alive for the audience.

Imagine a report about a new police helicopter with no background helicopter sounds to be heard. What would you think of a piece about stormy weather wrecking boats in a harbour if the only sounds your could hear were seagulls and ice-cream sellers? So, how are you going to create your atmosphere, and where in the piece will it occur (beginning and/or end; all the way through)?

FIGURE 2.51 *Creating the right atmosphere for your piece is very important.*

You also need to decide which production facilities you will need. Will you mix sound effects or music in with the other audio material in the studio, or will you just edit the audio together? Will you record additional voice links while out on location, or back in the studio when you have had time to select the material and have decided how to structure the content?

Bear in mind that you can change your schedule for production if it is necessary, but the more carefully you plan, the less likely it is that you will meet unforeseen problems that will prevent you from meeting your deadline.

Remember

The deadline for production can very rarely be moved. Working to deadlines is something that everyone working in the media has to get used to. If you are working in radio and there is a slot reserved for your feature, you miss it at your peril!

Whatever the recording format that you are using, microphone technique is basically the same. You must record the correct amount of sound onto the tape or minidisc – not too much or it will overload the system and distortion is likely to occur; not too little or the wanted sound will be lost in the background noise (or hiss) and turning up the volume will only make the background noise worse.

Theory into practice

You will have noticed how you need to move the microphone closer to a quieter person's mouth in order to record them at the same volume (or 'level') as your own voice. Likewise, you will need to hold the microphone further away from a louder person's mouth.

Recording a drama involving groups of people may mean experimenting more with the microphone position. Try placing it between all the different actors. If it is closer to some than to others, it will make them seem further away than the rest.

FIGURE 2.52 *A microphone set-up for recording.*

Always listen carefully for unwanted background noise before you record and turn off the source of the noise if you can. If you can't, try moving to somewhere quieter and do the recording there.

Background noise can cause problems of continuity when you are editing. For example, a ticking clock in the background will make your editing task difficult, as it will be very hard to remove sections so that the ticking sound remains even in the background. So prepare your working space in advance – remove the clock, take the telephone off the hook and put a 'do not disturb' notice on the door, to prevent unwanted interruptions. Keep an eye on your recording level during the recording and check the time, so you are sure you know how much you have on tape or disk and how much space is left.

Always check the recording after you have finished, just to make sure the equipment or your own technique hasn't let you down. You can record again if you are still there – but if you have returned to base, it will take a lot of effort to fix up the recording all over again.

If there is background noise in the room, bring the microphone closer to the person who is talking, and lower the recording level – this will decrease the amount of background sound heard when you play your recording back.

Remember

Always make a test recording before you leave for a location recording – and make one when you get there to hear how the finished recording will sound.

Check the battery level before you set off, too, and make sure there are no loose connections in the microphone lead.

As we discussed earlier, some background noise is useful to create atmosphere, but there are times when the noise of a heater or a machine in the background is just a nuisance and will detract from the quality of the recording.

Theory into practice

Make sure you have recorded all you need to record, following the proposal, script and schedule.

It is industry practice to record a 'wild track' while on location. That is a minute or so of the background sounds to have at your disposal so you have the option of mixing it with other material later in order to create an effect.

Recording with a minidisc allows you a great deal of flexibility – you can even edit the recordings on the machine on the way back. If you are using a tape recorder, you can at least listen to your recordings on the way back, and begin to decide which pieces are going to be the most useful.

Some parts of the recorded material will stand out as being very usable, while others will be less interesting, and the quality of some sections might not be up to the required standard. Sifting through the recordings while they are fresh in your memory is always a good idea.

When you get back to base, carefully log all the material you have recorded. Label your disks or tapes straight away and store them in an organised way, so that you can easily locate any part of any recording. Having a detailed and well-organised log of all your material will make it easier to make decisions about what to put into the final production, and what to leave out. Check the material again for recording quality: if it sounds wrong in some way, you will probably have to leave it out, unless the problem can be sorted out in post-production.

Remember

Always bear in mind that you need to be compiling evidence for your portfolio to show your skill development. You may want to include some less satisfactory material from early on in the course to demonstrate just how much you have learnt.

Sound Material Log

Programme Title: Radio Commercial

Client: The Wooden Horse Toy Company

Writer: Briony Smails

Producer: Briony Smails

Director: Briony Smails

Date: 15th April 2006

Scene No.	Take No.	Time In	Time Out	Description	Comments
1	1	00.01	00.09	atmos interior factory	N/G plane overhead
1	2	00.10	00.19	atmos interior factory	good
2	1	00.19	02.45	interview MD	N/G noise in back
2	2	02.45	04.37	interview MD	good
3	1	04.37	06.44	interview Head of Design	good
4	1	06.45	07.10	sound of wood-turning machine	good
5	1	07.10	08.10	sound of paint spray machine	good
6	1	08.10	09.45	interview worker	N/G fans noisy
6	2	09.45	11.45	interview worker	good

FIGURE 2.53 *An example of a recorded material log.*

Post-production

Once you have checked your raw material, and done any replacement recordings you find you need to make, you are ready for the post-production stage. This is when you add any finishing touches to your script and prepare any additional material that might be needed so the finished product makes more sense to listeners. You should still be working to the deadlines in your production schedule. You may need to delete some material in order to run to time.

Think about the structure you originally planned, and whether it works as expected. It is not too late to make changes as long as the changes you make will mean that your finished product will match the proposal better. Think in terms of fitness for purpose – is the product going to do what you promised in your proposal?

Once you have done your 'paper edit' (deciding on paper what to include and what to leave out), you can begin to do the actual edit on computer (or perhaps tape) – assembling all the different parts of the production in the correct order.

Theory into practice

Your product will sound awkward and unprofessional if the sound levels jump up and down on playback, so at this stage you must make a great effort to ensure that the levels are as even as possible. Make any necessary adjustments to the level, to keep the needle on the meters peaking at around the same place, but without making any changes too quickly.

Record your voice links at the same level as you dub your interview clips. If you have recorded your links on a portable cassette machine, you can dub them across at the same time as the interviews, putting everything down in the correct order. If you are editing on a computer using audio-editing software, you will need to load all your audio onto the PC at the same level too.

The final edit is the stage at which you tidy up the tape, removing all the gaps between items so that it sounds as complete and as professional as possible.

Learning activity 16

- ✓ Experiment with operating the different equipment that is available to you and practise the basic production techniques that you have learnt.
- ✓✓ With further practice, extend the range of techniques that you can use.
- ✓✓✓ Try to develop a creative approach to your production techniques that you can use with confidence. Ensure that you fully record and document your skill progression.
- * Do not worry if your school or college does not have the latest audio production and editing technology available for you to use. Once you have learnt the basics you can easily adapt your skills and techniques to the different equipment and software that you will encounter as you progress.

To achieve marks in the highest mark band, you will need to show an ability to operate the equipment that you use with confidence and proficiency, and in a context in which you show increasing independence.

You also need to have made extensive progress in improving your skill levels throughout the duration of the course, and to have developed skills in a substantial range of techniques, using them with confidence and creativity.

Moving image production

Although this area of the media covers film and television as well as video, it is likely that you will only have access to the necessary equipment for a video-based project.

As with the other forms of media production, the research and planning stages are crucial to the success of your project, perhaps even more so with a moving image project, as it involves both audio and visual elements.

Remember

Time spent planning and preparing for your moving image production is time well invested and can help you to identify and overcome potential problems before they arise.

> **Key terms**
>
> *Proposal* – a concise written outline of your ideas, used to sell an idea to a potential client
>
> *Treatment* – a more detailed description of the content of the proposed production – including details of the storyline, the plot, characters and locations (or subject matter, themes, presenters), as well as an indication of the resource needs and the budget required

> **Key terms**
>
> *Script* – a detailed account of what is to be spoken in the product, as well as positional and movement information and details of any music or sound effects that are to be used
>
> *Storyboard* – a visualisation of the script that includes an image of how each shot will look, as well as information about the camera angles and movements, the sound, lighting and editing transitions that are envisaged
>
> *Production schedule* – a working plan of the shoot

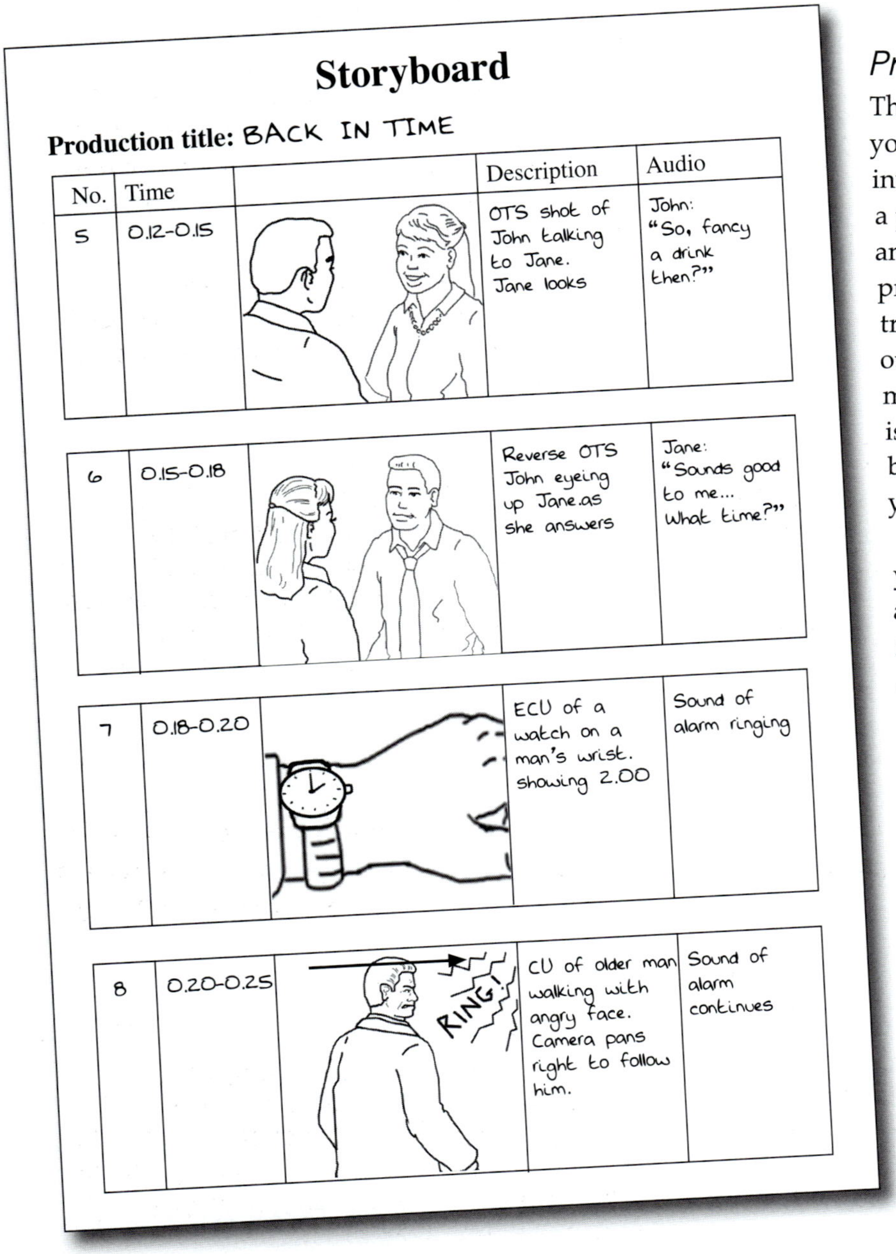

FIGURE 2.54 *An example of a storyboard.*

Pre-production

The pre-production stage of your moving image project will involve the initial writing of a proposal for your product, and the development of your proposal into a more substantial treatment. You will need to carry out research into the subject matter and the technology that is available to you, as well as the budget available and the costs you are likely to incur.

Once your have completed your treatment, you will be able to develop your ideas further by producing a script and storyboard. This stage will almost certainly involve a recce of suitable locations, so that you can plan the types of shot that you need, get a clear idea of what is possible in these locations and decide on the technology that you will need.

Remember

A storyboard is a visual representation of your planned production, and you will almost certainly make changes to these plans during the production and post-production stages.

What appeared to be a good idea at the planning stage might not be possible in reality, and every good production team is able to improvise and find a way around problems that they encounter when shooting and editing.

Production

Producing a successful moving image product can be a very complex task that involves lots of people undertaking a range of different tasks, so effective planning is crucial. But be aware that not everything will go to plan. As you work on your moving image projects and gain experience, you will acquire the skills needed to be able to adapt and change things as the production unfolds.

Think it over...

Having a contingency plan for some of the more obvious pitfalls is a good idea. For example, what will you do if it is raining on the day that you have booked the crew and equipment for a location shoot? Is your production schedule flexible enough so you can change the order and shoot an indoor scene instead? Can you think of other problems that you may face during production? And what might the potential solutions be?

During the production stage it is important to keep an organised and detailed log of the shots that you have completed so that you know where each shot can be found when you get to editing the footage. It is also important that you record in advance all of the footage that you need at a particular location, as returning later to record a missed shot could be time-consuming (and expensive in the real world) and may cause problems in terms of continuity.

It is always better to record too much footage than not enough, and don't forget to record **establishing shots** and some **cutaway** material – this can be vital when you come to editing the final product.

If you are recording an interview, it is always a good idea to include some 'noddy' shots – these are shots of the interviewer listening and reacting (for example nodding in agreement) to the answers given by the interviewee. Again, these can be inserted at the editing stage to provide a more varied and interesting product.

Key terms

Establishing shot – a long shot of a scene or location that shows the viewer where the sequence is set

Cutaway – an additional shot that is different to the main subject but still linked in some way – a cutaway can be used as a link or buffer between two shots that are very similar or to add an extra dimension to the narrative

Cut-in – this type of shot serves a similar purpose to a cutaway, but shows a specific detail of the subject, such as their hands to emphasise emotion

Theory into practice

Many of the more typical camera shots have been assigned specific names and abbreviations by those working in the film, video and television industries to help when communicating their ideas. Some of these shots are illustrated and described in Figure 2.55.

Camera control

The video camera or camcorder is at the heart of any video production and you need to ensure that you know how to use it effectively to get the right shots.

Remember

Too many good ideas are ruined by poor camerawork. You can make your product look more professional by paying careful attention to how you frame and angle each shot, to moving the camera smoothly and to using the zoom and focus functions correctly.

Extreme wide shot (EWS). This type of shot shows as much of the scene or location as possible and is often used as an establishing shot.

Wide shot (WS) or **Long shot (LS).** Here the subject is shot from a distance so that all of the subject can be seen as well as the location that they are in.

Mid-shot (MS). Here only about half of the subject is seen and you can see less of the surroundings.

Close-up (CU). With this type of shot, a part of the subject such as the head fills the whole frame and very little, if any, of the surroundings can be seen.

Extreme close-up (ECU). A very close shot of the subject, or some part of them, that is often used for dramatic effect.

Two-shot. A shot of two people framed like a mid-shot.

Over-the-shoulder shot (OSS). This is a shot of a subject taken from just behind a person who is looking at that subject. This shot helps to establish the positions of each person and is used a lot in interviews.

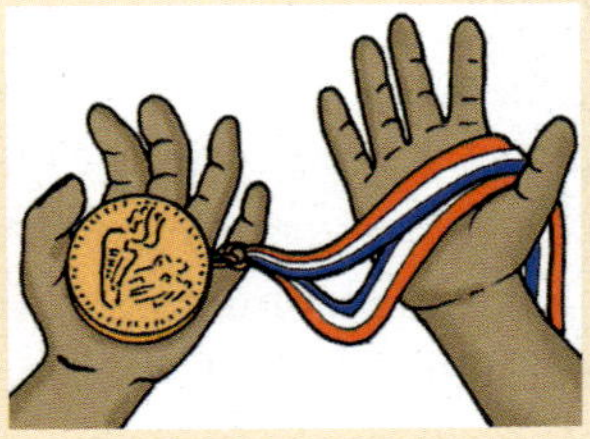

Point-of-view shot (POV). This is a shot that shows what a character is seeing, as if you are looking through their eyes.

FIGURE 2.56 *Eight commonly used types of camera shot.*

Key terms

Pan – a slow sideways movement of the camera around a central axis – if you are using a tripod, you will turn the tripod head slowly round on its axis to pan the camera either left or right

Tracking – the physical movement of the camera in any direction – sometimes the camera and tripod are mounted on a track to ensure a smooth movement, or stabilising equipment such as a Steadicam can be used

Tilt – an upward or downward movement of the camera to adjust the angle

Zoom – makes the image appear closer or more distant, and is used to frame the shot more effectively

Focus – how sharp the image appears – you can adjust the lens to ensure the correct parts of the shot are in focus

Becoming a skilled camera operator is a long and painstaking process that involves gaining a thorough knowledge of the camera and how it works. Practise with all of the camera functions and movements, and rehearse a difficult shot a number of times before recording it. Always play back the results to see if you need to record a second or third take.

Remember, it is better to have too much rather than too little footage, and it is often a good idea to have a number of different versions of the same shot to choose from when you come to edit the footage together.

FIGURE 2.57 *A camera operator performing a white balance.*

Theory into practice

On some cameras you will have to perform a **white balance** to ensure that the colours look natural and consistent.

You do this by pointing the camera at a white surface and pressing the white balance button to balance the colours recorded.

Post-production

Editing is also a very skilled job that requires a good working knowledge of the equipment and software that you are using, as well as a good understanding of narrative and the codes and conventions of the media genre that you are working in.

Before you start to edit you will need to produce an **edit decision list**, or a **paper edit** as it is sometimes known. This is a list of all of the shots that are required from the raw footage, in the right order and with an appropriate description or code so that they can be easily located. You will need to use the storyboard at this stage, but it will sometimes by necessary to deviate slightly from your original plans in the light of the footage that you were actually able to shoot.

Continuity is an important consideration at this point, particularly if you are editing together shots that were filmed out of sequence. Look for clocks in the background that suddenly go backwards, or drinks that rise and fall in the glass!

Remember

Some shots do not look good when they follow each other. As a general rule try to avoid:

- Cutting between two very similar shots. It is better to cut between different types of shot, or use a cutaway of some kind.
- Going from a very wide shot straight into a close-up, unless of course you are using it for dramatic or shock effect.

Also be wary of cutting from a still shot to a shot where the camera is already moving.

Another stage of the post-production process is adding any additional sound, music and special effects to the footage. Modern editing suites and software packages have an array of fancy transitions for you to experiment with and special audio and visual effects that can be added. These should be used sparingly, and only if there is a genuine reason to use them. You cannot disguise a poor product simply by adding a layer of special effects!

Learning activity 17

✓ Experiment with operating the different equipment that is available to you and practise the basic production techniques that you have learnt.

✓✓ With further practice, extend the range of techniques that you can use.

✓✓✓ Try to develop a creative approach to your production techniques that you can use with confidence. Ensure that you fully record and document your skill progression.

* It is not that important at this stage to have access to the latest technology. Once you have learnt the basic skills and techniques you can easily adapt them to the different equipment and software that you will encounter as your production skills develop.

To achieve marks in the highest mark band, you will need to show an ability to operate the equipment that you use with confidence and proficiency, and in a context in which you show increasing independence.

You also need to have made extensive progress in improving your skill levels throughout the duration of the course, and to have developed skills in a substantial range of techniques, using them with confidence and creativity.

Print production

Print is the oldest form of mass media and is still a vibrant and creative industry today. There is a broad range of print media products available to the public, and these include commercial products that readers can purchase, such as:

* newspapers
* magazines
* comics

as well as promotional and information materials, such as:

* flyers
* leaflets
* posters
* CD and DVD covers
* book covers.

The growth in electronic publishing has meant that there are now online versions of many of the newspapers and magazines that we see on newsagent shelves, and we will be looking at these further in the section on interactive media production.

In this section we will consider the skills and techniques needed to produce printed products.

Most print products consist of a combination of words and images, and once you have completed your pre-production planning, the next task involves the production of the text and images that will form the basis of the print product itself.

FIGURE 2.57 *There are many different types of print product.*

Copy

The words that are written for use in a print product are called **copy**, and the industry employs journalists and copywriters to produce those all-important words that are used to inform, educate, persuade and entertain the readers.

Producing original copy can be a demanding job, and it is often done to very tight deadlines. To produce copy that is both accurate and interesting to read, you will need to use a combination of your existing knowledge on the topic that you are writing about and the research that you have undertaken.

Think carefully about the audience that you are targeting, the context in which you will be placing your copy and its purpose.

The target audience for your writing needs to be at the forefront of your thinking throughout the planning and production process, and will have a fundamental effect on the words and sentences that you produce. The words and sentence structures that you would use in a comic aimed at primary school age children will be very different to those you would use in a lifestyle magazine aimed at young women. Similarly, the style of writing used in a news story in a tabloid newspaper will be very different from one that appears in a compact newspaper.

You also need to think carefully about the purpose of your print product, as this will also have an impact on the style and form of the writing that you produce. Are you trying to persuade somebody to buy something, or are you trying to inform them about something more factual? Are you writing a piece to entertain? To shock? To make somebody laugh?

All of these decisions will influence the language that you use, the style of the writing, the length of the sentences and the structure of the text. They will also have an impact on the number of words that you use. An advertising poster might have only one or two very carefully chosen words on it, whereas a newspaper or magazine article might consist of thousands.

ENGLAND'S new wonderkid Theo Walcott learned of his shock World Cup call-up on the day he took his driving theory test.

The jubilant 17-year-old — whose selection by Sven Goran Eriksson stunned pundits yesterday — PASSED with flying colours.

Last night Sven was keeping his fingers crossed that the teen sensation can put England firmly on the road to victory in Germany.

But even he confessed that including the Arsenal striker in his 23-man squad was a massive gamble.

SOURCE: www.thesun.co.uk

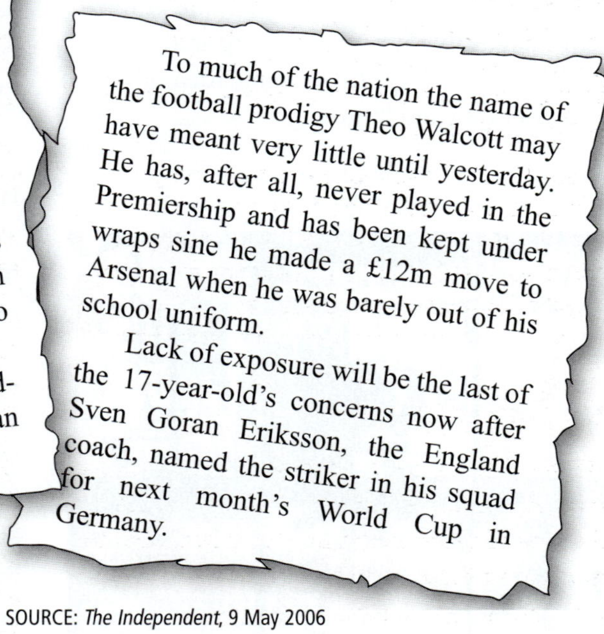

To much of the nation the name of the football prodigy Theo Walcott may have meant very little until yesterday. He has, after all, never played in the Premiership and has been kept under wraps sine he made a £12m move to Arsenal when he was barely out of his school uniform.

Lack of exposure will be the last of the 17-year-old's concerns now after Sven Goran Eriksson, the England coach, named the striker in his squad for next month's World Cup in Germany.

SOURCE: *The Independent*, 9 May 2006

FIGURE 2.58 *Different newspapers use very different writing styles, depending on the audience they are targeting.*

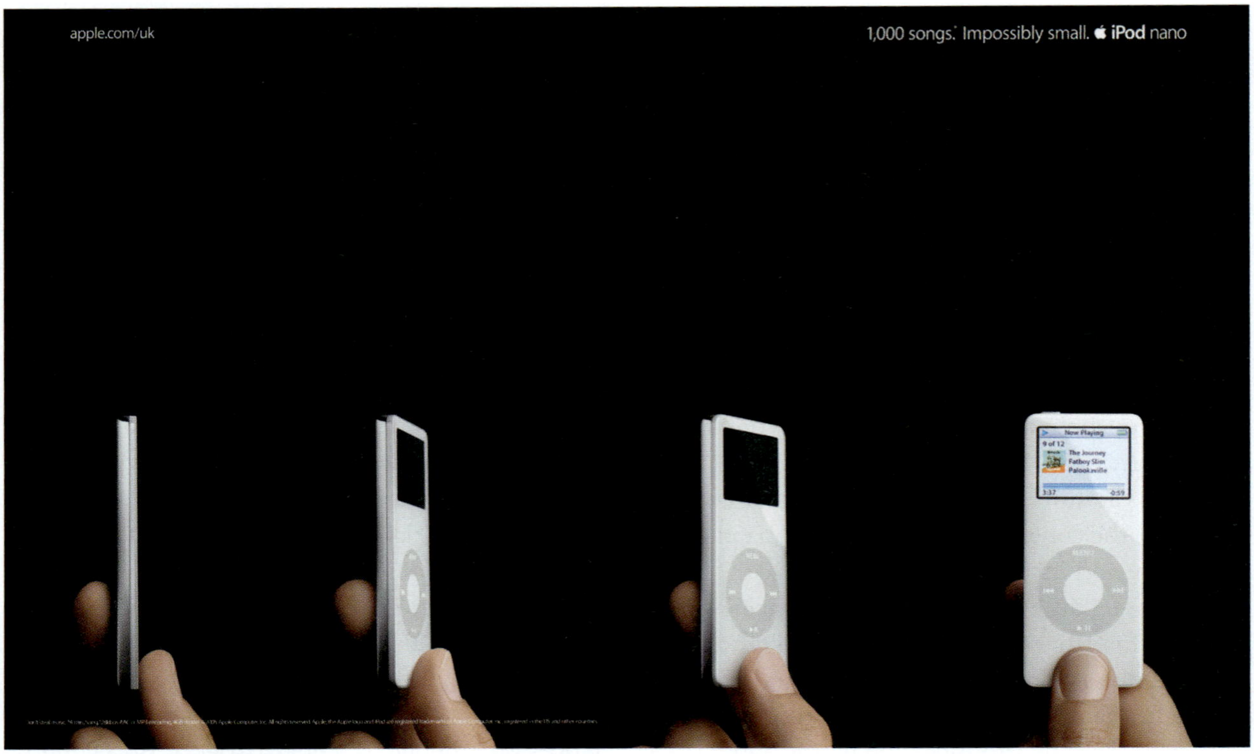

FIGURE 2.59 *Advertisements tend to use a very few carefully chosen words.*

Images

The inclusion of appropriate images into a print product is often crucial to its ability to attract the right audience. You only have to look at the different images that newspapers and magazines put on their front covers to get some idea of the audience that they are targeting.

FIGURE 2.60 *Cover images say a lot about the audiences the publication is trying to attract.*

Think it over...

Why are images so important in media products?

What information and messages do they give us about the world around us?

There is a saying that 'the camera never lies'. Is this true?

When producing your own images you have a number of different options. You can use traditional or digital methods to produce your own original photographic images, or you can use a scanner and picture editing software to copy and manipulate existing images. You can also use a scanner to convert existing images into a digital format.

Theory into practice

The use of digital images has almost completely replaced the use of traditional photographic techniques within the industry. However, some publishers still accept slides that are then scanned and converted to a digital format.

If you choose to use a digital camera to produce your own images, you need to ensure that the quality and resolution of the images will be sufficiently high to allow successful printing to take place. Once taken, it is then a simple procedure to transfer the images from the camera to the computer.

Once they are in a digital form, you can control and manipulate images using software packages such as *Adobe Photoshop*, and then import them into design software such as *QuarkXpress* or *InDesign* (as discussed in section 2.3).

When using a computer to design and put together a product such as a newspaper, magazine or poster, remember that what looks good on the computer screen can sometimes be disappointing once it is printed on the page. Checking for potential problems before you send a job for printing, using a program such as *FlightCheck* or *PitStop*, can save you time and money in the long run.

Graphics

Photographic images are not the only images that are used in printed products. Cartoons, line drawings, logos, charts and diagrams can all be used to illustrate a piece of copy and attract the attention of potential readers. You might have somebody in your team who is good at drawing and who can produce original illustrations, or you may want to use computer software to produce charts and diagrams from the data that you have collected.

> **Think it over...**
>
> What sort of graphics and images are you planning to have in your printed product?
>
> How are you going to produce them and ensure that they are of the highest quality possible?
>
> Think about what they will look like when they are printed.

Whatever type of images you include in your product, you need to ensure that they have a clear purpose, are of a high quality and are clearly captioned or labelled so that they communicate the intended message to the readers. Pictures are, by their very nature, more **polysemic** than words: they are capable of generating a wider range of meanings. A caption to a picture can help to narrow down this range of potential meanings and direct the audience to a preferred meaning.

FIGURE 2.61 *Some examples of graphics in printed products.*

Learning activity 18

Consider the picture of the teenager in Figure 2.62. In Unit 1 we looked at how different captions can change the meaning of a picture for readers; now you can have a go at this yourself.

✓ Write down the different meanings that this image could carry for different audiences. Is this boy somebody who could be famous? Is he somebody we should be afraid of? Look up to? Fall in love with?

✓✓ Try to think of different captions that could be added to this picture to direct people towards a particular meaning.

✓✓✓ Which types of publication might each of the different captions appear in and what effect might they have on the target audience?

* You might want to show the image to a range of different people to help you identify the different meanings that the picture can generate.

FIGURE 2.62 *Write your own captions for this photograph of a teenage boy.*

FIGURE 2.63 *A sub-editor in action.*

The editing process

Once you have produced and combined your copy and images, you will need to edit your product to make sure that it makes sense and is consistent, fit for purpose and of an appropriate length.

Theory into practice

The publishers of newspapers and magazines employ sub-editors to edit specific parts or elements of the publication.

A sub-editor might be responsible for checking the copy for accuracy, adding or deleting words to make it fit the space available, adding headlines and strap-lines, and structuring or sequencing the material.

If responsible for images, a sub-editor might scale a graphic or image (increase or decrease the size) to make it fit the available space, crop the image to exclude unwanted elements, or add a caption to make its meaning clearer.

Design

Putting the copy, images and graphics together in a way that is pleasing to the eye and follows the codes and conventions of your chosen media form is a skilled job. You will probably want to use one of the desktop publishing or design software packages identified in section 2.3 to produce the final draft of your product, and you will need to have a basic understanding of design principles as well as a working knowledge of the software chosen.

Experiment with the alignment of text and images, the use of columns and frames to structure the page, and the inclusion of headings, subheadings and strap-lines to break up the text and guide the eye of the reader.

Remember

Learning to use design software takes time, and you will need to learn about the basic controls and functions before trying more complex tasks.

Remember to save examples of how your skills are developing and your experimental work for your inclusion in your final portfolio.

Fonts

There are literally thousands of different **typefaces** or **fonts** available, each of which has its own distinctive style and is capable of generating its own set of meanings and connotations. The words 'typeface' and 'font' are used interchangeably.

Think it over...

Look at a range of different fonts. What sort of connotations does each font communicate to you? What sort of publication might you expect to see each one in?

The two main types of font are **serif** and **sans serif**. Serif typefaces have a decorative flourish to the letters, while sans serif typefaces are plainer. As a general rule, serif typefaces tend to be used in the main body of a text and sans serif tend to be used for titles and headings.

Times New Roman
ABCDEFGabcdefg

Palatino
ABCDEFGabcdefg

Baskerville
ABCDEFGabcdefg

Gill Sans
ABCDEFGabcdefg

Arial
ABCDEFGabcdefg

Trade Gothic
ABCDEFGabcdefg

FIGURE 2.64 *Examples of serif and sans serif typefaces.*

The choice of font and text size, and the use of such features as italics, underlining and emboldening of text, will all have an effect of the final look of your product and the extent to which it attracts the right audience and communicates effectively to them.

Take care not to introduce too many stylistic and typographical features into your product. A page, poster or flyer that is too cluttered and looks chaotic will often be ignored by the potential reader. Also, don't be afraid of white space. In terms of page design, less is often more, and you should strive for a well-designed page with clean lines and a consistent, coherent style.

The printing process

Once you have finalised your design, the copy and images are all in place and the whole product has been edited and signed off, it needs to be printed. In section 2.3 we looked at the range of printing technologies that are available to the print industry, and discussed how the choice is dependent on the type of product being printed, the quality of reproduction that is needed, the amount of money available and the size of the print run.

Theory into practice

Unless you are working in a school or college that has a dedicated print department, or have links with a printing company, it is unlikely that you will have access to anything more sophisticated than a domestic computer printer and a photocopier to print and reproduce your finished products.

However, whichever technology you use, the principles are broadly the same. The printing process involves the mass reproduction of text and images onto a substrate, usually some form of paper.

The printing process needs to be carefully monitored and controlled so that the same high quality is maintained throughout the whole of the print run. You do not want hours of careful planning, design and production to be ruined by a poorly printed final product.

FIGURE 2.65 *A student printing his finished publication.*

Remember

You will need to produce a number of test prints, and make any necessary adjustments, before beginning the print run proper. The test prints might be useful evidence to include in your portfolio.

Print finishing

Print finishing refers to the processes used to complete a product after it has been printed and before it can be distributed and used. As discussed in section 2.3, the finishing process usually includes cutting and trimming the product to the appropriate size using a guillotine. If the product is a book, leaflet, newspaper or magazine, then the pages will need to be collated together in the right order, folded, and then bound using staples, glue or stitching.

Think it over...

Think about how you will distribute your product to your target audience. You might like to consider the different ways in which newspapers and magazines can reach their target audience. If you are producing promotional material, what are the options available to you to access as many people as possible within the target audience?

Learning activity 19

- ✓ Experiment with operating the different equipment that is available to you and practise the basic production techniques that you have learnt.
- ✓✓ With further practice, extend the range of techniques that you can use.
- ✓✓✓ Try to develop a creative approach to your production techniques that you can use with confidence. Ensure that you fully record and document your skill progression.
- * Remember to keep examples of your work, even if it goes wrong! You can often learn a lot by analysing why something didn't work, and then doing it differently next time so that you get the result you were looking for.

To achieve marks in the highest mark band, you will need to show an ability to operate the equipment that you use with confidence and proficiency, and in a context in which you show increasing independence.

You also need to have made extensive progress in improving your skill levels throughout the duration of the course, and to have developed skills in a substantial range of techniques, using them with confidence and creativity.

Interactive media production

Whether you are planning to produce a website, an online newspaper, a computer game or an educational DVD-ROM, you will need to think carefully about the design of the product and, in particular, the way in which the potential user will use and interact with it.

> **Think it over...**
>
> Think about the different interactive media products that you have used. Which features and aspects helped make your experience a positive one and which simply got in the way?

Design

Usability is perhaps the most important consideration in interactive media design. You may feel very proud to have produced a beautiful, dynamic website, but if it takes too long to download or is difficult to navigate, then many users will simply give up and visit someone else's site instead.

> **Did you know?**
>
> The World Wide Web concept was developed in 1989 by scientists who were interested in making it easier to retrieve research documentation.
>
> In 1992 there were only about fifty websites in the world, but this grew rapidly to over four million by 1999, and then doubled again to over eight million by the end of 2001.
>
> The latest figures show that the number of websites continues to grow as more and more people are logging on to the World Wide Web.

There is an expectation that interactive media products will deliver the right information very quickly, and users will soon find another potential source of information in this highly competitive market if your product doesn't deliver fast.

One of the main keys to success for an interactive media product is good **navigation**. Navigation refers to the features built into a product that help users to find their way around, to know where they are in a product and where

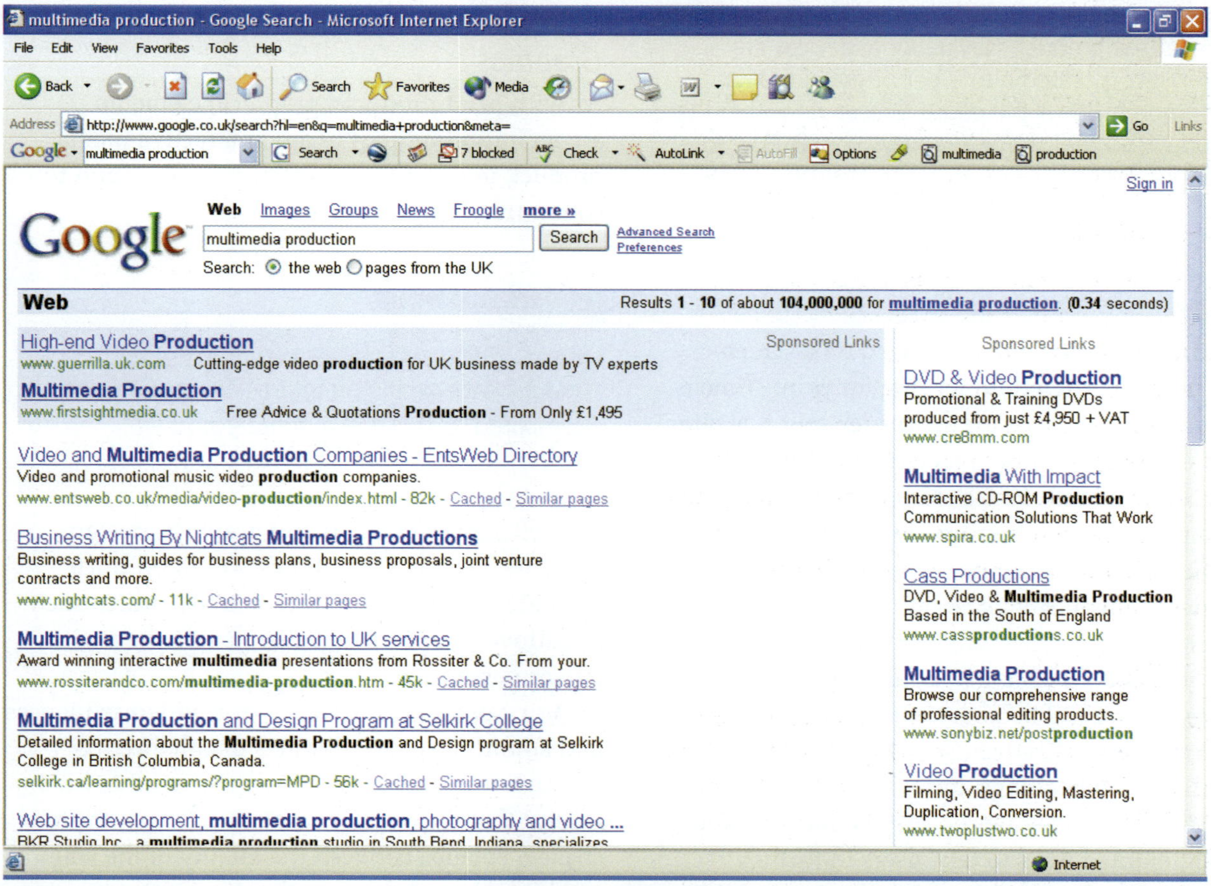

FIGURE 2.66 *Carrying out a search using any search engine will give you an idea of just how many websites there are.*

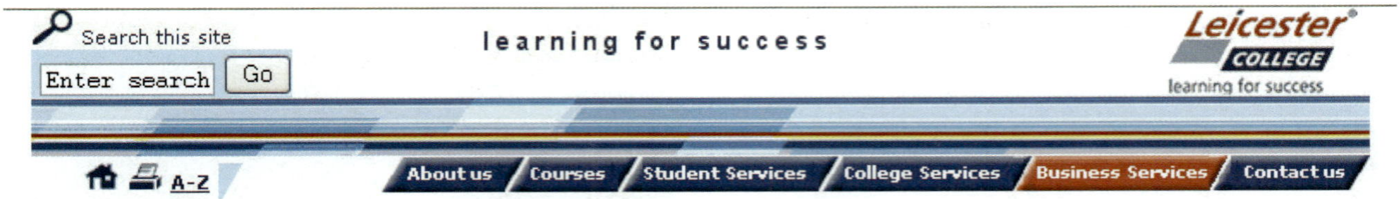

FIGURE 2.67 *Good navigation is essential to the success of a website or other interactive media product.*

else they can go within the product to get further information – menus and other buttons and links form the navigation. A well-designed interactive media product such as a website or DVD-ROM should have a logical hierarchy of information that is easily accessible using a clear and user-friendly means of navigation.

Theory into practice

Navigation within a website or CD-ROM can be via a text-based menu that is always present on the screen, or by a series of visual representations that direct users to a different part of the product. Navigational devices are often incorporated into a bar or panel that is common to all of the pages or screens within the product, so that the user always knows how to go forward or back or return to the main menu.

Copy

Writing copy that will be viewed on a screen can be very different to writing for print. Time is often a critical factor for the reader, and it is often harder to read text on a screen. People also tend to scan screen-based text, so you don't want to put reams and reams of writing in a product that will be viewed on a computer or television screen.

As a general rule of thumb, less is more in terms of copy that will be read on screen and you should keep it as concise as possible. Sentences should be kept short, with a simple structure, and effective use made of bullet points, headings, subheadings and white space. Frequent highlighting of key words and the incorporation of highlighted links to take users to further information can also help improve the readability of the text and overall usability of the product.

Learning activity 20

- ✓ Compare the differences in language between a paper edition of a national newspaper and the online version.
- ✓✓ Explain and account for the differences you have found.
- ✓✓✓ Assess the advantages and the limitations of the different techniques and forms you identified.
- * It will help your research if you print hard copies of selected pages from the online version and include these in your portfolio with your findings.

Graphics

As with print products, graphical elements are an important part of any interactive media product, in order both to attract the user and to communicate information.

Think it over...

What additional features can graphics and images have within an interactive media product compared to those in a printed product?

As well as static images and graphics, design software such as *Flash* allows you to produce **animated** graphics and **interactive** features such as **rollover** graphics that change as a mouse cursor passes over them.

You can also incorporate short **video** sequences and **sound** files into products to enhance the interactive experience, though you need to be careful that the file sizes are not too big – try to strike a balance between the quality of the sound or video file and the time that it takes to access or download the feature.

The overuse of gratuitous animated graphics, scrolling text or other moving items can put people off accessing your product and can draw attention away from the actual content.

Remember

Don't be tempted to use each screen or page of your interactive media product to showcase your creative talents. A busy, overcrowded screen with too much information and too many links can mean that the user won't know what to look at first and might result in them not bothering to find out what your product has to say!

Producing effective graphics, sound and video files for an interactive media product requires both creative talent as well as knowledge of the specific tools within the software program. The range of programs available, and the frequency of version upgrades, means that it is not practical to cover the different production techniques here.

Most software programs provide a tutorial and help section, as well as an accompanying booklet. There are also a number of online tutorials that you will be able to access for the particular program that you are using, as well as additional support from books and journals. You might also be able to enrol onto a short course that focuses on a specific piece of software, to further develop the skills and techniques that you need to learn as part of your media course.

Branding

If your product has several pages or screens that can be accessed in a nonlinear fashion, then you should also think about maintaining some form of branding across the whole product so that users can easily identify it.

Branding can take the form of a generic logo or title or the use of a distinctive colour or design, and is especially important for users who have entered your product from an external website and need to know which one they are in. Branding should also appear on any printer-friendly pages so that the original source can be easily identified.

Theory into practice

Visit a range of different websites and check out their effectiveness in terms of the following:

- download speed
- ease of navigation
- layout
- use of language
- use of interactive elements
- suitability of content
- branding.

Overall, which do you think is the most effective website and why?

Remember

As with all media products, you need to always think about what the needs of your target audience are and what the purpose of your product is if it is to be a success.

Learning activity 21

✓ Experiment with operating the different equipment that is available to you and practise the basic production techniques that you have learnt.

✓✓ With further practice, extend the range of techniques that you can use.

✓✓✓ Try to develop a creative approach to your production techniques that you can use with confidence. Ensure that you fully record and document your skill progression.

* Don't be afraid to make mistakes! You can often learn a lot when things go wrong, and you are more likely to get things right next time round.

To achieve marks in the highest mark band, you will need to show an ability to operate the equipment that you use with confidence and proficiency, and in a context in which you show increasing independence.

You also need to have made extensive progress in improving your skill levels throughout the duration of the course, and to have developed skills in a substantial range of techniques, using them with confidence and creativity.

UNIT ASSESSMENT

You have now reached the end of Unit 2 and will need to ensure that you have completed all of the required tasks and presented all of the assessment evidence in an appropriate manner.

Your work for this unit will be assessed internally by your tutor but will also be checked by an external moderator from the exam board at the end of the course, so you need to ensure that all of the evidence is clearly marked and labelled and presented in a logical and clear fashion.

- To summarise, your body of work must show evidence of:
- your understanding of the different research methods, techniques and procedures covered in section 2.1
- the research that you carried out for a media production and into an existing media product in section 2.2
- your understanding of and ability to operate the production technology covered in section 2.3
- your progress in developing your technical skills throughout section 2.4.

Media production brief

Unit 3

This unit contains four parts:

Unit 3 Introduction

Every one of the programmes you watch on television or in the cinema, every newspaper article you read and radio programme you listen to has been through a rigorous process of research, planning and recording with an audience in mind. For example, a programme detailing the features of the latest hatchback car probably won't appeal to a small child, while a comic strip cartoon is unlikely to appeal to a teenager thinking about purchasing his or her first car. The target audience for media products will have been carefully researched before any scripts were written or initial article drafts were developed. In broadcast television there is always a ratings war between the BBC and independent companies such as Granada. This is especially true at Christmas when each side tries to produce the best programmes to win audience share. Magazines undertake careful research into potential audiences before they commit to the development of a new title. Why do you think commercial television companies want to win the ratings war? Why do magazine publishers want people to buy their magazines? In some countries there is careful scrutiny of television viewer figures and if these drop, the programme is taken off air. Matching a media product to the audience is very important.

In this unit, you have the chance to produce a media product for a particular audience. The commission for this product is available from the Edexcel website. In order to complete your work for the unit you will learn about:

* pre-production skills and techniques
* production skills and techniques
* post-production skills and techniques
* how to evaluate your production.

In order to do this you need to read and understand the brief provided by Edexcel. It gives clear details about the client that is commissioning the work and the target audience. You have to choose which media format you would like to use to produce an appropriate product. When choosing the media format to use for your product you should consider:

* the skills you developed in Unit 2
* the resources available to you
* the time you have to make the product
* the needs of the client.

To help you understand the elements of pre-production, production, post-production and evaluation, have a look at the following scenario, about a project undertaken by a media production company for a client called Recycle.It. The scenario gives background information about the client and what they hope to achieve by creating media products. The scenario is accompanied by four briefs for you to consider, which are in the format specified by Edexcel and similar to the briefs you can find on its website. You can use these briefs to practise the skills you will need to plan and produce your own media product.

What you will learn in this unit

* How to undertake initial research into your chosen idea
* How to plan for a production
* How to organise your resources, time and people in order to successfully create your media product
* How to use your skills in production to produce appropriate and sufficient media material
* How to use your post-production skills to shape your final product
* How to review your final product and evaluate your work in producing this product

How you will be assessed

This unit will allow you to put into practice the skills you have developed in Unit 2. You will create a media product in response to a theme that is published on the Edexcel website in the autumn term of the year you are undertaking the AS qualification. The published brief will give you the theme for your work but you can decide which media format you are going to use to produce your product. It may be that in Unit 2 you found that you were particularly interested in moving image and enjoyed planning and producing a video. You may have enjoyed producing a print product and therefore choose to make a magazine or newspaper article on the given theme.

By working on this theme and planning and producing your chosen media product, you will demonstrate your skills in pre-production, production, post-production and evaluation. Throughout your work you will need to keep appropriate documentation that shows how you planned and produced your media product. Your work must include evidence of:

* an understanding of the production process
* the application of production techniques and skills to the creation of a media product
* the ability to work creatively to a brief
* evaluation of the media product

Scenario

Recycle.It *is an organisation that wants young people to think about the way that we recycle everyday materials. It has asked for your help in producing media products that will appeal to young people aged between eleven and fourteen years.* ***Recycle.It*** *has undertaken extensive research into the subject and has found that there are a number of issues that should concern young people.* ***Recycle.It*** *is inviting secondary schools and colleges to contribute to its campaign by planning and producing a range of media products aimed at the target audience. They are intended for distribution to secondary schools and colleges throughout the country.*

Choose one of the following briefs.

Brief 1: Recycle.It would like you to develop a moving image product. It should aim to raise awareness in young people of the benefits of recycling waste material.

The emphasis should be on producing an informative and educational moving image product, clearly targeting the intended audience.

There are no restrictions on the style, content or length of the moving image product. However, **Recycle.It** wants a moving image product that will motivate the target audience and make them think about the key issues.

Your moving image product must be accompanied by the appropriate documentation and an evaluation.

Brief 2: Recycle.It would like you to develop an audio product. It should aim to raise awareness in young people of the benefits of recycling waste material.

The emphasis should be on producing an informative and educational audio product, clearly targeting the intended audience. There are no restrictions on the style, content or length of the audio product. However, **Recycle.It** wants an audio product that will motivate the target audience and make them think about the key issues.

Your audio product must be accompanied by the appropriate documentation and an evaluation.

Brief 3: Recycle.It would like you to develop a print product. It should aim to raise awareness in young people of the benefits of recycling waste material.

The emphasis should be on producing an informative and educational print product, clearly targeting the intended audience. There are no restrictions on the style, content or length of the print product. However, **Recycle.It** wants a print product that will motivate the target audience and make them think about the key issues.

Your print product must be accompanied by the appropriate documentation and an evaluation.

Brief 4: Recycle.It would like you to develop an interactive media product. It should aim to raise awareness in young people of the benefits of recycling waste material.

The emphasis should be on producing an informative and educational interactive media product, clearly targeting an intended audience. There are no restrictions on the style, content or length of the interactive media product. However, **Recycle.It** wants an interactive media product that will motivate the target audience and make them think about the key issues.

Your interactive media product must be accompanied by the appropriate documentation and an evaluation.

Think it over...

In order to practise your pre-production, production and post production skills, you could use the Recycle.It scenario to produce your own sample paperwork.

If you do this, then be careful not to confuse this brief with the brief given to you by Edexcel in September of the year you undertake this unit.

3.1 Pre-production skills and techniques

The first thing you need to consider is which of the media formats you want to use to produce your work. Think about the issues raised on the previous page and then make an informed decision. To help you to make a decision use the planning template in Figure 3.1.

Which skills was I best at and did I enjoy the most in my work for Unit 2?
Which format would give me the most time to complete my work?
Which format would have the most impact on the audience?
What resources do I have available?

FIGURE 3.1 *A planning template will help you decide which format to choose for your product.*

Target audience

Once you have decided which media format to use, you will need to carry out some initial research activities. These will relate to your target audience and will help you to focus the design of your media product.

Learning activity 1

Choose a television programme or video that focuses on environmental issues. For the purposes of this activity, choose something that is quite short. Watch the programme or video and then complete the following tasks:

- Name the programme or video.
- Identify who made the programme.
- Identify the target audience.
- Did the programme or video give you a message?

Were you able to decide who the target audience was? Was the message clear and understandable for the target audience? Did the programme or video put over its message in an appropriate way? Remember that there are certain restrictions on what can be broadcast at particular times. You can judge the intended audience for different programmes or videos by the nature of its contents. A cartoon character that looks like a fluffy animal might not be appropriate for the eleven–fourteen age group, whereas a cartoon character such as Bart Simpson might be ideal.

Learning activity 2

Carefully examine the coverage of environmental issues in a national newspaper and a local newspaper. Note the geographical coverage of these two publications and, if possible, the nature of the environmental issues – whether of local, national or international concern.

Learning activity 3

Undertake the same exercise for a local and a national radio station. Make a note of the geographical area served by each radio station.

Learning activity 4

Using the Internet, find a variety of websites that provide information on the environment. Make a list of these sites and identify which of them have information that might appeal to the eleven–fourteen year old target audience.

All of the media products you examined in the above activities will have one main aim – to inform the target audience and to encourage them to do something. In order to satisfy your client, in this case Recycle.It, you will need to product a media product that fulfils its brief and addresses its target audience.

By now you should have developed an understanding of the target audience for an environmental awareness campaign. Now you need to consider the design of your product and how this will impact on the target audience.

Learning activity 5

If you have a school or college prospectus get hold of a copy. If not, find a prospectus for another school or college in your area. Read the prospectus carefully and think about its target audience. Does the prospectus have photographs and, if it does, what do the photographs show? Are there images of people who look unhappy? Is the school or college shown as being dirty and inhospitable?

The answer to the last two questions will probably be no: the target audience for a prospectus is students and parents who are prospective clients for the school or college. A great deal of planning will have gone into producing a publication that presents the school or college in the best light possible for its target audience.

Learning activity 6

See if you can find out who did the research and planning for the prospectus you looked at in Learning activity 5. If you can meet, ask them about the choice of material that appeared in the finished product. What informed their decisions about what to include?

If your school has a video or website that is available to prospective students, consider it in the same way as you did with the paper prospectus. What additional aspects can be included in a video or website that might be missing in a paper-based prospectus?

The proposal

Every media product starts life as an idea. It is important to refine your ideas to fit the needs of the client, your resources and the target audience. Generally all ideas for media products go through a process in which they are developed into a proposal.

The proposal is a document in which you set out to sell your ideas to a client. In this case you will want to sell your ideas for an appropriate media product to the organisation Recycle.It. An example of a proposal is shown in Figure 3.2, in which a company called Media Productions sets out its ideas for a video that fits the Recycle.It brief.

Throughout this unit, we will be looking at the production of the Media Productions video programme, and many of the examples given are specific to moving image production. You will be able to adapt the details to fit whichever type of media product you have decided to produce.

The proposal should include sufficient information for the reader to understand what you intend to do. It is a sales tool, designed to whet the appetite of a potential client.

The front page of the proposal gives details of the programme name, who the proposal is by, contact details and the date it was written. All of this information is important as it tells the client at a glance what the proposal is about, the name of the company making the proposal and how recent it is. You need to include your contact details so that a client can get in touch with you to discuss any details that need clarifying.

The second page of the proposal should give clear information to the client about your ideas for the media product. Try to make your proposal as exciting and informative as possible. The commissioner will need to make a judgement on your ideas and if the proposal does not 'grab them' they might not come back to you for further information. Generally a proposal should be short and succinct and give the client just enough information for them to want to find out more.

You should also indicate to the client the research you have undertaken when preparing your proposal. We looked at the different research methods in Unit 2. Now is your chance to put that learning into practice.

CASE STUDY

Media Productions has been asked to produce a proposal and treatment for a video programme. The client wanted a DVD that would be distributed to shops in the local area. The aim of the video was to demonstrate to shopkeepers what could happen if they sold knives to children.

The brief from the client arrived on the desk of the producer early in May and they wanted the finished product in June. Media Productions decided that there was insufficient time to produce a high-quality product in just over a month and declined to present a proposal and treatment.

Media Productions would have liked to work on this brief. However, it felt that its reputation might have been damaged if it had had to rush through this work.

- How long do you think would be a reasonable time scale to produce the video?
- List all the reasons why Media Productions declined this work.

media
PRODUCTIONS

Proposal
for
a video programme

Recycling and YOU

Prepared by
James Subrami

Media Productions
sally.ahmed@mediap.co.uk
21st May 2006

Client
Recycle.It

copyright © 2006

PROPOSAL

Prepared by James Subrami

Media Productions proposes to produce a ten-minute video programme aimed at encouraging young people to consider how they can recycle waste material. The programme will be aimed at an audience of 11–14 year olds and will be informative and educational. The programme will provide evidence of the effects on the environment of not recycling waste material.

The programme will feature material shot on location at a large school, a waste recycling plant and a large landfill site. It will be fronted by a well-known environmental spokesperson and will be accompanied by music from a chart band. We have approached Coldplay to provide an appropriate track and their initial response has been positive.

The programme will feature four young people who are all students at West Smethwick School. They are not concerned about the environment but after being shown what might happen to the planet they reconsider their views. We have contacted the school and they are willing for their pupils to take part in this programme.

We will include facts and figures concerning pollution levels and the effects of waste on the planet will be shown. We have obtained figures from Greenpeace and local authorities on the effects of waste material on the environment.

The spokesperson will appear on screen when interviewing the four young people about the choices they are about to make. Graphics will be used to reinforce the facts and figures about the effects of pollution on the planet.

The programme will be produced on digital format cameras and edited using the latest digital editing technology at our Birmingham editing facility.

The programme budget is subject to discussion but will be approximately £20,000.

FIGURE 3.2 *Your proposal should be succinct but contain enough detail to make the client want to find out more.*

FIGURE 3.3 *In the media world missing your deadline can mean that the product is out of date by the time it is completed.*

UNIT ASSESSMENT

Prepare a proposal for the media product of your choice using the scenario from the published brief for this year.

- Ensure that you include all the information needed to 'sell' this idea to your teacher.
- Give clear and precise details of the content, style and size of the finished media product
- Impress your client with your use of media language.
- Demonstrate that you have undertaken some initial research into your ideas.
- Give clear details of how you will produce the media product in the timeframe available.
- Reassure your client (teacher) that your ideas are feasible.

Once you have completed your proposal, give it to your teacher for their approval of your ideas. You must take careful note of the feedback from your teacher and make any changes that you agree with your teacher. Store both the initial and final versions of your proposal to be used for assessment purposes.

Theory into practice

Many professionals in the media industry have to 'pitch' ideas to a client.

You may wish to consider 'pitching' your idea to your teacher and your peers. You might decide to produce a PowerPoint presentation of your ideas. You could also give your audience a copy of your presentation as a handout.

If you do pitch your ideas in this way you must consider what you say and how you say it. Be careful to get your ideas across clearly and be creative with the language you use, using images and sound to enhance your pitch.

Think it over...

The example proposal given in Figure 3.2 is for a video programme. You may decide to produce another form of media product. The same principles for proposal writing apply whichever format you decide to use for your media product. You should make sure that your proposal clearly states the kind of media product you will be producing.

Remember

You could make:

- an interactive media product
- a short radio drama or news report on recycling and the environment
- a newspaper or magazine article on recycling, containing graphics (charts and diagrams) and photographs
- a video drama or documentary
- a poster or flyer.

The treatment

Once your proposal has been seen and agreed by a client, you can begin developing your **treatment**. The treatment is a written description of what your product will comprise, including the working title of the project, the proposed length of the product and the format of the product – for example, a video programme, a radio programme, a newspaper or a website. Your treatment must clearly identify the target audience and the ways in which the product will address this audience. It should also give your client a clear idea of the cost of the finished product. It must be written in a way that allows the reader to visualise the content of the product and to make an evaluation of its suitability for their purposes. Your treatment should be designed to encourage the client to ask you to develop the project to the production stage.

Your treatment should include:

* an outline of the ideas being developed for the product
* the details and results of all the research you have done
* depending on the format you have chosen to work in, your initial script/outline/layout/storyboard/mood board/thumbnails
* the outline budget
* your contingency plans
* the identification of 'talent' and production staff (talent refers to the actor or presenters to appear in your production).

Learning activity 7

Begin working on your treatment, making sure that you consider all of the following points:

- the feasibility of your chosen idea
- the audience for your product
- the time you have available for planning and production
- how you will meet your deadline
- the resources you have available for pre-production, production and post-production
- what you will do in the event of unforeseen circumstances (your contingency plans)
- how you will present the final product
- how you will review your product
- how you might make changes as a result of feedback from your client or target audience.

* In order to gain higher marks you must show an excellent understanding of pre-production, production and post production techniques using thorough documentation that is well organised and covers all aspects of the process.

Figure 3.4 shows an outline of a treatment document. In this case, James Subrami from Media Productions will complete the treatment with details of the Recycle.It video programme. When you produce your own treatment, try using the headings given in this example to structure your work. You may add further sections if you need them.

The **outline script** is sometimes called a scene script and it gives an outline of each scene without going into detail about each shot. This will be used for video and audio products. It can indicate whether a scene takes place at daytime or night, the characters involved and whether there will be dialogue or narration.

A **storyboard** is a paper visualisation of the media product. Producing a storyboard will help you to develop your ideas about the way that the visual and sound elements of a product work together. It is really useful when developing ideas for a video or interactive media product.

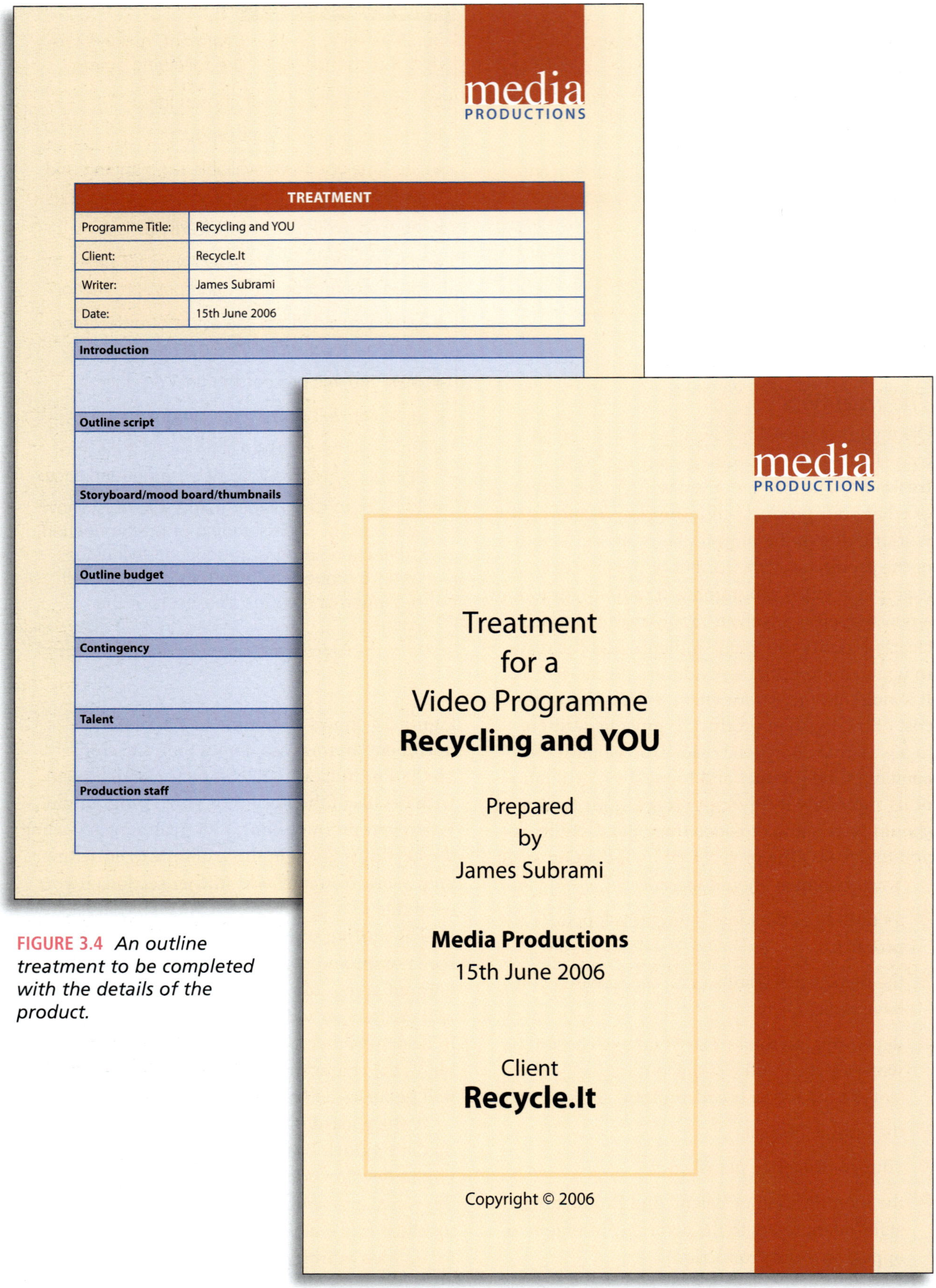

media PRODUCTIONS

TREATMENT	
Programme Title:	Recycling and YOU
Client:	Recycle.It
Writer:	James Subrami
Date:	15th June 2006

Introduction

Outline script

Storyboard/mood board/thumbnails

Outline budget

Contingency

Talent

Production staff

media PRODUCTIONS

Treatment
for a
Video Programme
Recycling and YOU

Prepared
by
James Subrami

Media Productions
15th June 2006

Client
Recycle.It

Copyright © 2006

FIGURE 3.4 *An outline treatment to be completed with the details of the product.*

A **mood board/thumbnail** is a useful tool when planning layouts for print products or pages of an interactive media product. The mood board can give a flavour of colour, text and images at an early stage in the development of the product.

An **outline budget** must give details of all the costs involved in the production of the media product. This will cover pre-production, production and post-production costs. The outline budget should be as realistic as possible and based on industry rate cards that can be found on websites for major retailers and equipment suppliers and producers. Your budget needs to make allowances for the contingency plan (see below) and for unforeseen costs.

It is important for you to have a **contingency plan** when you are developing your treatment. The contingency plan should indicate the plans for the production should there be unexpected delays, poor weather on location, staff shortages and changes required by the client.

The treatment should indicate the potential **talent** – the actors or presenters that you will be using in your product – and some idea of the **production staff** or crew who will be involved in making the product.

Theory into practice

You can use the example treatment format given in Figure 3.5 for whatever media format you have chosen for your product.

You may have to adapt some elements if your chosen format does not fit into the template given. For example, the storyboard for an audio product may be replaced by a script with notes on sound effects, narration, atmosphere and music.

You must ensure that you use appropriate headings for your treatment.

UNIT ASSESSMENT

Prepare a treatment for the media product of your choice developing your ideas from your proposal:

- Ensure that all the logistics in your treatment are accurate – for example, all the resources you need are available and there is sufficient time for production and post-production.
- Make it clear that you have a contingency plan if circumstances change.
- Demonstrate that you have researched thoroughly for your production.
- You should take note of the on-going feedback from your teacher on your treatment and incorporate any suggestions they make.
- You must keep all initial versions of your treatment and a final version for assessment of your work.

Think it over...

As you are working on your treatment, think about the following questions about your product.

1. After having carried out my research, is my idea still feasible?
2. Do I have enough time to complete my work?
3. Do I have sufficient resources to make my product?
4. Can I find the people I need to help me to make this product?
5. Will my product be 'fit for purpose'?

Once your proposal and treatment have been signed off by your teacher, you should commence the planning stage of pre-production.

Production planning

You may decide that you need help in the planning and production of your media product. Most media products are made by a team of people. Each of the team members has their own skills. You should consider who has the skills to help you with your media product and also be prepared to use your own skills to help other people with their products.

Roles

When you begin the planning and production stages of your media product, you will see that an individual working alone might find it difficult to produce a quality media product. You should investigate the different roles involved in producing the media product you have chosen. For example, in order to produce a video programme for a client, Media Productions will involve the following personnel:

- The **director** is responsible for turning the script into the visual medium of video.
- The **camera operator** works to get the best possible camera shots following their brief and under the guidance of the director.
- A **sound recordist** is primarily concerned with recording the best possible sound and working with the camera operator as a team.
- An **editor** works with the original material and links together the shots required for the finished video or film, working closely with the director in the editing suite.
- A **production assistant** is the vital link between the director and the crew, keeping notes of the requirements of the production and ensuring that everything runs smoothly.
- The **producer** is in charge of the logistics of the production; they hire the staff and manage the locations, materials and resources needed for a successful production.

Learning activity 8

Undertake some research into the personnel you will need to make your media product, bearing the following points in mind:

- You will have to take full responsibility for the media product you have chosen to produce but that doesn't mean you have to do all the work yourself.
- Remember that you probably don't have all the skills necessary or the time available to undertake all the roles yourself.
- Someone else may have specialist skills that you could use, for example drawing a storyboard or mood board, recording your music tracks or having a clear speaking voice for your voiceover.
- You may be able to demonstrate higher levels of skill by helping a colleague to complete their media product.

UNIT ASSESSMENT

Produce a staffing list for your product listing all the people you will need. Here is a checklist of what you will need to do to achieve this:

- Identify the skills you need and who might have them.
- Arrange to meet your team members and brief them on your idea.
- In consultation with your team members, clarify their roles and the timescale you have for production.
- Ask them to 'sign up' to help you.
- Ensure that they understand that you will help them with their work.
- Produce a clear list of personnel and the roles you have allocated.

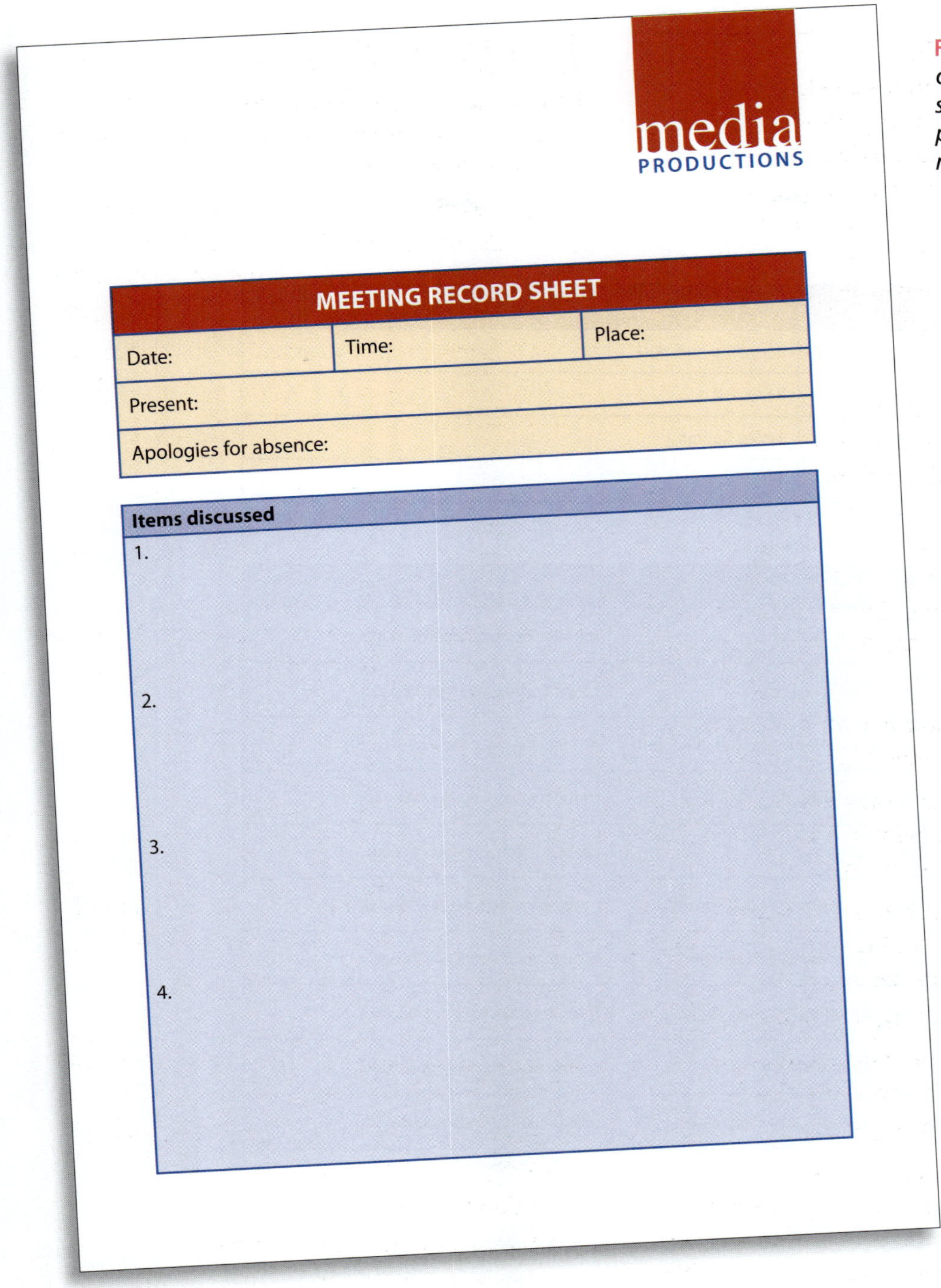

media
PRODUCTIONS

MEETING RECORD SHEET

Date:	Time:	Place:
Present:		
Apologies for absence:		

Items discussed

1.

2.

3.

4.

FIGURE 3.5 *An outline of a meeting record sheet for your production team meetings.*

Production team meetings

Holding regular team meetings will help to ensure that everything is on track and that all your team are aware of their roles and responsibilities. Keeping a chain of communication in place and having regular updates will keep you aware of any problems that are arising or any delays in aspects of the product being completed.

Keep a record of what is said in your production team meetings – you might like to use a version of the outline record sheet provided in Figure 3.5. List each item that is discussed as a numbered point.

Keep the list of personnel and the records of your production meetings to use in your **production schedule** – we will be looking at the production schedule next. Figure 3.6 provides an example of a staff list – you could use this format to help you keep a record of your crew.

media
PRODUCTIONS

STAFF LIST	
Programme Title:	Recycling and YOU
Client:	Recycle.It
Writer:	James Subrami
Date:	18th June 2006

Title	Contact Details
Director: Scott Mundy	mobile xxxxxxxxxxxxxxxxxxxx
Producer: Sally Ferguson	mobile xxxxxxxxxxxxxxxxxxxx
Cameraperson/Photographer: Bill Smith	mobile xxxxxxxxxxxxxxxxxxxx
Writer: James Subrami	mobile xxxxxxxxxxxxxxxxxxxx
Editor: Sani Samara	mobile xxxxxxxxxxxxxxxxxxxx
Production Assistant: Josh Zebrundra	mobile xxxxxxxxxxxxxxxxxxxx
Soundperson: Mandy Abrahams	mobile xxxxxxxxxxxxxxxxxxxx
Interactive Media Designer: Philip Jones	mobile xxxxxxxxxxxxxxxxxxxx
Graphic Designer: Mary Routh	mobile xxxxxxxxxxxxxxxxxxxx
Music Composer: Gary Hargreaves	mobile xxxxxxxxxxxxxxxxxxxx

FIGURE 3.6 *The staff list used by Media Productions for its work on the video programme for Recycle.It.*

Production schedule

This important document will include all your plans for your production, together with the details of what is involved and when. A production schedule will help you to plan effectively for pre-production, production and post-production.

The production schedule includes details of when the production started and when various activities are planned to take place. This information is important for your records as it will form a major part of the evidence required for the pre-production and the production stages of this unit. Your production schedule should contain:

* Details of the start and finish dates for producing the proposal and the treatment and when these were circulated to the client.
* Agreed dates for activities such as location shooting, editing and review by the client.
* Details of the production equipment you need to use and where you will obtain this from.
* Your transport requirements.
* Crewing requirements – with the names of the personnel.
* The talent (actors) required, with names.
* The properties required for the production and whose responsibility they are.
* Your post-production equipment requirements.

The production schedule helps to clarify all of the details of the production in one document. This document is a vital piece of evidence of your planning and production work, therefore you must store it carefully and have it available for the assessment of your work.

Monitor your production schedule regularly and record any changes as soon as they occur. Figure 3.7 shows the first part of a production schedule for the Recycling and YOU project undertaken by Media Productions for Recycle.It and includes all the key dates for this project. The schedule provides a clear picture of the way that the project is progressing.

For your own project, you might need to change some of the items included, depending on the type of product you are creating. For example, if you are producing a magazine, you will need to include dates for sample layouts, mood boards and copywriting instead of shooting script and storyboard.

Theory into practice

Communication between a production company and a client is vital. The client may wish to make changes to the programme, they may have to change their budget or they might want to add extra scenes to the programme.

Communication between the production company and their staff is also important. Everyone on the team needs to know what to do, where to be and what to produce.

It is essential that a communication chain is established in your production. Use a range of communication devices to keep your client and team 'up to speed' – meetings, e-mails, phone calls, etc. – whatever is most appropriate to the information you need to communicate.

Part 2 of the production schedule should provide a clear picture of the various requirements needed for the production, including equipment, personnel, talent, transport, props and post-production requirements, such as sound effects, music, etc.

Think it over...

Make sure that you identify all the requirements for your production when you complete your Production Schedule Part 2.

CASE STUDY

The producer at Media Productions had a limited time available to make the programme. Recycle.It decided, at the last moment, to bring their awareness raising campaign forward and publish the video earlier than originally planned. This meant that Media Productions had to rethink its plans.

It decided to continue with the project as planned but to bring the production dates forward. It was able to use its exisiting plans but change some of the dates on the production schedule. This, of course, meant extra work for the producer who is in charge of logistics – planning resources, crews and locations. It also meant having to contact all of the staff in order to keep them informed of all the changes.

- How do you think media companies come up with the dates for their production schedules?
- How do you think Media Productions will have decided which dates it could change?

media
PRODUCTIONS

PRODUCTION SCHEDULE PART 1	
Programme Title:	Recycling and YOU
Client:	Recycle.It
Writer:	James Subrami
Date:	21st April 2006

	Date		Date
Programme start:	**20/05/06**	**Programme completed:**	**22/08/06**
Proposal start:	20/05/06	Completed:	21/05/06
Agreement from client:	23/05/06		
Treatment start:	24/05/06	Completed:	15/06/06
Agreement from client:	16/06/06		
Shooting script start:	21/06/06	Completed:	30/06/06
Storyboard start:	04/07/06	Completed:	08/07/06
Production start:	23/07/06	Completed:	06/08/06
Post-production start:	09/08/06	Completed:	12/08/06
Rough cut to client:	13/08/06		
Agreement from client:	15/08/06		
Final version to client:	22/08/06		

FIGURE 3.7 *Part 1 of the production schedule gives all the key dates for the production of the media product.*

media
PRODUCTIONS

PRODUCTION SCHEDULE PART 2	
Programme Title:	Recycling and YOU
Client:	Recycle.It
Writer:	James Subrami
Date:	21st April 2006

Production equipment required
cameras lights microphones tripod
Crewing requirements
cameraperson sound recordist production assistant lighting technician props technician
Actors
1 male actor 1 female actor 3 extras
Transport requirements
Transport to 3 locations required for approximately 20 people
Props/scenery
1 large globe of the world
Post-production requirements (format, effects, music, voice-over)
Editing using Final Cut Pro Graphics for titles and credits Music throughout programme Sound effects where necessary

FIGURE 3.8 *Part 2 of the production schedule lists all the requirements for the production and post-production stages.*

Think it over...

The production schedule shown in Figure 3.8 is for a video project. List the items you would need to include if you were making:

- a radio commercial
- a newspaper or magazine article
- a poster or flyer
- a multimedia CD-ROM
- a website.

Remember

- You will need to keep careful records of your planning and production.
- Update your production schedule regularly to reflect any changes that occur.
- Make sure you record the changes to your production in an appropriate way. Keep a copy of the original schedule so you can comment on why any changes were necessary.

As well as the production schedule, moving image producers often use a daily schedule listing the resources required for each day of production. This is known as a **call sheet** and also details for the crew and actors of where to be and at what time. It can also contain details of transport arrangements, props needed, materials required for the day's work and location catering arrangements.

When you do your planning, remember to keep everyone informed about the schedule. If you give everyone involved a call sheet, people are much more likely to be in the right place at the right time and with the right equipment.

Think it over...

Try to answer the following questions about your own project:

- How will you ensure that you communicate effectively with your team?
- Do you have everyone's contact details?
- Do you know when and where you are going to a location?
- Does everyone know when and where you are going?

CASE STUDY

Media Productions has always kept careful records of its planning. But when the company first started it did not realise how important communications were to the successful completion of a project.

One of its first projects was a TV documentary that involved filming a short sequence in Spain. It arranged for the film crew to fly to Spain, but did not check with the crew that all of them had the necessary documentation for travelling abroad. In fact two of the crew members didn't have passports and were not able to leave the country. The project was delayed by several weeks while alternative arrangements were made.

The company now has a proper system of communication for each project – using production schedules and call sheets. It makes sure that everyone involved in a project knows where they will be going and any special requirements.

Clear and regular communication is crucial for the smooth running of a production.

- What communications procedures could have helped prevent the problem described in this case study?
- What communications procedures do you think will help you with your product?

media
PRODUCTIONS

PRODUCTION SCHEDULE CALL SHEET	
Programme Title:	Recycling and YOU
Client:	Recycle.It
Writer:	James Subrami
Date:	15th July 2006

Crew	
Camera:	Robin Williams
Sound:	Rory Smith
Lighting:	Jill Sparks
Production Assistant:	Kate Azhami
Technicians:	John Brown/Bill Bailley
Transport:	Just Cars
Props:	Gary Musazawksi
Meeting at:	Sponforth Waste Recycling Plant, Sponforth, Kent Meet at front gates
Location Venue:	Interior of reclamation plant

CALL DATE:	**25th July 2005**
CALL TIME:	**6.30am**
Transport:	leaving from Media Productions offices at 6 a.m. prompt
INSTRUCTIONS:	Crew to wear sturdy boots or shoes

Actors:	Bill Foreman	Jane Smith	Extras: to be confirmed
Wardrobe:	Bill: 7 a.m.	Jane: 7.30 a.m.	Extras: from 8 a.m.
Make-up:	Bill: 7.30 a.m.	Jane: 8 a.m.	Extras: from 8.30 a.m.

Location catering:	Breakfast required for 30 people from 7 a.m. Lunch required for 30 people from 12.30 p.m. Evening meal for 10 people from 6 p.m. Coffee/tea available at all times Chuck Wagon caterers on site at all times
Properties:	1 large globe of the world – Day 1

FIGURE 3.9 *An example of a call sheet used by Media Productions for the first day of the Recycling and YOU video shoot.*

UNIT ASSESSMENT

Produce a production schedule for your media product. Include as much information as possible.

Include call sheets for each day of production and include all your other paperwork, such as permissions gained for shooting or recording on location, confirmation of transport arrangements, etc.

Budget

So far all your work has involved the practicalities of developing your ideas and scheduling. Now you need to consider the costs involved in producing your media product. Once you have finalised all the requirements for your media product, you can begin to create a realistic budget.

In order to come up with a realistic budget, you will need to research the costs involved in producing your chosen media product. For example, you will need to know the costs of hiring the equipment you will need – one way of doing this is to contact a local media equipment hire company and ask them for rates for hiring equipment. This will give you a good idea of the rental costs for the equipment that you will be needing.

You must also consider the cost of the personnel you use in your project. Try to find out how much it will cost to hire your crew and actors for the time needed to produce your product. Try getting realistic costs for this, from sources such as BECTU, the union for moving image, radio and information design industries, which will have a rate card for various roles within the industry.

Making your budget as realistic as possible will help you to gain an understanding of the sort of costs involved in media production. It is always a good idea to include some contingency in your budget to allow for any extra costs that might arise.

UNIT ASSESSMENT

Produce a realistic budget for all the elements of your media product, including pre-production, production, post-production and contingency costs. Remember to include costs for all of the following:

- hire of equipment
- cost of materials
- crew payments
- actors' fees
- location charges
- travel
- subsistence (i.e. meals, hotels)
- contingency (e.g. equipment breakdowns, bad weather delays).

CASE STUDY

Media Productions always includes a contingency amount in the budget in case of unforeseen circumstances. It needed to use its contingency in a recent corporate video project for an electronics business with offices all around the world. The client wanted the video to include footage of all their branches in different countries.

During the pre-production stages of the project, the client bought another company in Ireland. This meant that the Irish offices now had to be included in the video. The contingency costs were enough to cover the filming at this extra location.

- What do you think would have happened if Media Productions didn't have any contingency allowance in the budget?
- Can you think of any contingency that might be needed for your media product?
- What do you think is a reasonable amount to include for contingency?

media
PRODUCTIONS

BUDGET	
Programme Title:	Recycling and YOU
Client:	Recycle.It
Writer:	James Subrami
Producer:	Amanda Phillips
Director:	Barry Norman
Date:	25th June 2006

MATERIALS	COST	TOTAL
3 x DVCAM tapes	£20 each	£60
Equipment		
Hire - Sony DVCAM camera	£150 per day × 3 days	£450
Hire of 1 tripod	£20 per day × 3 days	£60
Hire of lighting kit	£50 per day × 3 days	£150
Hire of microphone kit	£75 per day × 3 days	£225
Actors		
1 male actor	rehearsal £50 × 3 days	£150
	shooting £150 × 3 days	£450
1 female actor	rehearsal £50 × 3 days	£150
	shooting £150 × 3 days	£450
3 extras	shooting 3 × £50 × 1 day	£150
Props/scenery		
1 large globe of the world	purchased price	£30
Post-production		
Editing suite	£150 per day × 3 days	£450
Editor	£100 per day × 3 days	£300
Graphic designer	£100 per day × 1 day	£100
	TOTAL	**£3175**
Contingency @ 10% of budget		£318
	Total Budget	**£3493**

FIGURE 3.10 *The initial budget produced by Media Productions for its Recycling and YOU video. (All production crew are on the company payroll and have not been included in the budget.) Remember to adapt the budget to fit the requirements of your own media product.*

Location reconnaissance

Once you have completed work on your budget and all your other planning documents, you can begin to plan for the production of your media product. For moving image products, and perhaps also audio products, carrying out a location reconnaissance (usually known as a **recce**) is the next step in the process.

This is where you can visit any locations or the studio that you are planning to use and check out the lighting, power supply and accessibility for your crew and cast. You may have to organise a contact person to let you in early to set up your equipment. You will also be able to find out if there are any health and safety issues to overcome.

Always make sure you gain permission to film on location and notify the police if you are planning to film in a public area. It could ruin all your plans if you turn up on the day planned for filming only to find out that the location is closed or the owners of the location don't allow you to carry out your shoot. And make sure you don't plan to film in a place where you could cause an obstruction for the people using that location for their everyday activities.

FIGURE 3.11 *Gaining permission in advance to film on location can prevent all kinds of problems!*

There have been cases of students filming mock hold-ups outside bank premises without having obtained permission or notified the local police. In one such case, teams of armed police arrived at the scene as they thought a real robbery was taking place. Not only was this a waste of police time, but it also put the students and members of the public at risk. This is an extreme example but it does highlight the need to prepare properly for your location shoots.

Theory into practice

Media Productions takes health and safety issues very seriously. It understands that the safety of its production team and the public are important.

The producer and assistant visit all locations prior to filming to check on any hazards to the production team or the public.

The company always undertakes a thorough **risk assessment** procedure before any filming takes place – this involves identifying any potential hazards, the likelihood of any problems occurring because of each hazard and how the danger can be minimised.

There is more on health and safety issues in the next sections of this unit, and an example of a risk assessment sheet is given in Figure 3.14 on page 173.

Use a **location visit sheet** to record all of the information you gather during your recce – an example is given in Figure 3.12. Then attach this sheet to your production schedule.

Safe working practices

You must follow safe working practices at all stages of work on your media product. When producing media products you have to work with equipment, with other people and sometimes working with an audience. No one wants to work in a dangerous situation if this can be avoided. Your location recce can identify potential hazards so you can begin to compile a risk assessment document. This document is a vital piece of evidence for your work in this unit.

media PRODUCTIONS

PRODUCTION SCHEDULE LOCATION VISIT SHEET	
Programme Title:	Recycling and YOU
Client:	Recycle.It
Writer:	James Subrami
Producer:	Amanda Phillips
Director:	Barry Norman
Date:	2nd July 2006

Rough sketch of location including electricity points:
Sponforth Waste Recycling Plant

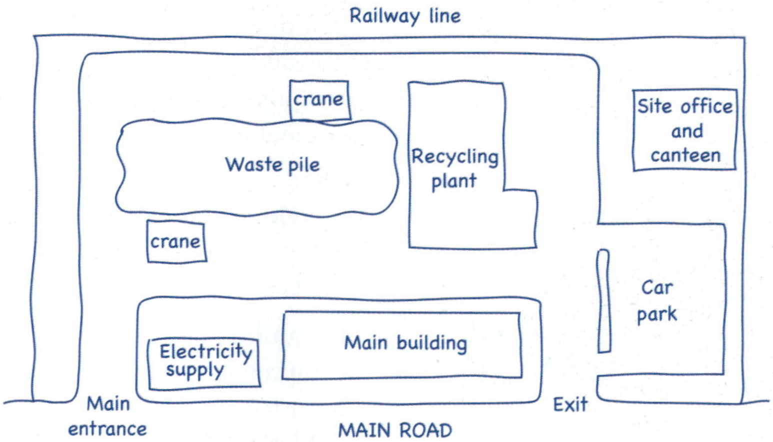

Access to location via:
Main road and through access gates via security

Name and number of location contact:
John Williams, Site Manager

Health and safety issues to note:
- Working machinery
- Some toxic substances stored on site
- Close to main road
- Railway line in proximity
- Slippery paths and working areas
- Potential hazard from airborne waste
- Location of emergency services
- Availability of first aid

Potential filming problems:
- Lack of electricity supply
- Close proximity of road and railway line
- Machinery working in location
- Noise when recording live interviews
- No cover for crew if inclement weather

Notes:

FIGURE 3.12 *The location visit sheet for one of the locations used by Media Productions for its Recycling and YOU programme for Recycle.It.*

UNIT ASSESSMENT

Produce:

- a comprehensive location reconnaissance record for your production (see Figure 3.12 for an example)

or

- a risk assessment of potential hazards when working in a studio (see Figure 3.14 for an example).

Keep this document safely with your production schedule.

Theory into practice

There is a wide range of health and safety issues you need to consider when planning your production. You may need to refer to the following regulations when undertaking your planning:

- Health and Safety at Work Act 1974
- The Management of Health and Safety at Work Regulations 1999
- The Manual Handling Operations Regulations 1992
- Display Screen Equipment Regulations 1992
- Control of Substances Hazardous to Health Regulations (COSHH) 2002.

Speak to your teacher to find out the relevant parts of each set of regulations and guidelines.

Production checklist

Before you start the production cycle of your media product, use the following checklist to make sure you are ready. If your answer to all of these questions is yes, you are ready to start with the production stage:

* Have I completed all of the pre-production paperwork?
* Do I have enough information to allow me to start producing media material?
* Is there enough evidence in my folder to demonstrate that I have done my pre-production thoroughly?
* Have I undertaken a risk assessment?
* Do all my crew understand what I am doing?
* Is my client happy with the planning?
* Do I have enough resources to undertake the production work?
* Do I have sufficient time to complete the work?

3.2 Production skills and techniques

Recording your material

In this section we will be looking at the techniques and technology you will use to produce material for your media product. You have now planned the production and you will have firm ideas about the content and look of your finished media product. The next step is to turn your ideas and planning into a reality.

Before you can start to create the content for your product, you must ensure that you have the right equipment for the job. Choosing the right equipment depends on the nature of the media product you have chosen to produce:

* For **video** you will need: studio or location equipment – including a video camera, tripod, lights and microphones.
* For **audio** you will need: studio or location equipment – including a cassette or minidisc recorder and microphones.
* For **print** products you will need: a camera, a computer, a scanner, a printer, software.
* For **interactive media** products you will need: a computer, a scanner, software.

You may need to consider how to record on location. For video, you will probably use one and move it around to shoot from different angles – this will make it look as if you have used two or more cameras. If you try to use two cameras you will have many technical issues to deal with, such as balancing the colour of the two cameras. Likewise, with sound recording you will use one recorder and one microphone to ensure that the quality of the sound recorded is consistent throughout. For print and interactive media, the new generation of still digital cameras can produce excellent images that equal the quality of film-based images.

If you are working on an interactive media product, you will be using a variety of media including text, graphics, photographs, and perhaps video and audio. You will want to ensure that all the media you use is of excellent quality, so that you will be happy with it and it will be acceptable to a client.

In order to successfully record material on location or in a studio you must plan carefully to ensure that everything runs smoothly. You should ensure that:

* the crew and cast are aware of the time and location of the recording
* equipment has been booked in time
* you have purchased or borrowed all the materials you need – for example, tapes, minidiscs, cassettes, CD-ROMs, memory sticks, data disks
* all the batteries have been charged
* the props you need are available.

Keeping a record

Once you start to record your material, it is useful to keep a careful record of everything you have recorded. This job is normally undertaken by a production assistant, where one is available, but for your product you will probably do it yourself.

For video and audio, your record should include a brief description of the action and the timing of the action. It could also indicate whether there was more than one **take** (this means the actual footage recorded) and which take you will be using for the finished media product.

Many digital video cameras have 'time code' recording, in which the running time is included in the recording and can be displayed in the monitor. With a digital still camera, you may have the option to use a built-in log, which identifies each shot by a discrete number. Audio recorders using cassettes have limited ability to log the takes on tape. However, digital recorders do allow you to log the start and finish of recordings.

Think it over...

Whichever type of media product you have chosen to produce, you should keep records of all the material produced. Consider the records you would need to keep if your were:

- producing a poster or flyer
- writing an article for a newspaper or magazine
- recording a radio commercial
- developing pages for a website
- producing an interactive media product, for example a simple game or information CD-ROM
- recording a short drama for television
- producing a press pack for the media.

Theory into practice

Keeping careful records can help with the post-production process. Imagine trying to locate the material that you want to use if you have twelve hours of video footage or seventy-five pages of notes for an article you are writing with no record of the material you have created.

All media professionals keep records in their own particular way or in the way required by the company they work for:

- A video producer might employ a production assistant to keep a record of every scene they shoot and how long this scene lasts.
- A writer might keep a box with file record cards or a database that details what is on each numbered sheet of their research.

Later, in the post-production section, you will see how keeping careful records can help to find material for the editing stage of your work.

Figure 3.13 shows the record (the 'shot material log') from a Media Productions location shoot. Next to each scene number, the production assistant has kept careful records of the number of takes for each scene, as well as a brief description of the scene and a comment to indicate whether the scene is good or not.

media
PRODUCTIONS

SHOT MATERIAL LOG	
Programme Title:	Recycling and YOU
Client:	Recycle.It
Writer:	James Subrami
Producer:	Amanda Phillips
Director:	Barry Norman
Date:	2nd August 2006

SCENE NO.	TAKE NO.	TIME CODE IN	TIME CODE OUT	DESCRIPTION	COMMENTS
1	1	00.01	00.09	exterior waste site	good
2	1	00.10	00.25	C/U pile of waste	out of focus
2	2	00.26	00.35	"	good
3	1	00.37	00.55	workers on tip	good
4	1	00.57	01.10	C/U workers	poor lighting
4	2	01.16	01.25	"	good
5	1	01.26	01.59	L/S whole site	OK
6	1	01.60	02.45	M/S whole site	good
7	1	02.46	03.59	C/U sign	good
8	1	04.00	04.50	interview site manager	good sound
9	1	04.51	05.58	interview worker	poor sound
10	1	05.49	07.35	interview manager	good

FIGURE 3.13 *The records kept by the production assistant on the location shoot at the waste recycling site. The abbreviations C/U, L/S, M/S stand for types of shot. Look back at Figure 2.56, page 132 and see if you can work out what each type of shot is.*

These records will be invaluable when the producer goes into the edit suite. The notes could form part of an initial **paper edit** that will save time at a later date. Imagine having twenty different disks with footage you need for your programme. There will be footage you need at some point on all of the disks. You could spend many hours going backwards and forwards through the disks to find the footage you need.

It is advisable to use a consistent style of logging whatever the product you have chosen to make. The log should include:

* scene/take/image number
* brief description
* comments
* time code, where appropriate.

If you have taken photographs on a number of memory cards, you will need to log the location of each one and number each memory card. The same is true for all the recorded material you produce, whether it is for an audio recording or material for an interactive media product.

If you were to be working on the material for a newspaper or magazine article you would have to use a slightly different version of this sheet that will contain records of all the copy, graphics and photographs that you have produced.

Whatever style of form you use, try to ensure that your logging is accurate and presented in a way that you will find easy to use at the editing stage.

UNIT ASSESSMENT

You must keep careful records of all your recorded footage, images or files. This will enable you to make decisions about the editing of your media product. Use a format that will enable you to log the time code, a description of the scene and whether it will be useful or not.

For photography, use a format that allows you to record the photographs you have taken and some details of their content.

Content considerations

In your pre-production work you will have looked at factors that might influence the material you record. Factors involving location work are sometimes the most problematic. Imagine arriving at a location to record a radio interview only to find that the owners do not want you to record on their premises. Do you continue with the interview and ignore the landowner's wishes? Do you offer to pay to use the location even though you haven't budgeted for this?

Filming in the street can create many problems for producers and camera crews. If people appear in your recording, you should ask their permission before using the shots in which they appear in your programme. Taking photographs in the street can present similar problems. You may need to produce release forms for people who appear in your product to sign, granting you permission to use the images you have taken of them. You may also need to pay a fee. For example, there may be a busker playing in the background of your shot. Would you pay him a fee for his performance and what about the copyright of the music he was playing?

There are many pitfalls involved in recording on location – make sure that you have all the angles covered. If you prepare a release form in advance and take a few copies along to your location recording, it will help ensure that everyone who appears in your project has agreed to it. You could include a brief description of the programme you are making so that the people concerned understand what it is they are appearing in.

CASE STUDY

Media Productions was filming a sequence for a programme for young children. The scene required footage of children playing in the sand on the beach.

The producer initially planned to simply go to the south coast and find a location. She would then ask the parents' permission to film their children playing on the sand and jumping through the waves. This could of course be problematic, as the parents might not agree for their children to be filmed or they might have wanted payment. Some parents might even have phoned the police if they weren't sure what the film was to be used for and were suspicious.

After careful consideration, the producer decided to hire several child models and take them to the beach. Although this might seem like an expensive option, it meant that no money was wasted in turning up to the location and not being able to shoot. This option meant that all the expenses were already in the budget and the parents' permission could easily be obtained.

Media Productions still had to get permission to use the beach for filming and had to take care to avoid filming other people who were using the beach.

- Why do you think that permission needs to be obtained from the people who appear in media products?
- What permissions might you need for your product?

Think it over...

Consider the possible issues that might be involved in producing the material for your media product.

Always ensure that you gain permission to use a location and that people who appear in your product have given you their permission – in the case of children, the parents must give their permission.

Safe working practices

You have already investigated safe working practices in the pre-production stage of this unit. In the production stage you have to put this into practice, by working safely with equipment and people. You will need to consider when to record material and under what conditions. There are a variety of restrictions you will find when recording material in a studio or on location, for example not using electrical equipment in the rain. The following are some examples of things you need to be aware of when undertaking your recording:

* handling recording and editing equipment safely
* being aware of trailing cables
* handling hot lights
* organising teams to work together in a safe environment
* recognising the dangers of prolonged use of VDU screens
* working in a sensible way and responding to directions.

UNIT ASSESSMENT

Keep an up-to-date record of all the safe working practice issues you encounter and how you managed to work safely. Store this document safely with your production diary.

Producing material

By now you have identified appropriate recording equipment, booked out the equipment and ensured that the batteries are charged, purchased sufficient recording material and made sure that everyone knows where to go and at what time, as well as ensuring a safe working environment and safe working practices.

You now need to ensure that you can record the material accurately and that all the elements

media
PRODUCTIONS

RISK ASSESSMENT SHEET	
Programme Title:	Recycling and YOU
Client:	Recycle.It
Writer:	James Subrami
Producer:	Amanda Phillips
Director:	Barry Norman
Date:	25th July 2006

FILMING AT SPONFORTH WASTE RECYCLING PLANT	
Possible hazards	
Risk	Level of risk
1. Waste material on floor making it dangerous for crew and equipment	High
2. Machinery operating in the area	High
3. Visibility of crew when on site	High
4. Contamination of equipment by waste materials	Medium
5. Close to dual carriageway and access road	Low
Solutions	
1. Ensure someone checks that area is clear for filming.	
2. Have a look-out person to ensure that crew are aware of operating machinery.	
3. Crew to wear high-visibility vests at all times when on site.	
4. All equipment to be covered, where possible, by protective covers. All equipment to be cleaned before being returned to base.	
5. Film well away from the roads.	
Contacts	
• Site Safety Manager Bill Brown xxxxxxxxxxxxxx	
Emergency Services	
• On-site services xxxxxxxxxxxxxxxxxxxxxxx	
• Local police xxxxxxxxxxxxxxx	
• Local fire xxxxxxxxxxxxxxxxxxx	

FIGURE 3.14 *An example of a risk assessment sheet. As well as identifying the risks and how to avoid them, lists of contacts and emergency services are included so that the appropriate people can be contacted if anything does go wrong.*

of the recording are included. For example, it is no good recording brilliant video footage if the sound is so poor the audience will not be able to hear it. When you produce photographs, you have to make sure that the image is well lit and that, when using a digital camera, you capture it at an appropriate file size. Sound recordings can easily be ruined by the sound of the equipment being handled or extraneous background sounds.

You must ensure that you have a clear understanding of all the elements that make up your recording.

UNIT ASSESSMENT

Undertake the recording of the material for your media product:

- Make sure that you have all the resources you need.
- Keep your planning documents with you to ensure you have covered everything.
- Keep careful records of the whole production process.

3.3 Post-production skills and techniques

In this section you will consider the post-production process involving the various techniques used to manipulate and amend your original media material. Almost all media material needs to be edited before being released, whether it is video footage that needs to be joined together or photographs that have to be cropped or colour corrected. The post-production process allows you a measure of flexibility by providing an opportunity to correct or improve the original material to make a finished product.

You can, for example:

* correct errors in recording by omitting them from the finished product
* choose to use alternative shots from the ones you thought would be appropriate
* shorten sequences that are uninteresting or repetitive
* control the overall length of the finished product by shortening or lengthening individual scenes or adding more information
* introduce special effects in moving image and audio products
* change the colour of images and manipulate them to alter their meaning
* reduce or enlarge file size to make an interactive media product run more effectively
* cut or add text to fill the page better, or add or remove images.

Safe storage

It is very important to keep your recorded material safe. You will need to access this material throughout the editing process so all tapes, memory cards and files must be kept in a safe place. You must follow the following guidelines:

* Label the source material clearly with programme title, date recorded, location/studio, tape/disk/card number.
* If the material has been transferred to a hard drive, you must have a clearly labelled space on the drive where you are storing the source material and a backup alternative in place.
* Keep the tapes, memory cards and files in a safe place.
* Ensure that no one can record over the source material by removing the recording tab or making the file disk 'read only'.

Losing your source material will mean that you have to re-record all of your material – which is clearly not desirable. It may be impossible to recreate some of the original material and it will certainly put you behind with your planned deadlines.

Figures 3.15 to 3.18 give some examples of labels that you could use to identify the different elements of your product. These could be physical labels, or descriptions attached to computer files.

Use a material storage log to keep a record of where you have stored all the material for your product. See Figure 3.19 for an example. Keep a backup of all files stored on a computer hard drive – on a CD-ROM for example.

FIGURE 3.15 *A label for a video tape containing original material that was shot on location or in the studio.*

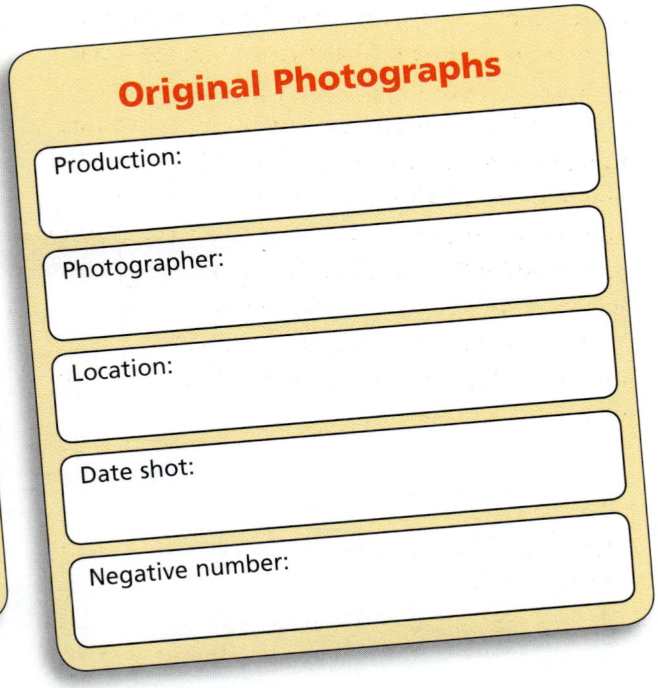

FIGURE 3.16 *For photographs you might use this type of storage label.*

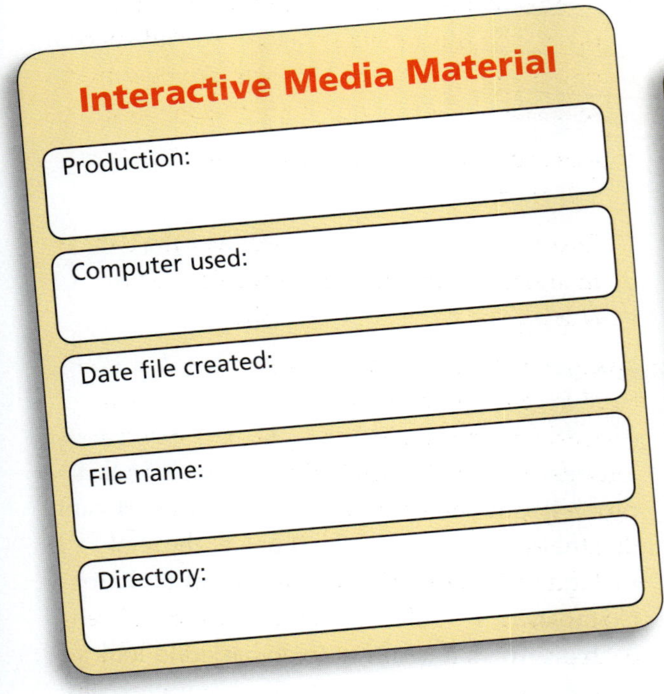

FIGURE 3.17 *This type of label might be useful for storing interactive media material on a CD-ROM.*

FIGURE 3.18 *You could store audio material using a label like this one.*

media
PRODUCTIONS

MATERIAL STORAGE LOG	
Programme Title:	Recycling and YOU
Client:	Recycle.It
Writer:	James Subrami
Producer:	Amanda Phillips
Director:	Barry Norman
Date:	8th August 2006

Tape number	Located
1	Tape storage locker – Edit Suite 1
2	Tape storage locker – Edit Suite 1
3	Tape storage locker – Edit Suite 1
Computer files	
Graphic designs for Titles	Hard drive – folder: Recycle.It / file: titles
Graphic designs for Credits	Hard drive – folder: Recycle.It / file: credits
Music tracks	Hard drive – folder: Recycle.It /music
Voiceover	Hard drive – folder: Recycle.It /voiceover
Backup files	CD-ROM labelled Recycle.It stored in filing cabinet

FIGURE 3.19 *Some of the material for the Recyling and YOU programme is stored in lockers and some of it is stored as computer files. You can adapt this log for your own product.*

UNIT ASSESSMENT

Create a material storage log for all the material you produce. This should clearly indicate where the material is stored.

Produce a clear labelling and storage system for all your source material.

Editing

The editing process involves reviewing all the material you have created and putting together the pieces you will be using in the final product. Your shot material log will be invaluable in this process, as it will allow you to locate the relevant material quickly and easily. (Look at the shot material logs shown in Figures 3.13 and 3.20 for examples.)

It is always interesting to go back and look at material you shot days or even weeks earlier. This will refresh your memory as you may see or hear things you had forgotten, which can be very useful when starting the editing process. It may give you new ideas about the best way of putting the different elements of your product together.

Video

There are various ways in which you can shape your video product during the editing process:

* You may want to change the order of the visual material from the camera original material. Perhaps you want to make the sequence more logical or remove poor footage.
* You may need to edit the sound you recorded on location or in the studio, perhaps to take out unwanted passages or instructions from the director.
* You may wish to add a title at the front of the product or credits at the end.
* Maybe you are going to add graphics, such as animations or pictures. The editing process will allow you to make room in your product for these to be added.
* You might need to correct the colour of your images or the level of your sound recording.

In video, the initial editing process is called the **off-line edit**. This process involves editing together the sequences and making a version that can be viewed by colleagues and the client so that they can suggest changes. The final editing process is called the **on-line edit** and this is where the final effects and finishing details are included.

Sound

There may be a number of reasons for editing sound material:

* Sometimes you will have recorded more than you need and so you will need to remove any excess audio.
* You may have recorded your material out of sequence. The editing process will allow you to rearrange the sequence.
* You may wish to delete recordings that are of a poor quality.
* You may want to add sound effects or music to complete your product.

Photographs

These are some of the ways in which you might edit your photographic material:

* You may need to crop or stretch photographic images in order to fit them into your layout.
* Or you may want to change the colour or contrast of an image.

This can be achieved in the editing process using the appropriate software.

Text

When working with text, you will use the editing stage to do the following types of tasks:

* You may wish to change the font or type style.
* You might need to make amendments to columns or spacing on a page in order to fit in your material or for aesthetic reasons.
* You might add captions to your photographs and illustrations.

Interactive media

An interactive media product will contain some or all of the elements listed above. You can edit the text, images, video and sound separately and part of the editing process will be combining them all in effective ways to create your finished product. File size will be an important consideration as you make your editing decisions:

* You may need to change the format of a photograph or video in order to improve download times.
* You may need to shorten the length of video or sound extracts so that the file size is not too big.

It is good practice to prepare for editing by undertaking a **paper edit** exercise. This will give you a clear picture of the shape, size and form of your media product. It will also save you time in the editing suite or when using your DTP package.

Figure 3.21 shows how Media Productions used one of the shot material log sheets from the location shoot as the basis of the paper edit. The best takes have been selected based on the comments recorded at the time of the shoot. The Effect column has been added to show how the scenes link together, and the type of sound to be used with each scene has been listed in the final column. You can see how the paper edit can be done quite easily by copying and pasting the shot material log sheet document and changing and adding information as necessary.

Once you have done your paper edit, you can carry out the edit itself using it to guide you.

(a)

media PRODUCTIONS

SHOT MATERIAL LOG	
Programme Title:	Recycling and YOU
Client:	Recycle.It
Writer:	James Subrami
Producer:	Amanda Phillips
Director:	Barry Norman
Date:	2nd August 2006

SCENE NO.	TAKE NO.	TIME CODE IN	TIME CODE OUT	DESCRIPTION	COMMENTS
1	1	00.01	00.09	L/S of crane	good shot/clear sound
2	1 2	00.10 00.26	00.25 00.35	M/S of crane M/S of crane	slightly out of focus good shot/good sound
3	1	00.37	00.55	3 men digging waste	good shot
4	1 2	00.57 00.16	01.10 01.25	C/U digging C/U digging	good shot – poor sound good shot – sound better
5	1	01.26	01.59	M/S digging	good – waste site in back
6	1 1	01.60 02.46	02.45 03.59	interview with worker interview with worker	OK – poor background better background
7	1	04.00	04.50	L/S workers	good
8	1	04.51	05.58	M/L/S workers	good – large crane in shot
9	1	04.59	07.35	interview with manager	good shot/sound good

FIGURE 3.20 *For video, the shot material log (a) forms the basis for the paper edit (b).*

(b)

media PRODUCTIONS

PAPER EDIT	
Programme Title:	Recycling and YOU
Client:	Recycle.It
Writer:	James Subrami
Producer:	Amanda Phillips
Director:	Barry Norman
Date:	9th August 2006

TAPE	SCENE NO.	TIME CODE IN	TIME CODE OUT	DESCRIPTION	EFFECT	SOUND
2	1	00.01	00.09	L/S of crane	fade in and cut to	atmos
2	2	00.26	00.35	M/S of crane	fade to	atmos
2	3	00.37	00.55	M/S 3 men digging waste	cut to	atmos
2	4	00.16	01.25	C/U digging	cut to	atmos
2	5	01.26	01.59	M/S digging	cut to	atmos
2	6	02.46	03.59	interview with worker	cut to caption (name)	live interview
2	7	04.00	04.50	L/S workers	fade to	atmos & music
2	8	04.51	05.48	M/L/S workers	fade to	atmos & music
2	9	05.49	07.35	interview with manager	fade out caption (name)	live interview

Reviewing your editing

Once you have completed the initial edit of your product, you will have the **rough cut** or **trial layout** version of your media product. Try this out on a sample of your target audience to get reactions to your product. Show it to your client too to get their feedback. It is important that you understand that even at this stage you can still make changes to your product if it does not meet the needs of your client or audience. You can incorporate any useful suggestions into your final edit.

It is very likely that you will have to make changes as a result of the feedback you receive. Don't be offended or discouraged by this. It is all part of the process of producing a successful media product that is fit for purpose and popular with its audience.

Many major feature films have had to be re-edited because the feedback from an invited audience has been negative. Imagine that you have spent several millions of pounds on making a film only to find that audiences stay away because they cannot understand the film or because the editing has left them confused. It is much better to get their comments before release when there is still time to make some changes.

One example of this involved a scene in one of the *Star Trek* films, in which Captain Kirk was shown dying a horrible death after an alien attack. The initial reviews showed that the audience reacted very badly to this scene, so the film makers decided to re-shoot the whole scene, this time showing Captain Kirk returning to fight alongside the new Captain, Jean-Luc Picard. Imagine the cost of doing this! But if the film were to be a success it was essential that both the audience and film critics would be happy.

You won't need to go to such great expense to make changes to your media product, and any changes you do make in response to audience feedback will mean that people are more likely to enjoy your product.

One way of getting feedback from your client and target audience is to hold a focus group in which you show all or part of the product in order to get valuable feedback. Develop a questionnaire to use in the focus group that allows your participants to review your product in an appropriate way. You may want them to concentrate on certain aspects of the product more than others. A questionnaire is useful because it provides you with some written feedback that you can analyse afterwards and help you to identify any changes you need to make.

Remember that it will not help you if you choose people to review the product who would not want to offend you. You must include a good cross-section of people from your target audience.

As well as trying out the product on the target audience, carry out your own review, considering aspects such as:

- the length of the product
- the quality of the visual or sound elements in the product
- how well the product conveys the storyline
- consistency of style.

UNIT ASSESSMENT

Present your edited product to a client or focus group that includes members of your target audience.

Devise an appropriate way of getting feedback on the product, such as a questionnaire, and analyse the results.

Keep all evidence of your review.

Produce evidence of the changes you make to your product as a result of the analysis.

3.4 How to evaluate your production

Keeping a log or diary

You should keep a comprehensive diary or log of the work you have undertaken during the pre-production, production and post-production phases of your work. This diary or log will help you to reflect on the work that you did and the help you had from colleagues. The following is a list of the points you could cover in your diary:

- How you thought of your idea.
- How you developed the idea into a proposal.

* How the proposal developed into a treatment.
* A breakdown of the primary and secondary research methods you used.
* Notes of meeting with team members.
* Notes on the way that your team members worked.
* Notes on the work you undertook for others.
* Ongoing notes of the skills you are developing.
* Reflections on the quality of your work.
* An analysis of your media product as compared to a professionally produced product of a similar nature.
* Your understanding of the fitness for purpose of your own media product.
* An analysis of how well your media product meets the client's brief and audience needs.

You might choose to keep a written diary or to use an appropriate format such as a PowerPoint presentation or a video or audio evaluation. Whichever method you use for your diary or log, you should use appropriate media language.

Remember

Always keep a careful diary of the key dates, times and actions you took during the pre-production, production and post production process.

Make a careful note of decisions you made and agreed with the client.

Keep this diary in a safe place.

FIGURE 3.21 *Finding time to keep a production diary is important – even when you are very busy with other tasks involved in your production.*

Figure 3.22 shows an extract from the production diary of Amanda Phillips, the producer of the Recyling and YOU video for Recycle.It. This extract shows the entries she made regarding the location shoot at Sponforth Waste Recycling Plant.

CASE STUDY

The producers at Media Productions always keep a comprehensive diary of their work. This helps them when they are reviewing the finished product with their client and enables them to provide evidence should any disagreements arise.

The producer's diary was very helpful on one occasion when the client decided, at the last minute, that they did not like a particular sequence in the video. They tried to claim that they had not given approval for this scene to be included.

The producer was able to find the date and time of a discussion with the client when the content of this scene was agreed. Of course, if the client wants a scene to be deleted that is fine, but it is good to be able to prove that it had been agreed in the first place.

- How did the production diary help in this situation?
- What might have happened if the producer hadn't kept a diary of her meetings with the client?

media
PRODUCTIONS

PRODUCTION DIARY

Name:	Amanda Phillips (Producer)
Production:	Recycling and YOU

Date	Action Taken
17th July	Met with client to discuss the location shoot at Sponforth Waste Recycling Plant (SWRP). Client agreed to contact SWRP to clear the location shoot.
19th July	Met with cameraperson to discuss issues with camera safety when working on waste disposal sites. Agreed that the camera must be protected against waste material and that this was the responsibility of the camera crew.
23rd July	Met with the director to discuss the location shoots. There was agreement on the length of time required for each location shoot – this was set at one day for each location.
30th July	Met with camera crew to brief them on the locations we will be using. Discussed the health and safety hazards when working on a waste materials site. Each member of the crew took a risk assessment document and agreed to read and follow the instructions on the form.
2nd August	Location day at SWRP – weather good. Camera crew arrived thirty minutes late at the location. The management at SWRP were expecting us but were unsure just what we were doing. Contacted client to ask them to confirm with SWRP the nature of location shoot and what the footage would be used for. This was carried out and confirmed by SWRP senior management.

FIGURE 3.22 *In your production diary it is important to keep a record of all the discussions that you have had regarding the product, and what decisions were taken.*

UNIT ASSESSMENT

Complete a production diary that records all of the activities you have undertaken for your product. This should include your pre-production, production and post-production work. Keep this diary in an organised way with clear references to your own work and the work done by others for your project.

Comments on your work

As part of your product evaluation, try to get a number of people to see and comment on the finished product. In this case of the Recycle.It programme, it would be a good idea to get some eleven–fourteen year olds to comment on the effectiveness of the product for the target audience. You should also get feedback from your client, in this case it may be your teacher, and ask them to comment on its effectiveness.

If you want to get a wider range of feedback, consider making multiple copies of your media product and sending it to people outside your school or college. This might include finding a group of eleven–fourteen year olds from a school or college who could give you some good and impartial feedback. If you send your product in the post, make sure you include a stamped addressed envelope to make sure they return it to you. If your product is an interactive media website, you may be able to post the pages up on the school or college website to make it available to a wider audience.

Include a questionnaire with your product so that the audience can provide structured feedback to inform your evaluation. Put some thought into the design of your questionnaire. Providing options with tick boxes makes it much easier for people to respond than asking them to write answers to each question. However, you may want to include some questions that require short written answers in order to gain more detailed feedback. It is good practice to have a mixture of the two question types in the same questionnaire.

Do not be disheartened by any negative views of your work. See them as a pointer to doing better next time. You could always use their comments to re-edit the programme or even re-record some of the material.

It can also be useful to sit down with an audience after a viewing (or reading or listening) of your product and ask for their immediate responses. You could record their views on video or audio and transcribe them (write or type them out) later. Some people will be more forthcoming in a face-to-face situation than in a written questionnaire.

UNIT ASSESSMENT

Arrange a viewing/reading/listening of your media product by an invited audience.

Ask people to reply to your invitation in order to ensure that sufficient people will be attending.

Produce appropriate feedback materials (such as questionnaires or pre-prepared questions to record on audio or video) to ensure you have appropriate responses.

Once you have obtained sufficient feedback, you will need to analyse and record this information in a way that gives a representative view of what the audience thinks of your media product.

Maybe the product is too short or too long, the sound might be indistinct or the pictures might be blurred. Maybe the interactivity doesn't work in some places or some of the navigational buttons do not go anywhere. With a website, you are able to keep updating the product after it has been released and correct any mistakes.

CASE STUDY

Media Productions generally undertakes a review of its work with a client.

A programme it was making for a famous pottery was in the final stages of production. The client agreed to review the product with the director. The programme was a short promotional video that was shot in the pottery and followed the making of a teapot from the initial cast to the finished product.

The client had a very firm idea that the programme should show the exact process involved in making a teapot and didn't always agree with the 'poetic licence' used by the director in order to make the programme more interesting.

The director tried to persuade the client that in order to make the whole programme flow there had to be some compromise in the sequences shot and how they were edited together.

The client finally agreed and the programme was released.

- Why do you think that it can sometimes be hard to balance the artistic requirements of a media product with how things really are?

Evaluating your work

As the final stage of your project, you will need to carry out a comprehensive evaluation of your work on this media product. In order to do this try to answer the following questions:

* What did I do?
* What skills did I learn?
* What went wrong?
* What went right?
* What would I do if I could start again?

Remember to sell yourself in this evaluation. If you have done really good work then say so, and if you had problems remember to say how you overcame them.

If you have problems writing down your evaluation, consider how you could record your thoughts in other ways.

Remember

You could use video or audio to record your evaluations.

You may be able to evaluate your work by using a PowerPoint presentation.

You may be able to hold a discussion with your teacher and record this conversation in either written or audio format.

UNIT ASSESSMENT

Undertake a review of your own work. Use:

1 your notes from the production diary
2 the records of your planning and production
3 comments made by your teacher or client
4 notes made from your production meetings
5 comments from a focus group or questionnaire
6 feedback from your team members.

Checklist

Below is checklist of the material you need to produce for the assessment of your work in this unit:

1. a proposal
2. a treatment
3. production meeting minutes
4. storyboard/mood board/thumbnails
5. a production schedule
6. a budget
7. a script/shooting script/running order
8. a production diary
9. the finished product
10. an evaluation of your work
11. a review of the fitness for purpose of the finished product.

You should store safely all of your paperwork, initial designs, finished product, evaluations and reviews. This evidence will be required by your teacher when assessing your work.

Finally

Remember that you can find the brief for the year you are undertaking the qualification on the Edexcel website. Your teacher may have already printed out the brief for you.

As you embark on your product, ask yourself the following questions and give some thought to the answers:

* What was I good at in Unit 2?
* Which of the media skills would allow me to get the best grade in Unit 3?
* Do I have the resources to enable me to make a good media product?

Remember

The assessment for this unit will be based on all of the pre-production, production, post production and evaluation work you do.

It is essential that you keep records of all your work – this will help your teacher to award you the correct grade.

In order to attain a higher grade, have a look at the assessment criteria grid in the specification book to see what is required.

Ask your teacher to explain how you can attain higher grades.

Remember

In order to achieve higher marks, you should show through your documentation that you have an excellent understand of pre-production, production and post production techniques:

- Your documentation will be well organised and cover all aspects of the process.
- You demonstrate an extensive range of production and technical skills.
- Your product successfully achieves its aims.
- You have demonstrated creativity in your work.
- Your product fully addresses the brief and engages the audience.
- You can critically review your own work and the fitness for purpose of your product.
- You use well-chosen examples to support your review.

Glossary

Actuality Real sound from a location, which helps listeners to imagine a scene or illustrates what is happening.

Alternative reading A meaning that is different in some significant way from the producer's preferred reading.

Anchorage A means of 'tying down' the meaning of some part of a media text.

Audience A group of people targeted by a media product because they share broadly similar characteristics and interests.

Authoring Assembling an interactive media product.

Average hours How long the station or channel is consumed over a fixed period; this figure indicates how long audiences are listening or viewing.

Back light A light placed behind the subject to light them from the rear and make the subject distinct from the background.

Balance Equal emphasis given to all sides of an argument, so no one side has an unfair advantage over the others.

Barn doors Moveable flaps on lights used to control the direction of the light and restrict the width of the beam.

Bias An unequal stance or representation, which gives one side an advantage over another.

Bidirectional Microphones that can pick up sound from two opposite directions.

Blogging People posting their own reports and views on a particular topic or event on the Internet.

Bollywood A term used to describe the Indian film industry, and a play on the word 'Hollywood'.

Boom microphone Directional microphone that is mounted on a boom arm and positioned just out of camera frame.

Brand An identity, used to help people recognise a particular product and to encourage them to want more of it.

Closed questions These are limited in terms of the potential responses possible, and are often answered by yes/no, or an answer picked from a range of given options.

Code A system of conveying meaning to audiences without having to use words to explain what is happening.

Commission A formal request for a product to be made, in return for payment.

Conglomerate An organisation that is made up of several different parts, each of which may appear to be separate.

Content analysis A research method that involves the counting of distinct elements or features within media texts.

Contract A legally binding agreement for a commission, usually in writing.

Convention An accepted, even expected, way of doing something; in the media industry this means the usual way of creating a particular type of product.

Copy The original writing that is used in a print product.

Cutaway An additional shot that is different to the main subject but still linked in some way; it can be used as a link or buffer between two shots that are very similar or to add an extra dimension to the narrative.

Cut-in This type of shot serves a similar purpose to a cutaway, but shows a specific detail of the subject, such as their hands to emphasise emotion.

CV Stands for *curriculum vitae*, which is a Latin term for a detailed list of information about your life so far.

Diaphragm A thin piece of material (such as paper, plastic or metal) inside a microphone which vibrates when it is struck by a sound wave.

Digital printing A form of printing that is capable of producing high-quality colour work using variable data.

Edit decision list A plan of the edit of a media product.

Editing Selecting from one source, or from a number of different ones, an appropriate amount of material that fits the brief and enhances a finished product.

Establishing shot A long shot of a scene or location that shows the viewer where the sequence is set.

Fill light The secondary light that is placed on the opposite side to the key light; it is used to partially fill in the shadows created by the key light and is usually softer and less bright than the key.

Floodlight A broad beam of light that is less directional and less intense than a spotlight.

Focal length The distance from the lens to the point behind the lens where the light entering it will converge; the focal length defines the angle of view and how magnified an object appears.

Focus How sharp the image appears; you can adjust the lens to ensure the correct parts of the shot are in focus.

Focus group Pre-selected panels of people used in research studies to represent the target audience.

Franchising The selling of permission to use a particular brand on a product.

Freelance contract A legal document agreeing a fee for the completion of a particular task or project.

Freelance work Casual or one-off work that is paid on a per item basis.

Frequency The way in which a microphone responds to different frequencies of sound.

Gels Coloured filters placed on lights.

Genre A type of media product within which most examples share a large number of characteristics.

Globalisation The increasing concentration of political and economic influence in the hands of a few people, in a way that ignores international boundaries.

Gravure A print process used for large-quantity runs where the set-up costs are high, but the unit cost is low.

Hegemony The dominance of a society by a ruling elite; in media terms, this would mean mass communication being controlled by just a few powerful organisations, thereby restricting access to alternative views.

HTML Hypertext markup language; the hidden coding behind any web page.

Human resources department The part of an organisation that deals with staffing issues, such as recruitment, employment contracts, pension contributions and pay.

Icon The most basic type of signifier, for example on radio the sound of a siren could be an icon representing a police car, simply because that is a sound police cars sometimes make.

Image manipulation The use of computer software to alter images so they look their best on the page.

Impartiality The state of being unbiased.

Impedence The amount of opposition a microphone has to an audio signal.

Income The money earned through the organisation's regular activities.

Index A secondary level signifier, for example the sound of the same siren may suggest police officers are present, not because officers sound like sirens, but because a siren often indicates their arrival.

Key light The primary light that is placed to one side of the subject so that one side is well lit and the other side has some shadow; normally a strong light.

Layout The way different items are positioned on a page.

Likert scale Rating system used in research that asks the respondent how strongly they agree or disagree with a series of statements.

Linear editing A process in which the recorded footage is copied from one tape onto a master tape in the order required for the completed product.

Loudspeaker A type of transducer that converts the energy back into acoustic energy.

Market The area in which customers for a media product may be found.

Media company An organisation, either privately or publicly owned, which is mainly concerned with communication through one or more of the mass media.

Media industry The prime focus of the economic activity of this industry is on communication through the mass media.

Microphone A type of transducer that converts acoustic energy (in the form of sound waves) into electrical energy (in the form of an audio signal).

Multinational An organisation that operates in several countries at the same time, owning parts of the media in each one.

Multi-skilling Having enough expertise in a number of different roles to be able to do all of them to a satisfactory standard.

Navigation The means by which the users of an interactive media product are helped to find their way around it.

Niche A specialised, and sometimes very narrowly defined, market segment.

Nonlinear editing A method that uses a computer and editing software to edit the footage.

Offset litho One of the main commercial print processes, used to produce media products such as newspapers, magazines and books.

Omnidirectional Microphones that can pick up sound evenly from all directions.

Open questions These allow the person answering to give his or her own view of the subject.

Outgoings The money spent by an organisation in order to meet all its costs, including: wages, salaries and fees for staff, as well as rent, heating, lighting, vehicle costs, power, materials and taxes.

Pan A slow sideways movement of the camera around a central axis; if you are using a tripod, you will turn the tripod head slowly round on its axis to pan the camera either left or right.

PDF Portable document format; type of interactive media file.

Pixel-based programs Used to control and manipulate photographic images.

Pixels A series of small coloured squares which overlap to produce millions of colours.

Pluralism The availability of a diverse range of opinions, perspectives and information.

Post-press or **print finishing** The processes such as cutting, trimming, folding and binding that take place on the printed material before a product can be distributed.

Preferred reading The meaning the producer intended the audience to make from the text.

Pre-press The generic term for all of the design and preparatory work that takes place to get a product ready for print.

Press The term for the actual printing process.

Primary research Original research to obtain new data, using such methods as interviews, questionnaires, focus groups and observation.

Production schedule A working plan of the shoot.

Propaganda Material designed to persuade people that one or other side of an argument is correct.

Proposal A concise written outline of your ideas, used to sell an idea to a potential client.

Qualitative data Focuses on people's feelings, impressions and reactions to what they have read, seen and heard.

Qualitative research Research that is based on opinions, attitudes and preferences rather than hard facts and figures.

Quantitative data Information that tells us how many, how long or how often; it uses numbers to describe things, like the consumption of media products, and it can be presented in tables, charts or graphs.

Quantitative research Research based on measurable and quantifiable facts and information, producing numerical and statistical data.

Rank order scale Rating system used in research that asks the respondent to indicate the order of preference from a list of given answers, usually through the use of numbers.

Reach How many people the product 'reaches'.

Reading The act of making meaning from a media text.

Recce A visit to a location to check its suitability for the production work being planned.

Reflector boards Reflective board used on location and in studio settings to provide a secondary light source and to act as a fill light.

Respondent Someone who provides responses in a survey.

Sans serif typeface Plain typeface that tends to be used for titles and headings.

Screen printing A print process that allows for greater control over the application of each individual colour and is used for a range of promotional materials.

Script A detailed account of what is to be spoken in the product, as well as positional and movement information and details of any music or sound effects that are to be used.

Secondary research Research using pre-existing data and information that has already been gathered by other people or organisations; often available in books, journals or via the Internet.

Segment A part of a market.

Semantic differential scale Rating system used in research that uses a sliding scale between two opposing words and asks respondents to indicate where on the scale their opinions lies.

Serif typeface Has a decorative flourish and tends to be used in the main body of a text.

Share Put simply, how large a slice of the market that product takes.

Shooting script A working plan of a moving image shoot.

SLR Single lens reflex camera.

Spin-offs A brand can be applied to different products to associate them with the main one.

Spotlight A strong, focused beam of light targeted at a specific subject.

Staff contract A legal document between an employer and an employee, which sets out the employee's set hours, pay and conditions and annual leave entitlement.

Storyboard A visualisation of the script that includes an image of how each shot will look, as well as information about the camera angles and movements, the sound, lighting and editing transitions that are envisaged.

Sub-genre A sub-division of a wider genre.

Symbol The third level of signification, for example the siren may be symbolic of crime, not because crime has a sound like a siren, but because police sirens are generally associated with a response to criminal activity.

Synergy The advantages obtained by different parts of an organisation sharing resources and working together to enhance each other's output.

Text Any media product that is 'read', or consumed, by an audience; a text may include written copy or it may consist entirely of sounds and/or images.

Three-point lighting Standard form of lighting used in moving image production involving the use of a key light, fill light and back light.

Tilt An upward or downward movement of the camera to adjust the angle.

Tracking The physical movement of the camera in any direction; sometimes the camera and tripod are mounted on a track to ensure a smooth movement, or stabilising equipment such as a Steadicam can be used.

Trade union An organisation formed to protect the interests of staff when dealing with their employers.

Transducers Devices that convert energy from one form to another.

Transitions Way of moving from one shot to another when editing a moving image production, such as wipes, dissolves and fades.

Treatment A more detailed description of the content of the proposed production, including details of the storyline, the plot, characters and locations (or subject matter, themes, presenters), as well as an indication of the resource needs and the budget required.

Turnover The total amount of money passing through an organisation's accounts in a year.

Unidirectional Microphones that can pick up sound predominantly from one direction to allow a specific sound source to be targeted.

Variable data The different information that can be sent to a printer when printing the same job.

Vector-based programs Used to produce logos and graphics.

WYSIWYG An acronym that stands for 'what you see is what you get'; it refers to the fact that when you use the appropriate software to edit the file on the screen, this is what it will look like when published as a web page.

Zoom Makes the image appear closer or more distant, and is used to frame the shot more effectively.

Index